BEST SERMONS

Books by G. PAUL BUTLER

Editor of

Modern College Readings, 1936, co-editor
Best Sermons, 1943-44 (Vol. I)
Best Sermons, 1946 (Vol. II)
Best Sermons, 1947-48 (Vol. III)
Best Sermons, 1949-50 (Vol. IV)
Best Sermons, 1951-52 (Vol. V)
Best Sermons, 1955 (Vol. VI)
Best Sermons, 1959-60 (Vol. VII)
  (Protestant Edition)

Co-Author of

Butlers' South America
Butlers' Mexico
Butlers' Caribbean, and
  Central America

Advisory Committee for Best Sermons, Volume VIII

Dr. Paul E. Scherer
Dr. Joseph R. Sizoo
Dr. Thomas S. Kepler

Adviser for Europe (Especially for France)

Dr. Clayton E. Williams

BEST SERMONS

VOLUME VIII

1962

PROTESTANT EDITION

EDITED BY G. PAUL BUTLER

Foreword by

BISHOP GERALD KENNEDY
Bishop of the Los Angeles Area of the Methodist Church

D. VAN NOSTRAND COMPANY, INC.

PRINCETON, NEW JERSEY

TORONTO NEW YORK LONDON

D. VAN NOSTRAND COMPANY, INC.

120 Alexander St., Princeton, New Jersey (*Principal Office*)
24 West 40 Street, New York 18, New York

D. VAN NOSTRAND COMPANY, LTD.

358, Kensington High Street, London, W.14, England

D. VAN NOSTRAND COMPANY (Canada), LTD.

25 Hollinger Road, Toronto 16, Canada

Published simultaneously in Canada by
D. VAN NOSTRAND COMPANY (Canada), LTD.

To
RALPH W. SOCKMAN
Preacher
Friend
Man of God

FOREWORD

When I was a seminary student many years ago, I had two chief worries concerning the ministry. The first was the fear that a man could not preach week after week without running out of fresh and relevant material. It seemed to me that in a little while a man's life would be a desperate search for something that had not been said a thousand times. The second concern was that if a man were a preacher, he would find himself in such strange company. I had known a few old boys whose dress and manner stamped them as archaic leftovers from another generation.

Regarding the first worry, time has revealed the miracle of the inexhaustible depths of the Gospel. I have been preaching for thirty-five years and I will be as excited next Sunday morning when I enter my pulpit, as I was at the age of eighteen when I preached my first sermon in my first student appointment. If I should live to be a hundred, there will still be a wish for more time to tell more of the old, old Story. There is no other subject in the world a man could discuss several times a week for a lifetime without any sense of repetition or fatigue.

The second problem has proved to be equally unreal. Preachers are the greatest fellows in the world and I am always proud of my calling when I am with them. When the going is hard and the pressure is on, it always lifts up my heart to think of my colleagues in all churches. It is a delight to be with them and it is an honor to be one of them.

Now BEST SERMONS has been a favorite source of study and inspiration for many years. I do not know any other volume of sermons which has the same breadth and variety. Preachers come from many lands and from many communions to bear witness to the universality of the Gospel. Yet there are common qualities which all of them possess.

For one thing, preachers are dedicated men. There is apparent in all good sermons a conviction and a belief that Christianity and truth are one. There is sometimes a feeling that men are only half sold on what they are saying, so they are lacking in fire and enthusiasm. But these are the second-raters, and those who are heeded have achieved that state of power which comes from the complete surrender of their lives to the One they call Lord.

Another thing obvious about great preaching is the mark of wide reading. The preacher's convictions are not the result of narrowness or ignorance. These men have ranged widely in their intellectual pursuits so that their ideas are big and their faith is broad. Hand-to-mouth preachers are soon recognized and no surface brilliance can cover up the lack of intellectual preparation. I know of no exceptions to the general proposition that good preachers are great readers.

The men who make their mark on a generation are also men of compassion. They feel the pain and misery of the disinherited. Some may try to cover their essential selfishness with sentimentality, but the covering is too thin and the selfishness shows through. The great ones have not become professionalized in their human relationships and their sermons have something of our Lord's anguish for the poor and the suffering. They make their congregations see the hungry and suffer with the lonely so that their churches place their resources back of Christian efforts to serve all of God's people.

Finally, great preachers are men of courage. They speak with the prophet's scorn and indignation. A layman wrote to me one time, very troubled about preachers. Why is it, he wanted to know, that the men in our leading pulpits are always stirring up their society? I could have replied that it is this very quality that has made them worthy to fill the great pulpits. Those who play it safe by keeping silent, have their reward, no doubt. But it is not the privilege of playing a leading part in the struggle to bring this world to the feet of Jesus Christ.

I have never been more convinced than just now of the central significance of preaching. I pay glad tribute to all the many ways in which ministers and churches serve the present age. But it becomes clearer to me with every passing year that when a man stands up to preach, this is the great moment in the Church's life. It is by this means, that God releases His power and works His miracles.

GERALD KENNEDY,
Bishop of the Los Angeles Area
of the Methodist Church

viii

INTRODUCTION

After reading sermons for eight volumes of BEST SERMONS during the last twenty years I still believe that preaching is a vital function in the Protestant church. Liturgy, worship, and preaching all are important. Some denominations make the liturgy the essential element of worship. But even in the liturgical churches, as well as in the evangelical churches, preaching is of great importance in reaching entire congregations with the Word of God.

In a very real sense preachers today are still prophets and the voice of the pulpit has to be a prophetic voice if it is to be effective. A sermon, therefore, affords the minister a chance—as a dedicated servant of God—to speak to his congregation and to his fellow men as the voice of God. God could speak directly to men if he wished, of this I am sure, but he uses men whom he has called to speak for Him. Thus, the highest spiritual message most men ever hear in this life is the one delivered to them from the pulpit. The minister, then, can be virtually the voice of God Sunday after Sunday, if he will.

This requires that the gifted minister live a life of prayer and devotion, of reading and meditation. Reading will occupy many of the minister's "free" hours day after day. Unless he loves reading he is likely to run dry before he gets far in the pulpit. The good minister of Jesus Christ will spend thirty hours a week in his study in sermon preparation. Then he can stand in the pulpit and speak each week as though he were standing in the very Presence of the Living God. The greatest minister never rants, never scolds at his congregation, never lets them down. Rather, the man who achieves greatness in the pulpit speaks to his people as though he were addressing the children of God who need to know—to be told and retold—God's way for the world and them.

Taken in this way, preaching is a divine task and makes going to church an event of deep spiritual value to both the people of the congregation and the man in the pulpit. It makes attending church important—and it makes preaching the most important work any man can do. Such devoted, scholarly, carefully prepared preaching will give the preacher a consciousness of pulpit power, but it should never give him a false sense of superiority or self-importance. There is a vast difference between confidence and ability and the emptiness of egotism, self-adulation or pompousness.

When—and if—men realize the importance of a sermon they put more of themselves, more work, more thought, more prayer into preparing each sermon as the capstone of their calling. In my travels in recent years I have visited many churches and have always taken particular pains to observe the pulpits. The architects of three hundred years ago built pulpits as an integral and vital part of the church, standing to itself, where the preacher stood alone as he faced the congregation in the place of God. Many of these pulpits were done in fine marbles, rare woods, most were carved with beautiful designs. A half dozen were overlaid with pure gold. A Pulpit of Gold! We may not have churches which can afford the luxury and beauty of such a pulpit, yet we can make every pulpit a symbol of the glory of God and vital to His people and His church.

Recently a well-known leader asked, "Is the church still necessary? Has the pulpit ceased to be of value in the world today?" In Russia and iron-curtain countries the Christian church has been curtailed wherever possible and the pulpit is closely censored or watched. Thank God, our pulpits are still free.

Yet—in our world today with all the discords of cold wars, fixed TV programs, juvenile delinquency and other problems that clamor for men's minds, when we see school boards misappropriate funds, highway departments or state governments use gas tax money for other purposes, when politicians make a mockery of race and educational problems for the sake of re-election, when men running for office make promises to reduce taxes and initiate reforms, then fail to keep their promises when elected—when all these things happen on all sides there *is* a definite need for the preaching ministry, for a man in each pulpit with something to say to help men to find God and the right answers to temptation and tax problems and personal and national and international questions.

The minister may remember that there is meanness in the world, but there is also kindness and goodness; there is sin and there are sinners, but there is also forgiveness and there are saints, and his preaching must be for all kinds and conditions of men.

There are times when some problems seem insurmountable. Right now we are in a period when parents are afraid to train their children, when discipline is not properly enforced. Race problems cause harsh reactions on the part of black and white men. The example of Nannie Helen Burroughs, the Negro educator and Baptist leader for fifty years, demonstrates how problems of race can be settled—by Christian understanding, goodwill, kindness, true brotherhood on the part of both Negro and white.

The chaplains of the Army, Navy and Air Force, have done much to bring the Gospel to men of the armed services. Men like Chaplain Carpenter, Jim Claypool and a hundred other consecrated service chaplains make preaching and ministry to service men and their families a worthy Christian task.

In the midst of divisions today, the ministry is preaching Christian unity, unity of spirit and purpose, unity in the love of God. Whole denominations have united with others these last ten years. There was a time when Greek, New Testament, church history, Hebrew, Old Testament and preaching were the basic courses in our theological seminaries. Preaching is still important. Some of our seminaries make it a strong course. But today at least a hundred American seminaries barely recognize homiletics as a subject. We need a new emphasis upon the pulpit and the teaching of sermon preparation, construction, effective delivery, public speaking.

Gathering these sermons has been one of the most satisfying tasks in my life and I believe this volume of sermons is one of the best ever assembled in a single book. It is representative of the best preaching being done in our time. Not all the best sermons preached are in the book, but those included are sermons worthy to stand with the best being preached anywhere in the world.

There are sermons by men of a number of different theological and denominational persuasions—Presbyterians, Methodists, Baptists, Protestant Episcopalians, Congregational-Christians, the Church of England, the Church of Scotland, Lutherans, the Reformed Church, Greek Orthodox, the Church of Canada; there are evangelicals, conservatives, liberals, ritualists, Trinitarians, Unitarians, men in great churches, middle-sized churches and small churches. North, South, East, West, France, England, Scotland, Canada are all represented.

Most sermons are by men in the pulpit, active pastors, but several distinguished sermons are by men in theological seminaries who are training young men today to be the preachers of tomorrow; some are by bishops, officers of denominations; New York, Washington, London, Edinburgh, Los Angeles, New Orleans, the Middle West—all different sections were given a place if the sermons received made it possible.

But—above everything else, the selection was based upon the quality and content of each sermon. The man's name or position did not influence the choice. Even the most important ministers had their sermons read on the same strict standards of excellence as the men from smaller pulpits. All sermons were selected on the basis of their merits—for homiletic excellence, a spiritual message for our own time, word choice, structure.

It is my sincere attempt to make each volume better than the preceding one. In twenty years I have sent invitations to more than 100,000 clergymen in 198 denominations in the United States and to 65 foreign countries. Sermons have come from 165 denominations and from 55 foreign countries in 15 different languages.

We have tried to find the greatest preaching by the world leaders in the pulpits, but we have also endeavored to discover the new men whose preaching is excellent but who have not yet won recognition on a large scale and to give them their first publication. As I indicated above, it is a source of real satisfaction to be the first to find a young man of promise who is destined to be one of the great pulpit leaders tomorrow. As the editor I believe in the importance of sermonizing and delivery; men who will read a book a week, sermonize faithfully for twenty to thirty hours, practice on their delivery and public speaking are bound to win recognition. I know of no man who has failed in this respect if he followed such a personal program of improvement in his pulpit ability. A man's whole success can hinge on his effectiveness in the pulpit. This does not mean that he will not faithfully visit and plan the other details of his congregation's welfare, but that his preaching will be his chief function. *The Christian Church will advance faster in this generation than it has for the past fifty years if thousands of ministers will adopt such a high preaching standard for themselves and their churches.* Laton Holmgren's sermon illustrates the necessity of such a preaching advance.

The Table of Contents and the Index have been arranged to be of assistance to busy pastors who want to find ideas or illustrations for sermons, hence we have classified sermons in the Contents under such headings as Easter, Church, Christian Life, Christmas, Faith, Evangelism, Marriage, Home, Missions, Sermons for Students, Baccalaureate, Stewardship. The index further classifies and cross-references such words or topics as education, Christ, God, important men. We hope this will all be valuable in stimulating men to find ideas to make their preaching both easier and increasingly effective. I believe, as Ralph Sockman has many times stated, that the pastor in the local church is the most important man in the life of the churches in every community.

G. PAUL BUTLER

APPRECIATIONS

This volume of BEST SERMONS could not have been done without the help and friendship of thousands of ministers all over the United States and in a number of foreign countries. As the editor of Volume VIII of BEST SERMONS, I am, therefore, most grateful to all the ministers—more than 7,785 of them—and a hundred or more leading laymen—who sent me their sermons or addresses for regular or special occasions so that I could read and consider them. To all those whose sermons were sent and whose sermons are included in this volume, as well as to those whose sermons could not be included, I want to express my deep appreciation. I am as grateful to those whose sermons were omitted as I am to the men whose sermons were chosen for publication. Without this opportunity for wide reading this book would not have its variety and inclusiveness. I believe it is truly representative of the best preaching being done today.

Men of many denominations helped me to find sermons of great beauty and power with a spiritual message for our time. Hundreds of denominational officers, bishops, presidents, executive secretaries, the Chicago Sunday Evening Club, church leaders almost everywhere have made nominations of their best preachers. In this way I was enabled to send invitations to more than 22,500 ministers. Dr. Franklin Clark Fry, Ralph Stoody, Tom Kepler and a hundred other friends made personal nominations of ministers they felt truly represented men who are doing some of the best preaching they know about in the churches today. Men have sent me personal letters from the Orient, Hawaii, India, our own country and many parts of the world with the names of fine preachers. Thus the book has grown month by month.

I am grateful to another group of men who have honored me with their friendship, their advice and their assistance month by month, men who have been my closest advisers. I want to express my appreciation to each of them, but they are in no way responsible for any mistakes I may have made as the editor: Joseph R. Sizoo of George Washington University; Paul Scherer of Princeton Theological Seminary (formerly of Union Theological Seminary, New York); Thomas Kepler of Oberlin College Graduate School of Theology; Ralph W. Sockman, Bishop Herbert Welch, Clayton Williams and a dozen other important religious leaders.

Various publishers of other books have given their permission to quote material from their volumes and I wish to express my gratitude to them:

To the Westminster Press for permission to quote material in the sermon *Christ is Alive* by Chalmers Coe, which will also appear in *Discovery*, April-June, 1962.

To Harper and Brothers for permission to quote *The Conflict of Loyalties* by Robert J. McCracken from his Harper book, *Putting Faith to Work*.

To Harcourt, Brace for permission to quote a selection from *Creed or Chaos* in the sermon, *The Struggle for Men's Minds* by William M. Elliott, Jr.

The sermon by Paul Scherer, *They That Wait for the Lord*, will appear in an entire volume of his to be published by Harper and Brothers.

To the editors of the religious and denominational press for their wonderful cooperation in my search for sermons (by making advance announcements and to afford every minister everywhere a chance to know his sermon is welcome for consideration) and in their reviews and announcements of my books as they are published I want to express my very personal appreciation.

To Bishop Gerald Kennedy another special appreciation for his excellent Foreword. His great ability as a preacher eminently fits him to write such a statement on preaching, which is his own greatest contribution to the church today.

To Norman Hood, my editor, my appreciation for his careful scrutiny of the sermons and my introductions. We have disagreed at times on editorial changes, but that is the function of an editor and author-editor.

And last, but not least, my gratitude to Erica Butler, wife, severest critic, and helper for her assistance in typing, checking, doing all the odd jobs no one had time to do.

G. PAUL BUTLER

Bookmere, Little Silver, N. J.
March 15, 1962

CONTENTS

CHRISTMAS

good

xvii

EVANGELISM

Sermon One

THE GOD WHOM CHRISTIANS WORSHIP

THE REVEREND JOHN BERTRAM PHILLIPS, M.A. CANTAB.

A Priest of the Church of England, Swanage, Dorset, England

During World War II the Reverend J. B. Phillips, meeting with a group of young people at The Church of the Good Shepherd in Lee (London), ended his discussion with a reading from St. Paul's Epistles in the Authorized Version of the Bible. Finding that many of his listeners did not grasp the meaning of the words of the Bible, Mr. Phillips decided to check the Greek and Aramaic and make his own fresh translations. When he read these the listening young men and women were immediately stirred to attention. So great was their interest that he showed his translations to C. S. Lewis of Magdalen College, Oxford, and was advised to publish them.

When *Letters to Young Churches*—as he called these translated books of the New Testament—was published in England more than a million copies were sold in a short time, showing that people were hungry for a Bible they could easily understand. The book was soon published in the United States and was an instantaneous success here as well. This first volume was followed by a translation of the four *Gospels*, then by *The Young Church in Action* (the Book of Acts) and *The Book of Revelation*. The four books form a complete translation of the New Testament.

John Bertram Phillips was born in 1906, entered Emmanuel College, Cambridge, majored in Classics and English and took both his B.A. and M.A. in these fields. He was ordained in 1930, became Curate at St. John's Penge, then of St. Margaret's, London. He was Vicar of the Church of the Good Shepherd, Lee, in 1940 and went through the blitz in this severely bombed part of London. His Church was destroyed. He became Vicar of St. John's, Redhill, in 1945, then in 1957 was made Canon Prebendary of Chichester Cathedral. He has since devoted himself largely to writing and speaking.

His other books include: *Your God is Too Small, Making Men Whole, Appointment with God, The Church Under the Cross, New Testament Christianity.* He is married and has a daughter.

1

This sermon was preached on the School Service Broadcast of B.B.C. on March 6, 1960. It is New Testament Christianity at its best.

THE GOD WHOM CHRISTIANS WORSHIP

Whether people are religious or not, almost everybody pours out love, admiration, devotion, the willingness to serve and make sacrifices for somebody or something, and that, naturally, is worship. The object of a man's worship may be a football team, it may be a "pop" singer, a film or T.V. star. In fact it may be anybody or anything that has skill or strength or talent beyond one's own, and that calls forth feelings of worship.

Now whatever we worship is bound to make a great difference in the sort of people we are. Our whole character and outlook is moulded, not by what we profess to worship but by what in fact we do worship, and we must be very honest with ourselves about it. The chief enemies of Jesus Christ, for example, were ostensibly worshipping God. But in fact, as Jesus continually pointed out to them, they were worshipping such things as power, privilege, position, wealth, and success. It's because worshipping the wrong things produces the wrong kind of people that Jesus spoke so sternly. It is, then, very important for those of us who want to worship God that we should see something of His true greatness.

Modern man does not, I believe, worship the living God very much. This is partly because he is seduced and blinded by the gods of the modern age —success, prestige, glamour, money, power and security. Such things loom so large in his reading and thinking, yes, and in his viewing and listening, that he has become spiritually short-sighted.

Apart from this, many people today find it difficult to hold a conception of God which they can honestly worship. I have talked with a good many people who don't believe in God, or who have given up their faith in Him. In most cases, I find that such people have thrown overboard childish ideas of God, and have found nothing to put in their place. Of course it's very common for adolescents, who are working their way from dependence towards independence, to rebel against authority. And this is very often the time when the childish faith is thrown overboard, along with everything else which is a reminder of childhood. But it is a tragedy if, after rejecting the childish, young people fail to discover a God great enough to command their grown-up worship and love.

We don't expect the ideas and loyalties of childhood in any other department of life to have the same significance when we grow up. And yet, to hear some people talk, you'd think that in advocating faith in God we were recommending a return to childhood! The truth is exactly the opposite. What we're trying to do is to get people to leave behind the childish and the inadequate, to look away from the distractions and false values of this world, and to rediscover the living God.

I've become more and more convinced that if we are to find a personal God we must accept His planned focussing of Himself in the Man Jesus Christ. If we don't do this, we're left with such a vast and overpowering idea of the wisdom and complexity of the Mind behind the universe that a personal God becomes impossible. Every good scientist feels a tremendous sense of awe and wonder as he discovers more and more of this amazing universe. But I don't believe that he discovers God as a person, not only infinite in His greatness, but infinite in His concern for the individual, unless he accepts Jesus Christ as what He claimed to be. You may be moved to wonder and awe at the infinite Mind behind all those things that we can observe, but you cannot easily love, worship and adore what is practically an abstraction. It is only when we see God expressed, as it were, in a human being, living under human conditions and limitations, that the springs of worship begin to flow.

Now let's be clear what we're saying. No Christian is claiming that the whole of God, so to speak, can be confined and compressed into one short human life, lived in Palestine some two thousand years ago. But what Christ Himself claimed was to reveal the nature and character of God. So that if we accept His claim, however immense our conception of God may be, the clue to His nature and purpose will always be found in Christ. In other words, we look out upon that immense mystery which we call "God" through a Christ-shaped aperture.

If we take the revelation of Christ seriously we may find we've been mistaken about the true greatness of God. As human beings, we're so made that we're bound to be impressed by size or great numbers, or by sheer power. And for this reason we tend to make in our minds images of God which are really no more than projections of man, enormously magnified in size, wisdom and power. Of course God is infinitely greater than we are, in wisdom and power and in everything else, but the greatness of God is not a matter of size!

There is, for example, His almost incredible humility. That quiet insertion of Himself into human history, which we celebrate at Christmas-time, is not a piece of pious legend. It's a sober fact of history. Anyone with any imagination at all can think of some God of righteousness and power

3

breaking through into the life of this sinful planet, in wrath and judgment, and displaying enough physical force to make the bravest tremble! But that was not the way of the God with whom we have to do. He came not to condemn but to save, and His humble means of entry is a strong clue to His character. No man's free will is interfered with; no man's personality is assaulted; no one is forced to do anything at all. God enters His world in humble circumstances, God lives life on the same terms as He expects all human beings to live it. God accepts no special privilege nor protection, and in the end God is betrayed and executed, without any superhuman intervention. On the face of it it seems a weak and feeble intrusion into human affairs, and it's that apparent weakness which we must never forget.

For the methods of God have not changed. He is still gentle and humble and apparently weak. The silliest chit of a girl can keep God at arm's length for as long as she wants, and the conceited man can do the same. It's a rather frightening thought, but it remains true that God does not interfere with anyone's freedom to choose. That's not to say that God is impotent and inoperative in His own world. He speaks, wherever men will listen, through conscience, through circumstance, and through the crying needs of other people. He's unceasingly calling people away from the life that leads to unhappiness and destruction to the life that leads to peace and co-operation with Himself.

There's a wisdom at work here, higher than any of our wisdom. Two thousand years ago you'd have said that the life of the field-preacher Jesus was an insignificant failure. Yet today there are millions who gladly serve and worship Him, and many who have proved their willingness to die for His sake. The greatness of Jesus, the greatness of our God, is quite different from the greatness which men usually admire.

I've already mentioned the very risky gift of free will which God gives to us human beings, and with which He doesn't interfere. We all have a personal responsibility in moral decision, which we cannot honestly evade. Now we may not like this freedom. Perhaps in our heart of hearts we would rather be guided and sustained by some infallible book of rules, or some infallible system. But God wants us to grow up, to learn to take intelligent moral decisions. And we only succeed in remaining childish if we cling to something which we think is infallible.

I am speaking tonight from a school, and if we look back to our own school days, we know that the teachers who did us the most good were neither the over-strict nor the over-lenient. It was those men or women who guided us and helped us, but who at the same time handed back to us a good deal of personal responsibility, to whom we are most indebted.

4

That's naturally only a human example, but it serves to illustrate how the real and living God, while always ready to help and guide us by His spirit, places in our hands a great deal of responsibility, so that we may grow up as His sons and daughters.

It is for this reason, I think, that Jesus asserted that "the Kingdom of God is within you." The Jews of His day were expecting a Messiah. They were looking for some leader to break in upon the pagan Roman conqueror with wrath and violence, with sword and fire. They were expecting God to rescue and vindicate His people in the sight of their enemies. It's not surprising that they didn't recognise Jesus as their rescuer, or appreciate His methods in founding a world-wide Kingdom.

The situation is much the same today. People say, in effect, "If there is a God, why doesn't he show himself in power?" "Why doesn't he put a stop to evil?" "Why doesn't he remove fear and sickness and want from the earth he's supposed to love?" Now we're not concerned with what we think God ought to do, but with what in fact He does do. And it appears that God hands back to man much more reponsibility than perhaps he bargains for. In theory and on paper, people are only too ready to see the fears and evils which afflict mankind removed. But how few are willing to act as God's agents, to work, at considerable personal cost, in the ceaseless battle against fear, disease, misery and want? "The Kingdom of God is within you," says Jesus, and it's really not the slightest good praying, "Thy Kingdom come, Thy will be done, in earth as it is in heaven," unless we're prepared to work and make that prayer come true. The moment we're ready to do this, the moment we seriously enlist on the side of the Kingdom of God, we find that there is spiritual reinforcement readily available from God. The greatness of God is there all right. But it's an invisible greatness, perhaps as different from our pre-conceived ideas as the Jews' idea of the Messiah was from the actual Christ.

Now I spoke a few minutes ago of the apparent weakness of God, but it is really a tremendous strength. You are at perfect liberty to defy God, to flout all His rules and make no attempt to co-operate with His purpose, and apparently there's nothing to stop you. But you and I live, as it were, "by kind permission of" God. We use bodies and minds and faculties which we had no hand in designing. We live in a world which we had no part in creating, and after the death of the body we pass on to a stage about which we know very little. So, although it remains true that God will never force our hands or overpower our wills, yet this is His world in which we live and move and have our being. In that sense God is quite inescapable.

Now sometimes it appears to us that goodness is a weak thing. The men

5

with a lust for power, the men with hard faces and tough consciences, appear to have the best time in this world, and the virtues of a Christ-like character appear to have little chance indeed against the tough, the violent and the evil. But in the end, whether it's in this world or the next, it will be plainly seen that goodness has a strange inner strength. What is more, goodness is permanent while evil is not. Goodness is part of the real and permanent because God is good, and although evil may survive in the mixed atmosphere of this world, sooner or later the game is up. There's no future in evil, only in good. People sometimes suddenly see this, even in this world. Saul saw it on the road to Damascus, when he suddenly realised that all his energies were being directed towards persecuting the real and good and permanent. He was travelling the wrong way in a one-way street. He was working against the very grain of the universe. And of course there have been thousands since those days who've seen, either suddenly or gradually, that God is in the long run undefeatable. It's a great day for anyone of us when we perceive that this world, despite its evils and imperfections, is a good world, part of a good universe under the ultimate control of a good God.

Nevertheless, no one, as I understand the teaching of Christ, is ever going to be coerced or frightened into the Kingdom of God. The Cross, the symbol of our faith and the very heart of its message, is not a sign of God's majesty and power conceived in earthly terms, but an unforgettable reminder of the lengths to which He will go to bring men to Himself. It has evoked love and wonder and the willingness to serve in countless thousands. Few indeed remain unmoved once they have realised who it is who suffered. "Christ crucified" is, as Paul once said, both the power of God and the wisdom of God.

How true a picture, then, do we hold in our minds of the real greatness of God? It's easy to magnify human characteristics to the nth degree and imagine that such a conception somehow resembles the Nature of God. Or we can imagine God as the Mind infinitely greater than any of the marvels He creates and sustains. All that is awe-inspiring, and its no bad thing to be awe-inspired. But size is not greatness, and awe is not love. And if we're to see the true greatness of God, and come to love and worship Him, we must look again at Christ. Perhaps we shall see the unfailing patience, the unremitting love and the invincible purpose which is the true greatness of the living God.

Sermon Two

TRUTH AND FAITH

Reverend Henry P. Van Dusen, Ph.D., S.T.D., D.D., L.H.D., Litt.D.

A Minister of the Presbyterian Church and President, Union Theological Seminary, New York, New York

As the President of one of the leading theological seminaries in America Dr. Van Dusen has an opportunity to direct the training of the ministers of today and tomorrow. Born in Philadelphia, Pennsylvania, in 1897, Henry P. Van Dusen studied at Princeton University, Union Theological Seminary, and Edinburgh University, Scotland, where he received his Ph.D. in 1932. His honorary degrees include the S.T.D. degree, from New York University, Columbia, Westminster Theological Seminary; the D.D. degree from Amherst College, Dartmouth, Colgate, Edinburgh University, Oberlin College, Yale University, Queen's University, Ontario, Harvard University; the Litt.D. from Jewish Theological Seminary; the L.H.D. from Bates College.

He began his career as an educator as instructor at Union Theological Seminary in 1926; he was Assistant Professor of Systematic Theology and the Philosophy of Religion from 1928 to 1931, Associate Professor from 1931 to 1936, and has been Professor of Systematic Theology since 1936. He is also Roosevelt Professor of Systematic Theology and Professor of Christian Theology. He was Dean of Students from 1931 to 1939, and has also been president of the faculty of Auburn Theological Seminary since 1945.

In 1924 Dr. Van Dusen was ordained to the ministry in the Presbyterian Church. He is a trustee of Princeton University, Ginling College, Nanking Theological Seminary, Yenching University, and the Little School. He is president of the United Board for Christian Colleges in China; a member of the Board of Foreign Missions, Presbyterian Church, U.S.A.; chairman of the Study Committee, World Council of Churches; president of the Union Settlement Association; and a trustee of the Rockefeller Foundation and the General Education Board.

He has written or edited more than twenty books, among them *In Quest of Life's Meaning, The Plain Man Seeks for God, Reality and Religion, For the Healing of the Nations, They Found the Church There, World Christianity, God in Education, Spirit, Son, and Father, One Great Ground of Hope.*

He has traveled around the world, visited South America, Asia, Africa, and China. This important sermon brings his philosophy and faith into vital perspective in a message for our day.

TRUTH AND FAITH

"You shall know the truth, and the truth will set you free."

John 8:32

"For this I was born, and for this I have come into the world—to bear witness to the truth. Everyone who is of the truth hears my voice."—"Pilate said to him, 'What is truth?'"

John 18:37, 38

"I am the way, and the truth, and the life."

John 14:6

This service, in this chapel, at this hour, marks the meeting-point of two of the most powerful and persistent concerns of the human spirit: the enterprise of learning, of education, in its tireless quest for Truth, in the conviction that "it is Truth which sets men free" and, the heritage of religion, in its claim to the trusteeship—not of all Truth, to be sure—but certainly of the key to Truth; the Christian religion focusing upon One who is not only the way and the life, but also, in some profound sense, the Truth.

However, these two—education and religion—may differ, however far apart their paths may at times seem to diverge, they are at one in their joint allegiance to a single sovereign—Truth. Moreover, it is obvious, isn't it, that if each rightly discerns that sovereign, and its claims upon them, they should discover themselves partners, yokemates, in a common battle against ignorance and error.

And so, it is altogether appropriate, indeed desirable, that from time to time these two great enterprises—education and religion—should be brought face to face, here in this university dedicated to the sovereignty of Truth, and in this chapel committed to the regnancy of Christ, the Truth. Here we may ask the question: "What is the right relation of Truth and Faith?"

8

I

But, to these general considerations, there is added a more immediate—what the current vernacular would delight to call a more "existential"—reason for taking this as the focus of our meditation this morning.

I have been much struck and disturbed by two recent, independent, comments on the state of religion in the U.S.A. at this time. They were made by two distinguished and unusually discerning European observers. Both affirm the widely recognized "return" to religion, and then, both go on to voice a misgiving, essentially the same misgiving!

After a year on the faculty of Cornell University, a brilliant young British philosopher, who had a marked influence among Cornell students, reported his discovery of a most surprising—in many ways, a most heartening—interest of American undergraduates in religion. He confirmed what is commonplace knowledge among those closely in touch with our schools and colleges and then confessed that there is one feature of this interest in religion which troubles him deeply: "students' almost total unconcern with the issue of Truth."

Perhaps the most perceptive and trustworthy European interpreter of the U.S.A. today, Professor D. W. Brogan of Cambridge University, summarized his impression:

"Religion in the U.S.A., like many other things, is booming. . . . That there is a genuine religious revival, I do not doubt. That the churches are not in retreat, I do not doubt. I do doubt whether the intellectual truce can be kept up indefinitely, in which few people dare to ask, 'Is this true?' Almost total unconcern with the issue of truth. Few people dare ask, 'Is this true?' "

It is not easy to say exactly what it is which these two commentators, from entirely different points of view and on the basis of quite different observations, are pointing to. But few of us would question that they are calling attention to something of real importance. At the least, they seem to be suggesting that in all the immense and favorable attention to religion in these days, no one is troubling—Professor Brogan says "no one dares"—to force the question as to whether the Faith which is so widely proclaimed and accepted is really true; whether its affirmations are grounded in reality. Behind this disinterest in Truth, beneath the surface, lies a hidden but debilitating, devastating, and ultimately disastrous scepticism as to whether

9

Christian Faith can stand up to rigorous scrutiny, can vindicate its beliefs as true.

Well, Dr. Brogan is certainly correct: if there be a truce between Intellect and Faith, between Learning and Religion, it cannot long continue; and, especially, in the centers of education. Here is added reason to re-examine the relations between these two great concerns which meet each other in this place to face Pilate's question "What is Truth?"

That that relationship has not always been one of easy and cordial partnership is obvious enough. How shall we think of the confrontation of Learning and Faith? What should be their right relationship?

II

We may well begin by recognizing that that relation must always be one of some tension, of strain. That tension is, in part, perennial, perpetual. It is, in part, immediate, particular.

The tension does not exist because these two elements are basically incompatible or contradictory, but because each always carries at its heart inadequacies, one-sidednesses, half-truths, to which the other is peculiarly sensitive; which it feels duty-bound to expose; which, ideally, it is its privilege to correct.

Learning in this modern age stands always under a three-fold temptation:

First, it is tempted to excessive contemporaneousness. In its preoccupation with new Truths, its glorying in genuine, authentic Truth, freshly discovered, it is forever tempted to disregard, if not deny, ancient, no less authentic truth. This is the essence of modernism: exaggerated confidence in the insights of the moment, disparagement of the wisdom of the ages. Learning in this country in our day always tends to be the unwitting slave of modernism, when it is not its proud exponent. Upon the superficiality and distortion of mere contemporaneousness, religion stands in perpetual judgment. It not only declares the larger Truth; it is itself a principal custodian and guardian of the wisdom of the ages. Moreover, so-called "new Truth" is never as wholly "new," never as completely "true," as is claimed.

On the other hand, Learning is forever tempted to premature finality, to declare not only "This new Truth is the only important Truth," but also "The new Truth is all Truth." Both of these temptations are, of course, enormously aggravated by the advance of modern science in its conquest of genuinely new Truth—in which broadly speaking, the latest is the truest. Over against this inadequacy, Faith should stand, not only as reminder of

10

the currently neglected Truth of ages past, but also as prophet of the fuller Truth of ages yet to be. Not that Faith itself has possession of that fuller Truth; not for a moment! But it should be alive to the large whole which forever surpasses and eludes man's grasp. The function of faith is to remind man with his limited and partial perspectives of the moment of the incompleteness of all men's fumbling grasp on Truth. But, it must be prepared to remind itself of that same Truth about Truth.

Again, Learning is forever tempted to an exaggerated estimate of the powers of human intellect, of reason alone, to discover and subdue all Truth. Intellectual pride and academic arrogance are among the most subtle, self-delusive, spiritually debilitating temptations which lure and mislead the human spirit. They are the pre-eminent temptation of the scholar, yes, and of the representatives of religion in centers of scholarship.

It is one of the functions of Faith to summon Learning to intellectual humility; to put scholarship in its place; and to do so, in part, by exposing the limitations of mere intellect, by insisting upon the wholeness of man— feeling and will, no less than mind—as alone adequate for the apprehension of Truth.

III

But, let us not suppose that the service of correction is one-way. Faith suffers its own distinctive temptations, temptations which Learning is peculiarly qualified to detect and expose:

One of these is the temptation to anti-intellectualism, the covert or open distrust of the mind, suspicion of clear, honest, critical thinking, which is inherently dangerous. Here, Learning summons Faith back to its own truer understanding of mind as a divine endowment, no less than feeling or will; Coleridge says, "He who loves Christianity better than truth will proceed by loving his own sect or church better than Christianity, and will end by loving himself more than all."

A second temptation is that of obscurantism, of uncritical traditionalism. For, if the standing vice of modern Learning is modernism, that of Faith in every age is traditionalism. Religion does not present itself to this confrontation clean and pure, the perfect repository of Truth. Its Faith is penetrated, permeated, and encrusted with superstition, like an ancient vessel which, in the course of its age-long passage down the centuries, has accumulated barnacles without and refuse within. From time to time, it must be dry-docked, scraped of its excrescences, purged of its dry-rot.

11

To this obscurantism, Learning brings the painful, humbling, but salutary catharsis of critical purging and cleaning.

Third, Faith is tempted to its own pride: pride of soul rather than of mind; spiritual rather than intellectual arrogance. If Learning often errs in its one-sided preference for understatement—affirming less of ultimate Truth than man actually possesses, Faith is perpetually guilty of the obverse vice—overconfident overstatement, pretence to more certitude than it actually has been given, and exaggerated claims to knowledge. Against this besetting sin of Faith, Learning brings the corrective of modesty in profession, spiritual humility.

IV

This perennial, inescapable tension has its special contemporary expression, determined by the historical background of our immediate "existential" situation. That background may be briefly summarized as: glorification of Learning and disparagement of Faith giving way to distrust of Learning and resurgence of Faith.

It should hardly be necessary to recall that historic sequence. It is within the memory of many of us when religion stood sore pressed, on the defensive, distrusted as to its claims to Truth, discounted as to its social utility—and nowhere so much as in the seats of Learning. Faith was branded an anachronism, a vestigial hangover from an earlier and less enlightened period in man's evolutionary advance, a kind of vermiform appendix of man's intellectual life. How often we listened, in those so recent days, to Learning's funeral dirge over Faith!

And yet, how long ago that day now seems—dim memories from an almost forgotten past. We have moved now into a new day. It would be an exaggeration to suggest that Learning is disparaged today; but its role as an all-sufficient interpreter of reality and guide for life is cast much more humbly. And, the other side of this picture, we have a "boom-day" for religion.

Yet, sad to say, the religion which seems on the way to reigning is rapidly slipping into all its traditional vices. Those vices from which religion's most conscientious exponents were being purged under the stern and stringent catharsis of modern knowledge, are reappearing: distrust of intellect, of the mind's painful quest for knowledge; discount of the achievements of modern thought; disdain of the issue of Truth; uncritical proclamation of a tradition still burdened and corroded with the deadweight of unexpurgated superstition; unjustified claims to more knowledge

12

than it really possesses; unjustifiable, and ultimately disastrous, spiritual arrogance.

How long will this situation persist? How long can the issue of Truth be evaded? Dr. Brogan is certainly correct: if there be a truce between Intellect and Faith, between Learning and Religion, it cannot long continue; especially in the centers of education. It is in the setting of these questions that we turn to inquire: What should be the Christian attitude toward Truth?

V

"You shall know the truth, and the truth will set you free." "Pilate said, 'What is Truth?'"

It would be interesting to know the inflection of voice with which Pilate's question was uttered. Was it scorn, as Francis Bacon supposed in his famous comment: "'What is Truth?' said jesting Pilate and would not stay for an answer"? Or was it, as another interpreter has suggested: "the cynicism of a disillusioned man of the world"? Or was there perchance in Pilate's voice at least an undertone of plaintive wondering, of wistful hope: "Is it possible that here, in this Jewish teacher of such majestic, commanding presence, there is light on life's central, unsolved enigma?" Or, most likely, was there in Pilate's voice a self-contradictory combination of derision and wondering, of cynicism and hope, with which the man of the world of every age, whether sophisticate or statesman, responds to this baffling enigma—to this Man who is Truth? No matter; Pilate uttered the world's poignant, ever-insistent, ever-thwarted question: "What is Truth?" He puts it to One whom Christian Faith declares, not simply to know the Truth but Himself to be, in some profound, mysterious sense, the Truth which sets men free.

VI

Well, in the conviction of Christian Faith, what is the answer to Pilate's question: "What is Truth?"

The mere mention of the word "Truth" inevitably suggests to our minds the meaning which we habitually associate with the term, the familiar dictionary definition: "agreement between statement and fact," such facts as science especially masters.

If we are really to comprehend what the word means, as Christian Faith uses it, we must undertake the difficult discipline of divesting our thoughts

13

of this conventional, accepted meaning, which we have inherited from the Greek philosophical tradition. It comes to us on the pages of the New Testament, this familiar word of five letters, worn thin and flat like a much-used coin, through familiarity. It is imbued with the heritage of a long history of development in the thought of the Hebrew sages and prophets which lies behind the New Testament. We shall never really come to terms with its meaning unless we have some feeling for that inheritance. It derived originally from a Hebrew word which means "to carry," "to support." Thence arose its richer meanings: steadiness, uprightness, steadfastness, faithfulness—all of them, you see, aspects of personal character, moral or ethical characteristics. And the source and ground of Truth is One marked, above all, by these same qualities: trustworthiness, fidelity, constancy; God Himself.

Truth is no mere acquaintance with, or description of, facts. It is apprehension of that which really is—of reality. And that reality in Hebrew certainty is God Himself, the living personal God, and for Christian Faith, the God and Father of Jesus Christ.

Truth is one of the great, central words of this gospel—this gospel whose determinative ideas and reigning convictions are embodied in a series of great words: light, life, love. Truth (with grace) is declared to be an attribute of Him Whom the gospel portrays: "The Word was made flesh and dwelt among us, full of grace and truth"; "Grace and truth came by Jesus Christ." At the end, looking beyond the end, there is promised the coming of the spirit of Truth, who will guide into all Truth. Midway between stands forth that amazing assurance: "You shall know the truth, and the truth will set you free"; and that even more astounding affirmation: "I am the way and the truth and the life."

To be sure, in the thought of this gospel there is an attempt to unite this mighty Hebrew tradition with the, to us, much more familiar Greek meaning: truth as correspondence with facts, a description of things as they are. Indeed, it is one of the writer's major purposes to make contact for the Christian gospel with the prevailing sophistication of Hellenism, to interpret that gospel in ways familiar to his sophisticated readers, to remint Hellenism's favorite words and ideas in the coinage of Christian Faith.

VII

And so, Christian Faith's answer to Pilate's question—the haunting question of the ages, and the plaintive query of our own time, and of this place with its central focus on learning—is given through this whole gospel, and

14

supremely in its central, pivotal declarations: Christ is the Truth. He is Way, and Truth and Life.

Yes; but what does that mean? Well, at least three things: G. K. Chesterton, with his penchant for paradox, once said: "The only important thing about knowing the truth is to know the really important truths."

Well, most of the most important Truths—what life is all about, its meaning and its destiny—what is worth knowing and seeking and having (what the philosophers call "values")—what is a "good life," a "good marriage," a "good home," a "good career"—almost all the really significant Truths— are personal, not only in the obvious sense that they concern persons and are known by persons, but also that they can be made known, disclosed, only through persons.

Just here is the major limitation of servitude to merely scientific norms and methods. As Clutton Brock once said of marriage, it is sheer common sense, but its implications are far-reaching. It is Faith's conviction that because Truth, all the Truth that matters most, is grounded in the reality of a living, personal God, it is disclosed—made known—to persons only through persons, fully only in a Person. If it is to furnish clear and sure guidance for human living, it must take flesh and dwell among us. Just that has in fact taken place, Christian Faith declares, in Jesus Christ. "In Him was life, and that life is the light (i.e. Truth) for men." He is the Truth because He is the life—the very life of God in the life of a man.

More than that. Because the ground of all Truth—God—is, above all, righteous and holy, the most important Truths are moral and spiritual. Yes, and for that reason, Truth must be morally and spiritually discerned. There are preconditions for its discovery—preconditions of the same qualities as Truth itself: uprightness, integrity, constancy, fidelity, steadfastness. Knowledge of Truth is through moral and spiritual kinship with Truth: "He who wills to do God's will shall know."

Finally, and by the same token, there are not only preconditions, moral and spiritual preconditions, for Truth's discovery. There are also consequences, moral and spiritual consequences. Because the deepest Truths thus discerned by the mind and soul of man are profoundly ethical and spiritual, they demand response in kind from those to whom they are made known. Truth, by its very nature, lays upon those who are privileged to enter within its presence the obligations of loyalty and obedience. They are primarily moral and spiritual obligations.

Here is the major word of Christian Faith to the world of Learning: the moral and spiritual preconditions and consequences of Truth. As one interpreter has put it: "Truth does not appeal solely to the intellect. That it

15

may be received, the moral dispositions of men must correspond with it; and its reception will further take effect upon character. If a certain moral attitude is a condition for receiving Truth, so also, when received, it has profound moral effects. It makes free."

What, then, is this freedom into which men are inducted by Truth? Formally, it is restoration to reality, to their real selves. Negatively, that means release from all that is false, unreal: insincerity, duplicity, hypocrisy; but also, fear, anxiety, self-preoccupation. Positively, it means kinship with Him who is Truth, glad obedience to His gracious command, participation in His life which is life indeed.

This freedom Christ has, in fact, bestowed, and continues to give to those who surrender themselves utterly to His sovereignty, His service, which is perfect freedom.

Sermon Three

BEYOND DISILLUSIONMENT TO FAITH

REVEREND JAMES S. STEWART, D.D.

*Professor of New Testament, Language,
Literature and Theology, New College,
University of Edinburgh; (Formerly Minister, North Morningside Church, Church
of Scotland), Edinburgh, Scotland. One
of the Chaplains to Her Majesty the
Queen in Scotland.*

This sermon takes up the problem of doubt and faith through reason.

For years Dr. Stewart was Minister of Morningside Church, Edinburgh, Scotland, before he was called to be Professor of New Testament, Language, Literature and Theology at New College at the University of Edinburgh. There his teaching helps to mold the thinking and careers of young ministers.

Preaching has been important in Scotland for at least four or five hundred years. The Scots grow up on good preaching, and the Kirk of Scotland has developed preaching of a high quality. From John Knox to James Black, John Baillie and James Stewart there has been a long line of great Scottish preachers who have spoken the gospel as they learned it in school and study and prayer.

When Dr. Stewart comes to America for his periodic visits, he is always sure of a warm welcome in New York or Boston or Chicago or Brooklyn or Los Angeles. He gave the Lyman Beecher lectures on preaching at Yale, adding stature to the long line of distinguished ministers who have given these great lectures.

His books have had wide influence on contemporary religious thinking: *A Man in Christ* (a discussion of the vital elements of Saint Paul's religion), *The Gates of New Life, The Strong Name, Heralds of God, A Faith to Proclaim* and *Thine Is the Kingdom.*

In 1959 he was invited to Australia to be guest preacher for three months in the Scots Church, Melbourne. In 1962 he was invited to give the Stone Lectures at Princeton.

17

BEYOND DISILLUSIONMENT TO FAITH

"The mirage shall become a pool."
Isaiah 35:7, R.V.m.

Israel in Canaan had come to terms with the desert. The desert bordered on Israel's lands, encroached on its fertile fields, marched right up to the roots of Olivet and the very gates of Jerusalem. The desert sent the terrible sirocco blowing from the east, carrying clouds of dust and sand across the sun. The desert was the breeding ground of fierce nomadic tribes which launched their hungry, harrying battalions across the Jordan. The desert had been the training ground of Israel itself during the forty terrible years when God was disciplining a rabble out of Egypt into a nation and a Church: those wilderness years had left a mark on them for ever. Out of the desert had come an Elijah, an Amos, a Jeremiah. In that same desert John the Baptist was to raise the standard of Messianic revival; and there Jesus, amid wild beasts and ministering angels, was to meet and rout the devil. It was against the constant background of this blistering, haggard wilderness that the people of God lived out their life. It fascinated their imagination, influenced their culture, haunted their literature, and colored their theology. The soul of Israel had come to terms with the desert.

This, in a deep spiritual sense, is still part of the human task. For we have to live our lives today—how well we know it in this atomic age—with chaos or the possibility of it just over the horizon. There are no wide comfortable margins any longer between civilization and the edge of doom. Ever since Hiroshima, the world has felt the breath of that sirocco full in its face. And indeed every man has to meet this issue in his own experience. For every pilgrim road to Jerusalem has its bare desolate tracts. Even here today there must be scores of personal stories of days of darkness and loneliness, barren days of grief and heartache and broken hope and paradise lost—and every story ending with the words "That was my desert day." It is immensely significant that all the great masters of the spiritual life—St. Augustine, à Kempis, St. Teresa—warn us repeatedly that we must reckon for the day when helpers fail and comforts flee and God seems to withdraw His face and the wilderness clamps down upon our souls. The Christian must come to terms with the desert.

Of all the desert phenomena the cruellest, the Jew would have told you,

18

was the mirage. Far away through the shimmering heat the desert traveller would see a bright oasis, tall green palm trees telling of living water. "Now God be thanked," he would cry, stumbling in the direction of his vision, "God be thanked for this great crowning mercy!"—only to find the vision receding, wavering, vanishing into nothing; and there on the bare rock at last he would lay himself down to die, mocked by that evanescent phantom, and perhaps even hearing in his soul the echoes of a more terrible mockery: "He that sitteth in the heavens shall laugh; the Lord shall have them in derision."

Israel had had this experience dramatically in her national history. Amid the desolation of the Egyptian bondage there was born a magnificent dream, the dream of freedom; and the day arrived when that dream came true, and out they went to taste of that living water, that intoxicating draught of liberty. What happened? Crushing disillusionment. "Liberty?" they cried to Moses bitterly, "Is this the prize we clutched at? We were better off as slaves. We have been fooled by life. The dream is illusion, the pool mirage. Lead us back to Egypt!"

This experience, the exact reverse of Isaiah's prediction here, is indeed one of the most familiar experiences of life. Sometimes the disillusionment is startling and crashing and overwhelming: Napoleon dreams of world conquest and empire, and ends crying:

> Great men are meteors that consume themselves
> To light the earth. This is my burnt-out hour;

Goethe contemplates at seventy-five the heaped-up prizes that the world has showered upon him, and writes "My existence has been nothing but pain and burden, the perpetual rolling of a rock that must be raised up again for ever"; Byron masterfully seizes life and compels it to stand and deliver the gold and jewels of the happiness he craves, but only to confess ere long:

> My days are in the yellow leaf;
> The flowers and fruits of love are gone;
> The worm, the canker, and the grief
> Are mine alone!

All this, indeed, is quite commonplace: the pool becomes a mirage so often. It has done this somewhere for every one of us. In fact, it is so familiar that if an Isaiah can come and reverse it, that really will be exciting. But it is well that we should first look this common experience in the face. "Good-bye to our day-dreams," wrote Captain Scott when he found himself forestalled at the Pole; and on less heroic levels hundreds of thousands have said the same. Good-bye to our day-dreams: perhaps they were too ethereal

19

for this rough, grudging world. Life so often refuses to play up to human desire, and the brave quest ends in disenchantment: so that Disraeli, with more than a touch of bitterness, could give it as his philosophy of life: "Youth is a blunder, manhood a struggle, old age a regret."

Many are feeling like this today about the quest for world brotherhood and peace. Humanity has seen that lovely vision from afar, the final oasis beckoning across the deserts of a world at war: not so very long ago it seemed quite near, and men were saying "We are almost there, just on the edge of it now! This is the dawn of the Golden Age, this is the birth of a brave new world." And then came such shattering disillusionment that thousands today have been left in the iron grip of pessimism and cynicism and despair. "What's the use of striving any more? Your dreams of a new world will always betray you in the end. Vanity of vanities, all is vanity!"

And often the experience is more intimate. Are you quite satisfied about your work to-day, the work you once thought was going to be so glorious and meaningful and worthwhile? And happiness? Has the fine flower of happiness not been buffeted by the storms and faded by the heat of the day? "Ah," wrote Thackeray, at the end of *Vanity Fair*, "which of us is happy in this world? Which of us has his desire? or, having it, is satisfied? Come, children, let us shut up the box and the puppets, for our play is played out." And what about character? How many of us are satisfied about that? We were going to construct something so strong and splendid and consistent, and what a poor shoddy thing it is after all—bits and pieces, nothing more! That dream of character which was going to lead us to living water—Oh God, it's just mirage!

Yes, if Isaiah can reverse this, it will be exciting indeed.

And religion? Even religion is not immune. The ultimate disappointment of life is the disappointment about God. "He trusted in God," jeered the rabble on Calvary, flinging its taunts up into the face of the dying Christ, "He trusted in God that He would deliver Him: let Him deliver Him now, if He delight in Him!" And the sting of it was that, to any on-looker there, God did nothing and no deliverance came and the tragedy dragged out to the end. "We trusted," said the two broken-hearted disciples on the Emmaus road to the unknown Traveller who had joined them, to whom they had been confessing their dreams about Jesus, "we trusted that it had been He which should have redeemed Israel"—and that is all over: it can never happen now.

> The Man upraised on the Judean crag
> Captains for us the war with death no more;
> His kingdom hangs as hangs the tattered flag
> On the tomb of a great knight of yore.

20

This is the ultimate disappointment, when God Himself disappoints, and the living water of divine grace becomes mirage.

It is a terrible hour when that final doubt assaults the soul. "How could I serve in the wards," cries the hospital nurse in Tennyson's poem, looking at the physical wreckage round her, "if the hope of the world were a lie?" But supposing the hope of the world *is* a lying mirage, what then? If Jesus Christ is mistaken, if His standards and interpretation of life are unfounded and illusory, then all our ideals and struggles are for nothing.

The man who wrote the Seventy-third Psalm knew something of the kind. I have done my best to keep straight and true, he cried, but what is the use of struggling for the right in a world that prospers the unscrupulous and sends virtue to the wall? "Verily, I have cleansed my heart in vain: in vain have I washed my hands in innocency." The fountain of life is mirage.

And if Jesus Christ is mistaken! If there is no Father of our spirits after all, no regnant and eternal scale of values, no everlasting differentiating standards to claim implicit sway, then we have taken the hard way needlessly, we have sacrificed so much for nothing, we have wasted time in prayer when we ought to have known that the heavens were as brass above our heads; we ought to have been eating, drinking and making merry, and the really wise people are the ones who have cast all Christian inhibitions overboard; our sins and repentances, joys and fears do not matter a straw. It is all one in the end. And the moral struggle is not worth the strain and effort. Not worth it!

There cannot be many Christians who get through life without meeting that fierce assault somewhere on the road. Perhaps we are meant to meet it. "My hosanna," declared Dostoevski, "has passed through great whirlwinds of doubt"; and many a man whose faith is impregnable to-day would say the same. Supposing I have been pursuing a will-o'-the-wisp in accepting the authority of Jesus? All very well for a religion to cry, "Whosoever will, let him take the water of life freely," but what if that offer is just an empty hollow mockery, and the living water a mirage? So thought Thomas Hardy, looking wistfully towards the fellowship of the Church in which he could not share:

> That with this bright believing band
> I have no claim to be,
> That faiths by which my comrades stand
> Seem fantasies to me,
> And mirage-mist their Shining Land,
> Is a strange destiny.

It is here that Isaiah breaks in so dramatically. With incredible daring he takes the cynical reading of life and the commonplace judgment of the

21

world which says that the pool will always turn out to have been mirage, he takes it and reverses it. "No," shouts Isaiah, "it's a lie! Hear the word of the Lord: The mirage shall become a pool!"

Life, he says in effect, is full of disappointments: wrecks of golden lovely dreams and broken bits of ethereal hopes: I know all that side of it, but—God is not mocked! In every situation, even when you are feeling disconsolate and desperate, grace reigns; and God's offer to your thirsty soul is not illusory; it really is living water. And it is running at your feet to-day. Oh taste and see how gracious the Lord is! Stoop down, and drink, and live. Indeed, it is the man who thinks he can find happiness in this world without God who is bound for the mirage, heading straight for disillusionment: the one thing certain about the dream of bliss that seeks to circumvent and bypass the law of God is that the dream will not come true. "Thou hast made us for Thyself, and our heart is restless until it rest in Thee." Do not fear, then, says Isaiah, to trust yourself to that wisdom and that love, even if the world thinks you a poor visionary and a fool: you are the true realist, and your hope will not deceive you in the end.

In that lovely poignant tale of African life *Cry, the Beloved Country*, Kumalo the village priest who has suffered much is speaking to Father Vincent. "It seems that God has turned from me," he says. To which Father Vincent replies: "That may seem to happen. But it does not happen. Never, never does it happen." If only we could trust like that!

Well, look at this. Was it not proved in Israel's own experience? They were carried away into exile, and they said, "This is the end. The glory is departed. Our hopes are finished. There is nothing left but heartache, misery, death. The pool is mirage." But there in Babylon the miracle happened. There, broken, prostrated and defeated, those homesick exiles discovered God, as not even in the shining days of David and Solomon and the Temple had they ever found Him before. "Yea, though I walk through the valley of the shadow of death and the shambles of Babylon, I will fear no evil, for Thou art there. Yea, though I make my bed in hell, behold, Thou art there!" So a new spiritual faith was born. "Israel went into exile a nation, and came back a Church." The mirage had become a pool.

All down the years this has been proved anew. The faith never glosses over the fact that Christ's call means sacrifice and discipline. But always it asserts that the sacrifice will be creative and the discipline transcendently worth while.

It is natural to tremble at the sacrifice Christ demands. It seems so often to cut right across life, till the heart begins to cry, "Don't demand this, Jesus! It is too much You are asking. Your yoke is too difficult, Your burden

22

far too heavy! You are surely forgetting that I am just common clay." But the miracle that came to Israel in exile happens again. And many here to-day could tell of it. The pain becomes creative. The thorns become a crown. You have a new power now for helping others. If it came to a choice, you know you would rather a thousand times be on that difficult road with Jesus than anywhere else in the world without Him. "O Jesus," your heart to-day is crying, "Your spiritual yoke that I rebelled against, Your moral burden that I hated—I know the truth about them now! If this is bondage, blessed be such bonds, and God forbid that I should ever seek to evade them. Your yoke is easy, and Your burden light!"

When you have reached this point, then indeed you have found the secret of all true zest and happiness and blessing. Here is a peace that is proof against the disappointments of the world: and the mirage has become a pool.

And we can trust it even though the world deride. St. Teresa in her day had a lovely answer to those who told her that her visions were delusion and mirage. She admitted she might perhaps mistake one person for an-other. "But," she went on, "if this person left behind him jewels as pledges of his love, and I found myself rich having before been poor, I could not believe, even if I wished, that I had been mistaken. And these jewels I could show them; for all who knew me saw clearly that my soul was changed; the difference was great and palpable." Teresa's hope in Christ was no imagination and mirage; it was a pool of living waters.

Was this not supremely the experience of our Lord Himself? Jesus set out from Nazareth with the dream of winning the whole world for God. And life took that splendid dream and seemed to shatter it to fragments. The world would not have His Gospel, the inquisitive thronging crowds soon dwindled into nothing, His best friends forsook Him and fled, and He died in the dark alone. The pool had become a mirage. But—and this is the victory—He died believing, sure that the shattered dream was still the very truth of God, that God would not leave His soul in hell nor suffer His hope to see corruption: and because of that, the Cross has veritably been the river of life for millions. "O Son of Man," cried George Matheson, "whenever I doubt of life, I think on Thee!"

> I came to Jesus, and I drank
> Of that life-giving stream;
> My thirst was quenched, my soul revived,
> And now I live in Him.

The mirage has become a pool.

Will you not trust it for your own life, with all your own particular problems and frustrations and bewilderments and disappointments? Francis Thompson, who more than most men had been fiercely buffeted by life, scourged by its apparent indifference to his dreams, and hurt callously and almost unbearably in the region of his emotions, had, like Job, felt the temptation to curse God and die and make an end. Everything he valued most seemed lost and every beckoning vision was mirage, but one day he heard a clear voice calling him from heaven:

> All which I took from thee I did but take,
> Not for thy harms,
> But just that thou might'st seek it in My arms.
> All which thy child's mistake
> Fancies as lost, I have stored for thee at home:
> Rise, clasp My hand, and come.

And will you not trust it too—that Christ's interpretation of life was based on no delusion, that He made no mistake when He called you to His service, that His offer to you today of happiness and peace and a satisfying life is really valid and substantial, and that the vision He has set before your eyes will never lead astray?

In our best moments we all know that. If only we could trust it always! I remember once near Interlaken waiting for days to see the Jungfrau which was hidden in mists. People told me it was there, and I should have been a fool to doubt their word, for those who told me lived there and they knew. Then one day the mists were gone, and the whole great mountain stood revealed. Next day the mists were back, but now I had seen, and knew myself that it was true. Men and women, let us trust the saints, the people who have a right to speak about the fellowship of Christ, because they have lived in that country all their lives. Yes, and let us trust our own moments of vision:what matter if there are days when the mists come down and the face of God is hidden? We have seen, and we know for ever that this is real, so real that by it we can live and die. And if you are in Church one day, even if you have brought a clamouring crowd of doubts and worries and perplexities with you, do tell yourself: This is the abiding reality of life! I have seen it with the mists off, and I know. It was valid once, and it is valid now and for ever. This is what matters most of all. This will stand when all the flowers of every primrose path that lures me from it have withered to corruption.

24

Sermon Four

BACCALAUREATE 1961

Nathan Marsh Pusey, PhD., LL.D., L.H.D., Litt.D.

*President of Harvard University, Cambridge, Massachusetts
and a layman of the Protestant Episcopal Church*

In this address Dr. Pusey reminds the Harvard graduating class of the significance of the spiritual life in every man's destiny. This is a time to believe, he says, and to act—"to act greatly." Dr. Pusey delivered this sermon in the Harvard Memorial Church on Sunday, June 11, 1961.

Nathan Marsh Pusey was born in Council Bluffs, Iowa, on April 4, 1907. At Abraham Lincoln High School in Council Bluffs he received the Charles Elliott Perkins Scholarship to Harvard, where he first met "the excitement of reading under the guidance of great teachers." Conrad Aiken, the poet, was his tutor there. Pusey's love of teaching grew out of his many associations with such people and with books. He received his A.B. in 1928, studied in France and Italy for a year, then returned to teach at the Riverdale Country Day School in New York City.

In 1931 he began the study of Greek literature and language, and subsequently entered graduate school at Harvard, where he received the Ph.D. degree in ancient history in 1937. In 1934 he won Harvard's chief literary honor, the Bowdoin Prize, and that same year went to Greece as an Archibald Cary Coolidge Fellow.

President Henry M. Wriston of Lawrence College engaged him to teach and help start Lawrence's "great books" course and later Scripps College asked him to develop a similar plan for them. He taught for four years in the newly instituted liberal arts program at Wesleyan University and in 1944 he was asked to become President of Lawrence College. At Lawrence he continued to develop the great books courses, and in 1953, he was named President of Harvard University.

Dr. Pusey explains his modern educational philosophy in this way: "Today the colleges and universities of America are inextricably embedded in and have become indispensable to our national life. . . . The variety of the ·services they perform and the dependence of more and more areas of our life on their activity and on their graduates now far transcend what was imagined even as recently as fifty years ago." He sees education not as a series of jumps, but as a continuous growth from nursery school through graduate school and beyond. He believes in better teachers and better paid teachers. With this in mind he laid out Harvard's advance program to raise $82,500,000 for additional endowment, new professors, new buildings, new educational developments.

It is clear from this thoughtful address that education and religion are a normal part of Nathan Pusey's own life and that he believes in their value for others.

BACCALAUREATE 1961

The baccalaureate service is an ancient Harvard tradition—perhaps almost as old as Commencement itself. Despite its antiquity—possibly because of it—it now presents special difficulties for us. I tried several years ago to suggest why this is so. I did this in part to clarify better the significance of the service, but also in the hope that bringing the difficulties into the open might blunt their prickles and so make the occasion less painful for the participants. I should like to make a somewhat similar beginning today.

The root of our difficulty is that by tradition this is a religious service, and in this generation in universities we are not at ease in exercises of common prayer. In this respect we may assume our situation contrasts sharply with that of our early predecessors who established the baccalaureate. Services of prayer were expected then and appear to have come naturally to our forebears; they do not come so easily to us.

Our inexperience with this kind of service is one source of difficulty, but there are others. Assuming that at least once in four years, at leave-taking, a class might like to come together in a service of worship, how today is this to be done? Three hundred years ago, two hundred, even more recently, a Harvard class may have been, if not a close-knit little band of Puritans, at least a relatively homogeneous group of New Englanders sprung from a common ethnic and cultural background. Now there are no longer such groups even in New England. Here we are Catholics and Jews as well as Protestants, and also Muslims and Buddhists, and all the rest. We come from all faiths—many of us from none at all—from various races, and increasingly from all parts of the globe. How under such circumstances can we worship together? I wish I knew.

The fact of cultural diversity has led to renewed efforts in our time to

26

find forms of worship which transcend ancient particularities, but at best these efforts have met with questionable success. Unfortunately, contemporaneously contrived liturgies do not have wide appeal, nor do they unite. If there is one thing which seems to be true of religious experience it is that it cannot be improvised or lived abstractly, but only concretely—in full involvement in the particularity of specific cultural and historical circumstance. This conviction underlies the program of the University's new Center for World Religions from which we hope much. Meanwhile we may dream of an empyrean of pure thought, but we are not born to such a realm. We are earth-bound creatures, and from this situation comes much of our present perplexity. In our cultural diversity, how today would it be possible to hold a universally acceptable and meaningful religious service in any hamlet or city of the world, or in any university for that matter? This is a very considerable part of our difficulty.

While our unfamiliarity with religious practices and our cultural diversity may hamper us, these barriers in the way of easy and moving participation by us in this baccalaureate service are but superficial compared with others which can be mentioned. Worship in our world is held back generally today by widespread spiritual rootlessness. Those who have moved from village to urban area in Africa or the East, those who have made the change from an agrarian to an industrial society in the West, even we ourselves in this restless, energetic, mobile America, have too often been torn loose from the roots of spiritual traditions. This difficulty has now been compounded in the West by the fact that we have had a series of consecutive generations neglectful of their spiritual inheritance. Indeed there are now many individuals who have had little or no help in understanding the nature and role of religion from either parents or grandparents. Here as in so many matters, it is difficult always to begin at the beginning, and yet in the area of religious experience this seems repeatedly what we must do.

A perhaps more immediate reason for our difficulty is a widespread failure of spirit in our time. President Kennedy and others trying to rouse peoples to action seem everywhere to meet a frustrating spiritual deficiency —perhaps even in themselves. For the confidence and hopefulness and eagerness to proceed which historically have been the fruits of faith are now too frequently simply not there—or too feebly there. All leaders are crying out for unifying purpose and direction and a will to push ahead. Everywhere these are the great desiderata of our time. Lacking them we find it difficult to come together in community of spirit in any enterprise. And failing this, we do not cleave together or move forward.

Ours is more a mood of dispiritedness than of despair. It is not difficult

27

to find justification for this. Consider only the impact on all of us of certain public events during the brief four years you have been in college.

When you came here in the autumn of 1957 a contention of will, not yet resolved, had closed the high schools in Little Rock simply because a few Negroes had wished to enroll in them. You were scarcely settled here when the Russians put their first satellite into orbit and plunged us, as a nation, into deep anxiety from which we have not yet fully recovered.

Your experience at Harvard began in a troubled season. Then as now the frustrating question of controlled world disarmament occupied a central position in the minds of thoughtful people—perhaps more hopefully then than now. Also we were much preoccupied with the baffling problem of a constructive organization of the several American nations. Castro was still in the hills. Souvanna Phouma announced a decision to take the Communist-supported Pathet Lao group into the government of Laos. But it is only fair along with these discouraging events to note that in the autumn of 1957 the late lamented Camus was awarded the Nobel Prize for literature. He has had much to say to people of this generation because of his persistent and stoical affirmation of the strength of the human spirit.

Such was the character of public events in the autumn of your freshman year. It has not changed dramatically since. Latin America, Algeria, East and Southeast Asia—these regions were much in the press then and have continued to be almost constantly ever since. Also, increasingly, Africa—South Africa, Ghana, the Congo, and now Angola.

In the spring of your freshman year Allen Dulles declared that the rate of economic growth in the Soviet Union was twice that of the United States. In the autumn of your sophomore year the Russians announced they had developed intercontinental missiles with sufficient thrust to bring us into range. And at the same time the Chinese, backed by millions of population, were being unpleasantly aggressive in the Taiwan Strait.

The spring of your sophomore year had a somewhat different tone. Batista was gone, and Castro had come to power. Before you had left for the summer, he was to appear—and be welcomed!—in Cambridge. Once again we were working toward a relationship of good feeling with the Russians. It had been decided that our nations should exchange professors, performing artists and other kinds of people. A congress of foreign ministers met in Geneva. The following fall, as you became juniors, Khrushchev came to America. Momentarily the general world situation seemed improved. Scientists of the U.S.S.R. and the U.S.A. were getting together—as to a degree they still are. But then suddenly came the exposé of the rigged quiz shows, and, in the spring, the shock which attended—rightly or wrongly—

the U-2 incident and the collapse of the Paris Conference. There have been other disillusioning experiences since, some so recent as to be fresh in everyone's mind. The apparently insoluble problem of Berlin remains. So do many other difficult international situations, and every month new ones are added. Meanwhile the number of refugees loose in the world is larger now than it was right after World War II, and the population menace races onward.

In a frighteningly disturbed world situation we continue uncertain in our behavior and in our will. We remain irresolute, and tend increasingly to quarrel among ourselves, while the Communists chant ever more loudly that they will win without war. In such a gloomy atmosphere the many recent advances in science and medicine, the growth of ecumenical activity among church groups, the achievements of the World Bank, the accomplishments of the International Geophysical Year, the recent adventures into space, the increasing opportunity for meetings of people across cultural barriers, the joys of your undergraduate life, the beauty of your choral groups and of so many of your achievements—these and other similarly hopeful acts weigh lightly in the scale. When we are serious, we can say of ourselves, as Shelley writes in "Adonais" that

> . . . . fear and grief
> Convulse us and consume us day by day,
> And cold hopes swarm like worms within
> our living clay.

The question we must ask ourselves is, how do we behave, or what stance do we assume in face of such a world?

A few weeks ago one of you asked me if an individual "reasonably idealistic" (I believe those were his words—at any rate, I like them) if an individual reasonably idealistic could go into politics and hope to hold to and care for the convictions which he had acquired here concerning people and how they ought to live. I am afraid I gave a very poor answer at the time, and though I have been brooding about his question since, I doubt that I can do much better now. It is an old question, asked in every generation—not just about politics, but about almost every one of the possible careers open to men. All one can say in reply is, "I simply do not know," or, "It depends."

It is wrong, of course, to begin by thinking either that goodness is firmly fixed in oneself or that wrong and corruption are necessarily lying in wait at every turn outside. Neither of these things is ever true; but despite these considerations, there is reason in each generation for a person embarking upon a career to feel apprehensive both about himself and about

29

the forces, the possibly very hostile forces he is bound to encounter. It may well be, as is so often said, there is more reason now for such apprehension than ever before; certainly there is as much. The Christians' low opinion of the unredeemed world has never been unsupported by evidence.

How does an individual, "reasonably idealistic," make his way in the world without being overwhelmed, defeated, or, even worse, corrupted by it? This is the big question, and the answer must be, in each individual case, that we simply do not know. But all along people have been doing it—people in all ages who have cared and loved and worked, and not been easily discouraged. The world has a crying need for such people now. Perhaps the answer the question calls for is only an artless resolve to face up to the task, to have the courage to be human—to face up to it despite the disheartening knowledge that even the best of those who have gone before us have done it only imperfectly.

We are now involved together in a very trying, a very frustrating, indeed a very maddening situation, where progress seems not only slow but almost impossible and where there appears to be almost no hope of order, permanence or stability in human affairs. More and more, our mood, as a consequence, is simply to try to hang on. Less and less do we expect advance. But in our hearts we know—and the thought will not let us alone—that what the world of men demands of us and is crying for is that we resist and overcome this debilitating inertia in our human condition. This is no time to feel sorry for ourselves. It is a worse time to blame or fear others. It is a time to act—a good time to act greatly.

But there is little encouragement to this kind of action. Also we learn as we go along that to make any progress at all we stand constantly in need of help. For this reason it is my opinion that the best answer which can be given now to the question asked is that one begin by ceasing to think of religion as something unrelated to contemporary life, as something "outgrown" since the time of those who founded Harvard College, or as an enterprise which in any way counsels withdrawal from life. Rather we should regard it as both an aid and a present necessity, and learn to pray for the strength to stand steadfast against both unconcern and, more deeply, despair.

Many of you came to hear Reinhold Niebuhr preach in this church each year during your time in college. Next year, at long last, we shall have him in residence for a term. Through a long generation he has offered an exceptionally profound commentary on our times. Recently I came on a summary statement from him quoted by another which I reproduce here as an admirably concise expression of what many, taught at least in part by him, would now agree is the deepest need of this time. Our need, he says, is for "religious faith and a humanism more profound than many extant varieties (in order to) make sense out of these terrifying facts of modern history, particularly those facts which prove that all historic responsibilities must be borne without the certainty that meeting them will lead to any ultimate solution of the problem, but with only the certainty that there are immediate dangers which may be avoided and immediate injustices which may be eliminated."

Perhaps this is only an attempt at restatement of the meaning of the Cross, but if so, it clearly comes not from rote, but from discovery.

Over and above knowledge, is it not true that what we want finally from Harvard—or perhaps I should say, what we should like to have grow in us while we are here—is an underlying, lifegiving faith of the kind defined by Mr. Niebuhr? Though we use different methods of expressions, different words, different mental images, is not this what those who have loved Harvard most deeply in all generations have felt to be her finest gift —a life-giving spirit to undergird and confirm the works of mind, and to purify them, at least partly, of the limiting corruptions of self? Surely it is something like this that "Veritas" connotes. Not syllogistic truth, not accuracy, not correct statement. These things yes, but deeper than them and encompassing them all, as the founders intended, the Lord's truth which makes men free. I can think of nothing more precious that one might take from Harvard than a glimpse of the deeper meaning of this word and at least the beginning of an allegiance to it. This is what I have wished to say to you today.

All round us are grounds for frustration and despair. And for cynicism. And they multiply every day. Problems do not get solved; they seem only to accumulate. Catastrophe follows catastrophe. One after another our instant hopes come to grief. The end of trouble and worry is not yet; nor will it be. The trial of nerve, announced long since, is now well underway. How in this world not just to survive, but how to remain "reasonably idealistic"? How to wish to go forward, to do something constructive, and to find the will to do it? These are our questions and our problem. I have no ready, convincing answer to give you concerning them. But it will be a great joy to all who have known you here and have become interested in you, if in this most difficult matter of how a man lives constructively in a troubled world you have decided to sign on for the duration. If this be so, Harvard has at least served to start you in a right direction where in time a hopeful answer may be found.

I can vividly recall the laudatory welcome which greeted you as freshmen

31

Sermon Five

A MOVING FORCE MADE FLESH

REVEREND W. GODDARD SHERMAN

Pastor, Melrose Park Methodist Church,
Fort Lauderdale, Florida

This sermon on Desiderius Erasmus, the Dutch humanist, scholar, theologian, priest, satirist and author, demonstrates the use of biography for sermonic purposes.

William Goddard Sherman was born in Jacksonville, Florida, in 1921, and began his career as a commercial artist, after graduating from the Art Institute of Pittsburgh. But feeling the call to become a preacher of the Word of God, he entered Brown University, where he took his degree in liberal arts, then did his theological work at Boston University School of Thelogy and Pittsburgh-Xenia Theological Seminary. Following graduation from the seminary he became a member of the Florida Conference of The Methodist Church in 1953.

He has had sermons published in the *Christian Advocate* and other periodicals and in books. His particular interest is in Transcendentalism. His artistic talent is still evident in the cartoons he has had published in national magazines and in the pen sketches he creates for church bulletins from Maine to California.

A MOVING FORCE MADE FLESH

No movement achieves vitality until its spirit becomes incarnated in human life. In a very real sense the deep core of meaning behind the Renaissance came to life in the person of the Dutch humanist, Erasmus.

Too little thought is given to this great forerunner of the Reformation, although he continues, if we will let him, to speak to our time. Men always build upon foundations which previously have been laid. In terms of the Reformation the name of Luther leaps from every common tongue; in truth he built upon ground which had been prepared by the prince of humanists. Indeed, it was said that Erasmus laid the egg which Luther hatched, though the Dutchman reputedly exclaimed, "But I expected a different sort of bird."

In the same year that Columbus discovered America, Erasmus was ordained a priest. His whole life was to be spent in interpretation and reformation, that the power of of the gospel should become known in the lives of people in every area. In a day when the Church was tarnished, even polluted, by corrupt men, here was a dedicated scholar who wished to approach as near as possible to Christ. "Above all," says one biographer, "he wished the world around him to be conformed to Christ in the inner man—to drink deep into His Spirit—to be in truth so one with Christ, as to judge by the same standard, and to appreciate at the same value, and to cherish the same feelings towards every object in earth and heaven, every interest both in time and eternity."

Erasmus speaks to our time because the questions which he asked of his own still shatter our complacency. He remarked that while men were seeking knowledge with so much eagerness, still the philosophy of Christ was ridiculed by some, and neglected by the majority. With biting sarcasm he pointed out that in all other branches of human learning "there is nothing so hidden and abstruse, that the sagacious intellect of man has not fully examined it." Then with sharp exactness he asked, "How then is it that this is the only philosophy which is not studied with equal earnestness, at least, by those who make a profession of Christianity?"

We need to be stirred by such questions, for there are many who cannot give reason for the hope that is in them. Why do we not show more zeal in the things of Christ? The communist knows what communism teaches, and is well versed in Marxist philosophy. Erasmus had observed that it

34

would be disgraceful for one who professes his belief in the philosophy of Aristotle to be ignorant of what Aristotle taught. Is it not also a disgrace and a tragedy that Christians are so vaguely conversant with the teachings of Jesus Christ?

The sixteenth century humanist brought out the first edition of the New Testament in Greek, in 1516. His purpose is found in his conviction that it is impossible to understand the Scriptures unless one can read them in the original languages. The translation was not completely accurate because, for one thing, it was written in great haste in order to see publication before a similar work by Ximenes. But it must be realized that there were no dictionaries available, and it was all but impossible to be certain regarding the precise meaning of some phrases and words.

The Church which Erasmus so sharply criticized and violently satirized opposed his publication of the Bible. The scholastics and monks in particular were opposed to making the Scriptures available to the people. The Church desired to remain the sole interpreter of the Bible. But Erasmus desired that "the husbandman should sing the verses while following his plough, the weaver while throwing his shuttle, and that the traveller should beguile with them the tedium of his journey."

One of the chief reasons the schoolmen opposed the Greek rendition was that they held the absolute inspiration of every letter of the Latin Vulgate. If the problem of inspiration were confined to the Reformation era this would be a matter only for theologians and historians. The fact is that this is still a controversial matter: "What do we mean by inspiration of the Scriptures?"

A radio preacher not long ago suggested that the biblical writers were merely tools in God's hands, and that they had no understanding of what they were writing. There are many persons who think of inspiration as being miraculous and unnatural. But the very word implies breathing, which is most natural. A miracle is a violation of, or a setting aside of, that which we describe as natural law. Breathing is a natural function, and it is a divine function to breathe into human spirits. The Bible cannot be termed a miraculous book, for it has come in fulfillment of natural law, not in violation of it.

Erasmus could not accept the dogma of verbal inspiration of the Vulgate. Because he saw more clearly than other churchmen, he rescued the Scriptures from the Roman Church, which had frequently interpreted them to favor particular Roman dogmas.

Martin Luther has been called the Great Reformer, but in actual fact he was more of a revolutionist. It is Erasmus who was the true reformer, for he always remained loyal to the Church and desired to make changes by leavening from within. Roland H. Bainton has remarked concerning Luther, "The church threw him out. He excommunicated the church."

Whatever can be said about these two in their relationship to the Church, it is important that we see their relationship to each other. All of the reformers, Luther not excepted, were deeply indebted to Erasmus. The great Dutch humanist relied heavily upon reason, and it was his conviction that reason condemned many Roman dogmas. Luther is famous for his theses posted against the sale of indulgences, but he borrowed his nails from Erasmus, who was equally firm against the practice. Erasmus wrote *In Praise of Folly* deriding those who "derive comfort from false pardons and indulgences . . . , who, having cast down a small piece of money, taken from that vast amount which they have gained unjustly, think that all their guilt is purged away."

Erasmus was stabbing at the very heart of something deeply imbedded in religious practice: the use of magic. Magic is man's attempt, by whatever means, to bend the natural forces to unnatural ends; to cause God to act in behalf of man. Erasmus wrote against images and relics, and the worship of saints and the Virgin Mary. His masterful pen described a shipwreck in which all addressed themselves in agonizing cries to the saints. Those who clutched images to their bosoms were pulled under by their weight. The one sane person, and the only true Christian, was one who prayed directly to God.

Again Erasmus speaks to our age, for reliance upon magic is surely not put away from us. Protestants ridicule Catholicism for its emphasis upon images and relics, but magic in a cheap and debilitating form is still present among Protestants.

Our emphasis upon magic stems from the fact that we want a God we can manage—someone has called it a desire for "a packaged God and a packaged religion, all nicely delivered in the large economy size." We need not look far to discover that we rely too heavily upon a Santa Claus-like deity who responds immediately to our whims which we breathe as prayers. The peace-of-mind cult is concerned too much with bending God's will to ours, so that when we push the prayer button we get a satisfying answer which frees us from our tension. Perhaps we need to remember that music at its best comes from strings which have tension, but those which are completely relaxed offer tones merely flat and dull.

The history of religion is in fact the history of man's attempt to control God; not always has it been a history of man's willingness to be yielded to

Him. But as Phillips Osgood has observed, "The ideology of magic is diametrically against truth; therefore it is *immoral*."

Erasmus of Rotterdam exclaimed, "You think that a lighted taper is a sacrifice. But David calls the sacrifices of God a broken spirit. Of what use is it for the body to be covered with a holy cowl, when the soul wears a filthy garment?" They called him a heretic, but it is a challenging thought to us within the stream of orthodoxy that flaming truth has burst upon the world through the channel of the way called heresy: Jesus, Plato, Socrates, Galileo, Servetus, Priestley, Emerson—branded as heretic every one, but they brought truth to the world. What is more, they were conscious of truth without resorting to the use of magic, for they saw more clearly than the orthodox that magic obscures God, but a pure soul finds Him real.

God is not a gimmick; He cannot be used. The pure in heart shall see God, as Jesus long ago promised, and this without the aid of magic. God will become a vital force in the lives of those who live according to His holy will, but no amount of hocus-pocus will make God active in the life of one who does not love Him.

Erasmus—a moving force made flesh. The spirit of truth gripped his soul and he gave his life to making truth known in every common life. Who can deny that such a man has something to say to our own time?

Sermon Six

THE CONFLICT OF LOYALTIES

REVEREND ROBERT JAMES MCCRACKEN, D.D., S.T.D., L.H.D.

Minister, The Riverside Church, New York, New York

Born in Motherwell, Scotland, Robert McCracken grew up in a Scottish Presbyterian home, went to the local school, and became a member of the Baptist Church in Motherwell. He graduated from Glasgow University and became minister of Marshall Street Baptist Church in Edinburgh. In 1933, he became lecturer in Systematic Theology at the Baptist Theological College in Scotland. Thus he became both preacher and teacher. In 1937, he was called to teach theology and the philosophy of religion at McMaster University in Ontario, Canada.

During 1937 and 1938 he took a special year of study at Cambridge University to prepare himself for his work at McMaster, then assumed his chair in 1938. In 1945 and 1946 he was president of the Baptist Convention of Ontario and Quebec. In 1946, he was called to the Riverside Church to succeed Dr. Harry Emerson Fosdick when he retired. In 1955, he became a naturalized citizen of the United States.

In this new post he again became both pastor-preacher and teacher, for he was appointed Lecturer in Practical Theology at Union Theological Seminary, New York and is now Associate Professor of Practical Theology there. He has lectured at Andover, Yale, Union (Richmond), Princeton Seminary, Southern Baptist Seminary, McMaster, Pacific School of Religion, and Auburn Seminary. He preaches on the National Radio Pulpit every year.

Dr. McCracken's books include *Questions People Ask*, *The Making of the Sermon*, and *Putting Faith to Work* (in which this sermon was included as one of a series).[1]

In 1957, he traveled to Japan at the invitation of the Japan Committee for Intellectual Interchange. While in the Far East, he visited Hong Kong, the

---

[1] Robert J. McCracken, *Putting Faith to Work* (New York: Harper and Brothers, 1960), used by permission of the publisher.

Philippines, Thailand, Burma, India, and Pakistan. He saw the U.N. at work and visited missionaries, State Department officials, and leaders in education and religion.

The importance of his work has been recognized by thirteen universities or colleges by the conferring of honorary doctorates: The S.T.D. by Columbia University; the D.H.L. by Bates College, Shurtleff College, Pratt Institute; the D.D. by McMaster, Bucknell, Glasgow, Colgate, Denison, Princeton, Vermont, Wake Forest, and Colby.

THE CONFLICT OF LOYALTIES

Loyalty is one of the royal virtues. He who is without it lacks a quality indispensable to true character. It is not just a personal quality. It is the cement of society. In every realm—the home, the church, the nation, the community of nations—loyalty is what holds human life together. Without it all these institutions would fall apart.

The problem for many, however, is not how to be loyal—faithful to love, to duty, to vows, to obligations—but how to deal with conflicting loyalties. Naaman, the Syrian, cleansed of his leprosy, swore that he would thenceforth be loyal to the God of Israel, but he had hardly done so before he realized that when he went back to Syria he would have to go with his master into the temple of Rimmon, and when his master bowed down to worship Rimmon, he would be expected to do likewise. One can sympathize with Naaman's dilemma. There was the duty he owed to the God of Israel and the duty he owed to his monarch, the king of Syria. "Bowing down in the house of Rimmon," has become a proverbial expression to denote the danger and dishonesty associated with compromise. Yet when loyalties conflict, how is compromise to be avoided?

It may be a conflict of loyalties in the course of the day's business. An employee is asked to do something that his conscience does not approve. Dependent on him and his earnings are his wife and children. What is he to do? Register a protest? Give up the job? Tell himself that the employer is responsible, not the employee?

In 1742, John Woolman, the Quaker, was a clerk in a store. He kept a journal and in it set down this entry.

"My employer, having a Negro woman, sold her, and desired me to write a bill of sale, the man being waiting who bought her. The thing was sudden; and though I felt uneasy at the thought of writing an instrument of slavery for one of my fellow-creatures, yet I remembered that I was hired

40

by the year, that it was my master who directed me to do it, and that it was an elderly man, a member of our Society, who bought her; so through weakness I gave way and wrote it; but at the executing of it I was so afflicted in my mind, that I said before my master and the friend that I believed slave-keeping to be a practice inconsistent with the Christian religion. This, in some degree, abated my uneasiness; yet as often as I reflected seriously upon it I thought I should have been clearer if I had desired to be excused from it, as a thing against my conscience; for such it was."

The conflict of loyalties may take place in wartime. In 1941, when I was teaching at McMaster University in Hamilton, Ontario, a student came to talk with me. He told me that he hated war and that, as a Christian, he didn't think he should have any part in it. But he loved Canada, and he felt that the whole democratic way of life was in mortal danger. Besides, he said, he could not endure to see so many of his classmates go off into the service while he stayed at home and, in comfort and security, made a study of philosophy and ethics. He enlisted in the Royal Canadian Air Force, got his wings, was shot down over the Irish Sea, was the last man (his comrades testified) to bail out, and he alone of the crew was never seen again. Stanley Gaudin, a fine upstanding lad, the only son of a widowed mother —I can see him yet as he discussed with me the problem of conflicting loyalties.

What a fierce and terrible conflict it is! There was the Christian member of the French Resistance Movement who wrote as he went underground:

"I ask God that He now forgive my sins, and the decision which I voluntarily take this day (for I know that recourse to violence has need of pardon). But I am leaving without hate and fully convinced that we Christians have not the right to leave it to non-Christians alone to offer their lives."

If only all that was asked were to offer one's life! Did that French Christian have to do what so many in the Resistance felt obliged to do—forge ration books, steal passports, liquidate traitors, come stealthily on an enemy from behind and knife him? There was a scene in the film "The Cruel Sea" in which the captain exclaimed in anguish of mind after sinking a U-boat at the cost of dropping a depth charge among his own men struggling in oily waters, "I suppose you must just go on and do what you have to do— and say your prayers."

Consider the conflict of loyalties to which thousands upon thousands of our fellow Christians on the other side of the Iron Curtain are being subjected right now. The issue of loyalty to one's country and government poses one of the most poignant and difficult questions in life. What does a Christian in one of the satellite countries feel about it all? For example,

41

what should be the attitude of a Christian when he sees a government in power that denies the spiritual basis upon which he himself interprets life, but at the same time is carrying through land reforms which, as a Christian, he has long desired to see? We ought not too quickly to come up with dogmatic answers to those pressing questions. We are not living there. We are not familiar with all that is at stake. We do not know at first hand the tension that such conflicting loyalties create. Nor are we forced to work out the problem as they must in concrete situations and personal relationships.

Thus far I have been doing no more than stating the case, showing how a conflict of loyalties may arise in the course of the day's business, in wartime, in a Christian's relation to his country or his government when violence is done to Christian principles. These are issues about which we should be sensitive and to which we should give careful thought. It is easier, of course, to pose the problem than to come up with solutions. There are no simple solutions. It is hard to be a Christian.

For instance, when should one obey, and when defy, a law which one in conscience believes to be unwise or even morally wrong? It is easy to say that the voice of conscience should be supreme. But is there no difference between an instructed and an uninstructed conscience? It is easy to say that no man-made law should override the dictates of conscience. But some deference is due to established authority. How and where should the line be drawn?

Is it ever right to tell a lie? Even as I raise the question, I think of Carlyle's thundering reply: "Truth! though the heavens crush me for following. No Falsehood! though a whole celestial lubberland were the price of apostasy." But I think, too, of the saintly bishop in Victor Hugo's great novel coolly fabricating a lie to save a thief from arrest, and saying to him: "Jean Valjean, my brother, you belong no longer to evil, but to good. It is your soul I am buying for you. I withdraw it from dark thoughts and from the spirit of perdition and give it to God." For the bishop, the virtue of truth was related to justice and mercy. Facts, he saw, could actually get in the way of truth. If you pass judgment not on the bishop's action but on his motives, you will let him go uncondemned.

Is it possible to do always what is ideally right? Stanley Gaudin, the Canadian student to whom I referred earlier, did not find it possible. And many another has found himself in a position where, through no fault of his own, there seemed no right course open to him but only a choice between evils. That was what going to war meant in the forties for countless young Americans, not a holy crusade but the lesser of two evils. So, rather than take his country into war Neville Chamberlain tried appeasement for

42

the sake of keeping the peace. It was a compromise and there is rarely anything idealistic about a compromise. You probably criticize him. So do I. After the event we can all do that. Yet Chamberlain, born and bred in Unitarianism, was probably no lover of compromise. A policy of appeasement is not heroic. Take the case of Hans Simons, former president of the New School for Social Research. Living in Hitler's Germany, the conflict he was torn by was between compromising for self-preservation or becoming a martyr for a cause. He was in a position where he had the choice of either challenging Nazism openly, or compromising to the extent of saving his own life. In the first case, he reasoned, he would have ended up in a concentration camp and been silenced. In the other, he could hold his tongue for the time being and try to get out, and from the outside fight Nazism. He recognized that there were strong arguments either way. He says that nobody who has not had to make them for himself can possibly know how irreconcilable they are. Repeatedly in life it is like that—the choice not between black and white but between differing shades of gray.

A Christian, however, will not make this an excuse for lowering his standards and conforming to the ways of the world. He will not give up trying to apply his Christianity to everyday life. He will strive to act as nobly as possible in every situation, in wartime, in race relations, in the fiercely competitive world of business, seeking always to select the better of two alternatives. By so doing, he will not only cultivate a worthy character but will do his part in building up a better state of society in the future, so that things impossible for him may be possible for future generations.

Maxims like "One step at a time" and "Half a loaf of bread is better than none" are not necessarily maxims of worldly prudence. Those who by nature are idealistic have no patience with them, are contemptuous of them. But doesn't it often happen that the idealist, after declaiming indignantly about an evil situation, withdraws into an ivory tower? Two global wars and the present state of the world ought to have taught us that the human conditions for an ideal solution of our national and international problems are not yet present. As Christians we shall serve our generation most by seizing on whatever of good the situation of the moment makes possible. By the vigilant detection and the practical use of each concrete opportunity of improvement and reform we can lift society to a higher level.

I know of no Christian of our time who was more concerned to apply his Christianity to everyday life, to business, to politics, to questions of war and peace, to national and international relations, than William Temple. But if he had his head in the air he kept his feet on the ground. He was a practical Christian statesman. He believed that Christian principles would

43

be workable if a sufficient number of people would get behind them, but he accepted the fact that people by and large do not get behind them, and he joined hands with them to secure the lesser good they were willing to support. He worked with his fellows for the second best when they were not ready to work for the best. He preferred to achieve in co-operation with them an attainable good, while at the same time he kept pointing them to the supreme good. He once said, "It is certainly a mistake to begin with the picture of a supposedly ideal system and try to establish it. The way of Christian progress is to ask where an existing system is breaking down and readjust it in the light of Christian principles." If this be compromise, it is, as with the bishop in Victor Hugo's novel, a compromise of action, not of ideals.

Even so, compromise has its limits. What those limits are each of us must find out in each case for himself, keeping before us continually the example and spirit of Christ. We shall be on our guard, prayerfully and constantly, against a lowering of standards and a cowardly compliance with the demands of self-interest and worldliness. We shall be on our guard, prayerfully and constantly, lest a minor loyalty lead us to sacrifice a major one. That is the thing especially to avoid: a little loyalty to one's family, one's profession, one's class, one's race, pressed at the expense of a larger one. Jesus has so much to say about that. Devoted to our family, but unconcerned about other families. Devoted to our nation, but caring little about other nations. Devoted to our denomination, but isolated from, if not critical of, our brethren in other denominations.

And first, last, always, we must remember that our supreme loyalty is to God. John Gunther tells us that whenever he visits a country and asks about the leading political personality and talks to him, he tries to focus on two questions: "What are the real sources of power behind the man? What does he believe in most?"

What do you and I believe in most? When the choice of loyalties finally narrows down, in what direction does it point? For that is the real source of power behind us. Is it our family? Is it our profession? Is it our nation? Is it God?

And now, as an illustration of the way in which a Christian can deal with the conflict of loyalties, I quote the tribute of a friend to Judge Augustus N. Hand.

Those who watched the victory of the spirit in Judge Hand gained new insight and new courage. They became convinced that beyond the clash of interests and the compromise of competing claims there can be found standards of rectitude and generosity, and that in the search for these standards and in the steadfast adherence to them lies the triumph of man. To quote the words that the poet Archibald MacLeish wrote in his honor, Judge Hand taught us that—

> We are neither weak nor few.
> As long as one man does what one can do—
> As long as one man in the sun alone
> Walks between the silence and the stone
> And honors manhood in his flesh, his bone,
> We are not yet too weak, nor yet too few.

Sermon Seven

THEY THAT WAIT FOR THE LORD

REVEREND PAUL E. SCHERER, D.D., LITT.D., LL.D.[1]

A *Minister of the Evangelical Lutheran Church and Visiting Professor of Homiletics at Princeton Theological Seminary, Princeton, New Jersey*

Born in Mt. Holly Springs, Pennsylvania, in 1892, Dr. Scherer studied for his B.D. at the Lutheran Theological Seminary, Mt. Airy, Philadelphia, and was ordained a minister of the Luthern Church at Allentown, Pennsylvania, in 1916. During 1918 and 1919 he was assistant pastor of Holy Trinity Church, Buffalo, New York. He taught at Mt. Airy Seminary from 1919 to 1929 and was pastor of Holy Trinity Lutheran Church, New York, from 1929 to 1945. For years he was Brown Professor of Homiletics at Union Theological Seminary, New York City. In addition, he has preached frequently at colleges and universities along the Eastern seaboard, in England, and on NBC's Sunday Vespers program. At the August Conference in Northfield he has served as vice-chairman since 1937 and as a dean since 1942.

He is the author of a number of stimulating books, including *When God Hides* (sermons), *Facts That Undergird Life*, *The Place Where Thou Standest*, *Event in Eternity*, *For We Have This Treasure* (the Lyman Beecher lectures for 1943), and *The Plight of Freedom*. In the recent edition of the *Interpreter's Bible*, he contributed the expositions of Job and of the last six chapters of Luke.

After his retirement, he spent 1960-1961 as Visiting Professor of Homiletics at Union Theological Seminary, Richmond, Virginia, and 1961-1962 as Visiting Professor of Homiletics at Princeton Theological Seminary.

---

[1] Sermons by members of the Advisory Committee were contributed at the special request of the editor and are included on his responsibility.

THEY THAT WAIT FOR THE LORD

"Thus saith the Lord God, . . . they shall not
be ashamed that wait for me."

Isaiah 49:22, 23

The Bible is very honest and outspoken about the times when God does not seem to be around at all; when every indication is that he has gone off stage and returned to his own place. "Why shouldest thou be as a stranger in the land," Jeremiah wants to know, "and a wayfaring man that turneth aside to tarry for a night?" And Habakkuk, as he stares out across the fields at the spoiling and the violence: "O Lord, how long shall I cry, and thou wilt not hear?" Every step of the way, from the beginning of the Old Testament to the end of the New, you would say that over here is a splendid faith which refuses to die, and over there a world which refuses to live by it; while in the place between men keep asking of us, "Where is now thy God?" And often enough we do not know. If anybody should shout to Him in the dark, as a sailor might shout, "Stand by!"—why then, there are days and weeks and months and years when one can only say that if He does stand by, apparently that is all He does!

And the sum of what the Bible has to offer at that point, it would seem, is this word "wait." So I want to begin with it, and get into the record right away the fact that it is a very disturbing word. The more you find out about what it means, the more troublesome it becomes.

For one thing, it is disturbing precisely because so often, to all intents and purposes, it does not get you anywhere. The Bible prescribes it, and you do what the Bible says, and what comes of it? Decent hopes are still crushed; and whoever it is up yonder is either too far away or too busy or does not care enough to do anything about it. During the desolate years of her exile, Israel was schooled in hope: it was her reading, writing, and arithmetic. "Thus saith the Lord God . . ." In this very passage one of the most stately and vibrant of all her prophets is speaking to her in the name of her God. Just listen to him. Listen to all of it now. "Behold, I will lift up mine hand to the Gentiles, and set up my standard to the people; and they shall bring thy sons in their arms, and thy daughters shall be carried upon their shoulders. And kings shall be thy nursing fathers, and their queens thy nursing mothers: they shall bow down to thee with their

48

face toward the earth, and lick up the dust of thy feet; and thou shalt know that I am the Lord; for they shall not be ashamed that wait for me."

Is there anybody who would like to go on with it? They got back home at last, but nothing was as they had dreamed it would be. There were no Gentiles anywhere that took very kindly to them: only dismal ruins to start with, and jackals prowling around in the moonlight. They built up the walls of their holy city as best they could; and when they were through, you must give them credit for being gallant enough to turn their waiting into a song. "I wait for the Lord, my soul doth wait, and in his word do I hope. My soul waiteth for the Lord more than they that watch for the morning: I say, more than they that watch for the morning." Every year they sang it as they made their pilgrimage to the temple that had to serve them now. But there was never a morning when anything looked very much like the Lord: instead, wave after wave of conquest swept over their land.

There did come a day, though, centuries later, when an old man whose name was Simeon came into the shining Temple which Herod had built, and took a little child up in his arms, and blessed God, and said, "Lord, now lettest thou thy servant depart in peace, according to thy word: for mine eyes have seen thy salvation, which thou hast prepared before the face of all people." And you think, Surely the waiting is over now! It isn't. The Child grew into manhood, called a few fishermen to be his disciples, trudged up and down the roads of Judaea and Galilee talking about the Kingdom of God, healed the sick; they said He even raised the dead, but of course there were enough to dispute that: all of it as long as people would let Him. It was not long.

His one pitiful hour of triumph the Church to this day fondly reenacts on the first Sunday in Advent, as she celebrates the eternal mystery of His coming. Through Introit and Collect the age-old yearning of the past moves up toward the Epistle and the dawn: "The night is far spent, the day is at hand." Then the stirring cadences of the Gospel, as once more that curious pageant winds its way, in the memory of the people of God, down the slopes of the Mount of Olives, up the steep ascent of Zion, to the sudden fluttering of palm branches, and the excited cries of "Hosanna to the Son of David: Blessed is he that cometh in the name of the Lord; Hosanna in the highest." And even as you listen you remember something more: that within the week He was whipped up by the storm like a piece of torn paper and placarded against a cross.

It is true, many said they had seen Him alive after that, and they spread their news all around the Mediterranean world, confident that He would come again soon with power and great glory; but He did not. The years dragged on interminably, while His followers were stoned and sawn asunder and slain with the sword, wandering in dens and caves of the earth. The very next to the last verse of the New Testament—which is the record they have left us—sounds like an intolerably weary sigh: "Even so, come, Lord Jesus." Did it never seem to you almost incredible that at that moment, just when you might well have been ready to write it all off as the epic of a God, if indeed there is a God, who has made it His business to promise more than He can deliver, that just then the conclusion of the whole matter should be set down in the sheer effrontery of a benediction? "The grace of our Lord Jesus Christ be with you all. Amen." It tries at any rate to wipe the tears from your eyes.

But this word "wait" is a disturbing word not only because so little seems to come of it. More than anything else it is disturbing because it does not mean what we think it means! In the Bible it keeps hinting that the postponements are not God's at all: they are ours. So that the waiting is not in the least as it was represented some time ago in a play on Broadway called *Waiting for Godot*—a thinly veiled title that meant waiting for God. The curtain went up on a huge outcropping of rock, to remind us I suppose of the rock from which all of us were hewn; with a scrubby bit of a tree at its edge, symbol no doubt of Eden, or of the cross, or of both: and two tramps waiting for Godot, with nothing to do but to wonder what to do next. It was an idle and hopeless business. One of them took off his shoes, and put them back on. They told stories, and waited. After an hour or so the curtain went down on a message from Godot: he could not come today, he would come tomorrow. The second act was only different enough not to be the same. The tramps called each other names. They talked of separating. They thought of hanging themselves; but the tree was no taller than they were, and the only belt they had between them broke. When the final curtain fell, another word had come from Godot, and it was the same word: he could not make it today, he would surely be there tomorrow!

Now that kind of waiting is bad enough; but the kind the prophets and psalmists are talking about is worse. They are talking about the kind which understands that there is something in us which makes the waiting necessary: something that forever insists on getting between us and God; something we want more, or like better, that keeps him at a distance. And they know we cannot deal with that by saying we are sorry: sorry for much that we remember, and for more that we have forgotten. We make quite a ritual of gathering it all up on Sunday morning, and confessing in unison

50

that we have done those things which we ought not to have done, and—for complete coverage—have left undone those things which we ought to have done. And there may well be no health in it! Tell me: how many of these "things" in you and me that mar the face of human life, how many of them do you think it would take to make Bethlehem worth while, and the Calvary that always stands beside it in the heart of God? Surely, whatever it is that is wrong with us, it must be farther down than that! "When thou passest through the waters, I will be with thee." What if the only peace you and I ever really seek were the peace of not knowing how deep the waters are!

Kafka knew. In *The Trial* his hero stands accused before a mysterious tribunal, but cannot for the life of him find out what it is he is supposed to have done. He runs over the past in his mind, every item he can remember, to discover for himself what they know who have pressed the charges against him; and he can think of nothing, nothing to account for the deadliness with which the indictment seems to have been drawn up. He wants desperately to defend himself; but there is no indication anywhere of the quarter from which the attack is going to come. And it ends that way, one grey dawn, with an execution which seems a kind of blessed relief, because he does not have to worry about any of it any longer.

Maybe God doesn't seem to be around because underneath everything else there is something in our hearts which does not want him to be, could not stand it if he were. Is that the nameless evil which called for Bethlehem, and cost God—Calvary? One thing is very certain: we will not sit it out! In the face of it, what the Bible means by "waiting" can scarcely have much to do with patiently letting the time pass: on the theory that it may all be for the best, there must be a silver lining somewhere, the night is always darkest just before the dawn—and a good deal more of the pious nonsense which "good" people so often like to scatter abroad when the going gets rough. The verb "to wait" speaks to us of our insecurity. It speaks to us of a God we do not already know, says Paul Tillich, and do not already have. We do not already have him in some doctrine or in some church. We do not already know him in some book or in some experience. "Wait, I say, on the Lord." It is a word which gives us solemn warning that we live all our days on the dreadful margin between knowing and not knowing, between having and not having.

Is that why the word in Hebrew is a kind of tortured word? It hopes you will see a man stretched out and straining, turning and twisting this way and that, weaving together the strands of all he knows, not about the God he wants, but about the God he has, into a rope strong enough to hold

51

him no matter what happens: probing the mysteries of God's dealing with him, of that will beyond his own, so much more gracious than any he could ask; looking for some sign of a Presence where he had never thought of looking before, among tasks he was sure were beneath him, and people to whom he had never paid much attention—knowing right well all the time that his search for God is bound to be out around the edge of things somewhere, and has to be watched, to keep it from shading off into idolatry at the drop of a hat, while at the centre is God's search for him, never getting tired, never washing its hands of him and letting him go. Because, you see, in the Bible the waiting is always double; it is never one-sided. Somebody is at the other end of it, and always has been: something on foot up yonder, fearfully intent, to match, and more than match, whatever it is that is on foot down here. And every muscle there too is taut, like his muscles who hangs on a cross.

Can it ever then be true, is it possible or even thinkable, that very little should come of it? We began with that, tossing it off, as if it were clear as a pikestaff. Now we must examine it. "They shall not be ashamed that wait for me." It is no puny assurance, I can tell you. That may be the reason we found it so disturbing in the first place: not because so little comes of it, but because we want so little what comes of it! Nothing here says you will not be disappointed any more, or that you will not be lonely ever again. You may indeed begin to wonder why you are lonely, with so many people about: troublesome, I can see that; but it could be sheer profit! Nothing says that you will feel needed all at once, with life chockfull of meaning everywhere you turn. You may start wondering why you ever felt unneeded, with as much need as there is at no more than arm's length from where you are sitting. That could be a little upsetting; but it might mean a new beginning where the wheels for you had ground to a full stop! There is nothing here about quick answers, or knots that come untied the minute you pull at them, or problems that solve themselves while you sleep.

The Bible operates on deeper levels than that. It never plays around in the shallows. It does not do much surface work. If you do not want to be disturbed by what it says, you must try not to understand what it means! When it talks of not being ashamed, it is thinking first and foremost of whatever it was that made Adam hide, back there in the third chapter of Genesis, when the Lord walked in the garden and kept calling to him in the cool of the evening, saying, "Adam, Adam, where art thou?" That's the religious, not the philosophical question. You can hear it as the shadows lengthen on Calvary, and the name becomes your name. When the Bible talks of not being ashamed it is thinking of what comes over a man when

52

for one reason or another he is brought face to face with himself as he is, and knows that he cannot stand naked like that, stripped of all his illusions, and hold up his head. How much of life's loneliness and anxiety do you suppose that accounts for? Jean-Paul Sartre says that this sense of ultimate guilt, the very guilt of being, which was what Kafka was talking about, is at the root of all our bitterness and resentment and dread of death.

Those of you who have seen Arthur Miller's play about Willy Loman, *Death of a Salesman*, will remember how it can drive a bare, plodding, desolate nobody, who cannot put up any longer with what he sees in the mirror, from one pathetic deceit to another, until he is so far away from his sons that they can only despise him, so far away from his wife that her love cannot reach him, so far away from himself, from what he truly is and ought to be doing, that there is no reason he can find anywhere for going on with the rotten lie he has become even in his dreams, and nothing is left for him as he sees it but his rendezvous with a gunshot and a grave and a woman's tears.

Well, to be free of that is what the Bible is thinking about—free of the shame that comes not so much from the wrong we do as from the wrong we are: and not just to feel free. Scripture wastes very little time on the way we feel. It sets a fact in front of you, not inside, outside, where you can lay your hands on it; and not just the fact of forgiveness, though you can document from many a modern drama and novel what goes on where there is none. It is not even the fact that some good at last can get in where the evil used to be. Rather it is this, for anybody who will take hold of it: the fact that life can come now where death was! The Bible is not interested in anything else.

In Edna St. Vincent Millay's poem, *Renascence*, she tells of a day when the world seemed to crowd in upon her from every side. Somehow, all sin was of her sinning, she thought; man's hunger was her own, and his suffering, and his death. At that strange word the earth gave way, and she sank gladly, deeply into its breast. But there still was the friendly sound of the rain above her, and she wanted so much to kiss its fingers again. The dripping trees, and the spring silver, the autumn gold—who could bear never to see any of it any more? Would not God please put her back? She would know so much better how to live if only he would! When suddenly to the sound of herald wings the startled waters plunged down the sky and washed her grave away. The winds blew and thrust the miracle of breath into her face. Up from the ground she sprang, and hailed the earth with such a shout as is not heard save from one who has been dead and is alive again. She understood now, her hair blown back, there on the hilltop

53

where it all began, how far away the heart could push the sea and land; knew, with a knowledge unlike any other, that the soul could cleave its way through the clouds and roll back the sky from God's very face!

It can happen whenever you like. That is what the Bible is about! Whenever you want to, you can stand again where life once stood before it was spoiled and knew that the only thing for it was to hide. You can stand where Christ is, free of the past and open to the future, that very inmost citadel and self of yours under another flag, stormed and ravaged by the love which stretched itself out on two beams of wood to die, lest living without that love be a chattering emptiness and dying without it a "cold horror."

That, and because there can be nothing beyond it, one thing more to follow: when the Bible talks of not being ashamed, it is thinking too of never being defeated, not really, never being driven off the field in headlong flight by the odds. It says that does not have to happen either, that there is not anything we can't face up to now and whip it to a standstill on its own ground. There would be no sense in saying that if times without number it had not been done. There would be no sense in saying it if you could not do it.

Jesus once spoke, as men remembered it, of building his church on the marsh-lands of a life which he called a rock. Peter it was, and a more unlikely bit of shifting sand you could hardly have found. Yet Jesus added, in his "humble, outrageous arrogance," that the gates of hell would never be able to prevail against it. Have you thought he meant that hell was making the assault? He did not. It was his church pounding at the gates. Hell it was that could not hold out! Will he then, do you think, find altogether beyond him the odds which happen at the moment to be staring you and me out of countenance? "Now that"—can you hear him answer as he looks at your outstretched hands?—"that I cannot possibly manage." He may very well tell you that he cannot do it as poorly as you want it done, that he can only do it far, far better: much as he has handled this vast and motley crew of his, this straggling company of his would-be kingdom, which is his Church, and written it, not as men planned, but as he planned, written it large into the text of human history.

Certainly there is no guarantee anywhere in the gospels that the issue will be tailor-made, according to our specifications. Paul breaks out into half a dozen doxologies: "O the depth of the riches . . ." "Thanks be to the God and Father of our Lord Jesus Christ . . ." But look them up and see for yourself: not one of them got itself put together on his terms! Three times he asked to be rid of some crippling infirmity, and the only answer

54

he got was, "It's enough for you to have my grace." So please—never call it rhetoric when he says that in a world where nothing is yours, if you are Christ's, then—because Christ is God's—life and death, and things present and things to come, all are yours! Poetry? Over and over again he turned it into prose: five times with the forty stripes he received save one, and the rods with which three times he was beaten; stones and shipwreck, hunger and thirst, cold and nakedness! Poetry for us, God pity us! Prose for him! A pageant, God's pageant, in overalls! I am told that a French skeptic of the last century one day put his finger at that place in the book, and looking away into the distance was heard to whisper, "Sometimes I wish I knew where the road to Damascus runs; I would go and walk there!" It's the one road in the world that runs wherever you want it to run! It runs through the place where you are sitting!

Wait, I say, in the Lord—"Didn't I tell again at the beginning that the waiting is troublesome? Only because it is so difficult to make out what God is doing—anywhere, at any time! Where would you have liked to live, and when, just to be sure that he had not given up and gone away? When Christ stood before Pilate? When Paul died under the sword? When Augustine watched the Roman Empire crumbling before his eyes while he was writing his "City of God?" When the Reformation cracked Christendom wide open? Now—in this riven world? Perhaps what is really troublesome is that God never leaves us alone!

Sermon Eight

THE TYRANNY OF WORDS

REVEREND JOSEPH R. SIZOO, D.D., LITT.D., S.T.D., LL.D.[1]

A Minister of the Reformed Church and Professor of Religion and Director of the Chapel at George Washington University, Washington, D. C.

Dr. Sizoo was born in the Netherlands and was brought to the United States by his parents. He graduated from Hope College and took his ministerial training at New Brunswick Theological Seminary. In 1910 and 1911, he was a missionary in South India. When he returned to the United States he was minister of churches in Malden, New York, and Somerville, New Jersey. In 1923, he was summer minister of the American Church at the Hague. He served the famous New York Avenue Presbyterian Church in Washington, D. C., from 1924 to 1936. In 1936, St. Nicholas Collegiate Church in New York called him to be its minister.

Dr. Sizoo was President of the General Synod of the Reformed Church in America and served a term as President of the Greater New York Federation of Churches. New Brunswick Theological Seminary elected him as President in 1947. In 1952, he was made Professor of Religion and Director of the Chapel at George Washington University.

His books—*On Guard, Not Alone, Make Life Worth Living, Preaching Unashamed,* and *I Believe in the Bible*—have won a secure place in religious literature.

During the Second World War and the Korean War, he traveled extensively to visit Army and Navy bases on the fighting front. He was voted the "Clergy Churchman of the Year 1958" by Religious Heritage. His work has been recognized with the honorary doctorate by Hope College, Columbia University, Rutgers University, and George Washington University.

---

[1] Sermons by members of the advisory committee of *Best Sermons* were contributed at the request of the editor and are included on his responsibility.

THE TYRANNY OF WORDS

The Sermon on the Mount, often called the Magna Charta of the Christian faith, concludes with this sobering judgment, "Not he that saith unto me Lord, Lord, but he that doeth the will of my Father."

It is becoming increasingly clear that the tensions, strains, misunderstandings, and dangers which haunt and confront our time arise out of words. The cold war is a war in which the weapons are words. Modern man has developed a demonic skill in juggling phrases and giving false twists to words so that they no longer have their original meaning. The result is that words are hollow and empty, and they become dangerous shibboleths.

When Mr. K speaks of the glory of democracy in Russia he has drained that word dry of its meaning and poured into its place ideas utterly foreign to it. He culls something out of every religion, every philosophy, every social program, and every psychological theory. He adds to them the dream of Mohammed, the trickery of Machiavelli, the genius of American advertising, the mythology of the Trojan horse, and the ruthlessness of underworld gunmen. He rolls them all up into a ball and calls it democracy. When the bearded Castro shouts himself hoarse about emancipating his people, it is not the kind of freedom for which our forefathers fought, bled, and died. When we pray "Grant peace in our time, oh Lord," a haunting, poignant hope and glory encircles those words. When the communist speaks of peace, he means a classless, godless society, enslaved by force and terror.

There are certain words like justice, truth, democracy, freedom, and good will which have gone deep into the hearts of people. Everywhere today apostate forces with satanic thoroughness are twisting them out of shape. They have stolen words by which the western world has come to be what it is and given them different meanings. The result is that the people of the world are bewildered and confused. Words no longer mean what they say or say what they mean. It is like a man emptying a bottle of honey and filling it with vinegar without changing the label. We live in a world which is tyrannized and terrorized by words.

This is also true in our national life. We have a passion for freedom. We take rather seriously the Declaration of Independence that "all men are created equal." But freedom seems like a lonely island in a sea of swirling hate and fear. Why is that? Freedom has always meant tolerance, good will, mutual understanding, and respect. The difficulty today is that we have so often emptied that word of its meaning that it has become a façade for self-interest, pressure groups, political double talk, indifference to education, and religious bigotry. This twisting of words out of shape has lost us many friends. Instead of being so deeply concerned about the gap between the West and the East, would it not be equally important to become a little more concerned about closing the dreadful gap between our words and our deeds. You can't put words like democracy, freedom, justice, and good will into a deep freeze or in cold storage for the duration and expect them to survive. Just because the name of God is engraved or embossed on our coins and stamps, just because we have added, rather belatedly, the words "Under God" to the pledge of allegiance does not mean that we have put into practice the meaning of freedom or that we are more welcomed and emulated by the people of the world. We are suffering from the tyranny of words.

What we need so desperately is a fresh new emphasis on semantics, the study of words. We must learn again that words have value in so far as they are true to the ideas which created them. The meaning of words is determined by the ideas behind them and a person's reaction to them. Dr. P. W. Bridgeman, the noted physicist and one-time Nobel prize winner, wrote this, "The true meaning of a word is to be found by observing what a man does with it, not by what he says about it." The definition of a word is more than more words about a word. The value of a dollar bill is determined not by the words that are written on a bit of paper, but on the integrity of the government behind it. If the government becomes irresponsible, the dollar bill is worthless. Words are empty if the ideas which have created them cease to be valid. They may become dangerous shibboleths.

All this is especially true and relevant in the area of religion. We make a great deal of the Book. Our religion is Bible centered. Our ethics, our language, and our theology all come out of the Book. The Bible is full of words; indeed, to be exact, it contains 773,692 words; but all too often the words are meaningless. We read them as Hamlet read when Polonius asked him, "What readest thou, my Lord?" And Hamlet replied, "Words, words, words." When you lose sight of the ideas behind the words, they become meaningless and a dangerous fetish.

We make a great deal of the cross, and we should. We carve it on wood, emboss it on prayer books, emblazon it from steeples, and smother it in roses; but it is hardly a way of life. Once upon a time when people sang, "When I survey the wondrous cross," they went out into the world to do something about it. It gave them a sense of urgency and commitment.

Today we make a long series of arguments about it and leave it where it is. The tragedy of so much of the attempt to build the Kingdom of God is to suppose you can advance it by words only. If words could save the world, this earth ought to be paradise. Christian discipleship for many means only intellectual assent to a series of phrases and clichés. There are unfortunate people whose religion turns on these word patterns. So long as they hear certain words, they are sure your religion is genuine; nothing else matters. If they fail to hear these words, although the ideas are expressed in your life and conduct, they think your religion is phony. When I was a boy, there lived in my community a man who had all the answers. He could argue every theological nicety to a hair-splitting finesse, he could quote endlessly from the Book and repeat page after page, but you couldn't trust him with a nickel. Some one has said that one step to the irreligion of modern man has been by way of religion itself.

In some respects organized Christianity has never been more prominent or received greater publicity: its membership has never been larger; its architecture has never been more aesthetic; its music has never been more appealing; its organization has never been more effective; its ministry has never been better trained; politically it has never been more powerful; socially it has never been more acceptable; and financially it has never been more prosperous. And yet, many think they have to go outside the church to find what the church was meant to bring. Too much of Christianity turns on clichés rather than conduct, words rather than action, and discussion rather than deeds.

A distinguished anthropologist visited a Bantu village in South Africa to make certain surveys of the customs and habits of the people. They were a primitive people without any semblance of western culture, but they welcomed and received him most cordially. When the anthropologist returned to the United States, he sent the people a sun dial, as an expression of his gratitude and appreciation, so that they might have some way of telling time. They were so grateful that they thought they could preserve the gift for a long time by building a thatched roof over it to keep it from wind and weather. Many treat their religion that way. When there is a divorce between what you say and what you do, when words do not match deeds, religion is a hollow and empty thing.

Occasionally you will come upon people who toss religion out of their lives just when they need it most. Once they were ardent and devoted to the church. They could always be counted on for any responsibility. But when some adversity swept over them or a great disillusionment crowded in on them, they turned their backs upon it.

60

When you try to analyze this behavior, you will discover they had a religion of a kind, but it was very shallow. Paul Tillich calls it a lost sense of depth. Their religious life turned on words. When the black camel kneels at your door, when loneliness lays its clammy hands on you, when adversity washes away some precious hope, it will require something more than the mumbling of a few pater-nosters to see you through. Words are worthless when the ideas which have created them cease to be valid or relevant. The true meaning of words is determined not by what you say about them but what you do with them. An American flag to some is only a piece of cloth of varied colors, worth only a few cents; but many of us who understand its symbolic meaning are willing to die for it.

That was the quarrel of Jesus with the Pharisees. They worshipped the letter of the law, rather than the spirit. They washed the outside of the cup, while inside it was foul and corrupt. The worship of words leads to fetishism, externalism, and legalism. It is on the surface. Everything is in the show window, but inside the shelves are empty. The greatest barrier to the coming of the Kingdom of God comes from those who give it lip service but do nothing about it. Words may be beautiful, but they are often so empty.

Words are never enough, not even God's words. Ever since the dawn of conscience men have cried out, "Oh that I knew where I might find Him." They turned to the prophets for an answer. These men saw what nobody else saw, felt what nobody else felt, heard what nobody else heard, and lived in such close communion with God that when they spoke it seemed as if God were speaking. So you read, "The word of the Lord came to Isaiah, the word of the Lord came to Amos," etc. But the question still remained unanswered and the problem was still unresolved. So "in the fullness of time God sent His son, and the Word became flesh and dwelt among us full of grace and truth." When men saw Jesus they said, "Immanuel, God with us." Jesus said: "He that hath seen me hath seen the Father also." The true meaning of a word is determined not by what you say about it but by what you do with it. Words have meaning only when the ideas which created them continue to be valid.

Not long ago Carl Sandburg addressed a joint seesion of the United States Congress on Abraham Lincoln. It was a moving occasion. The great interpreter of Lincoln held them spellbound. There is a part of that stirring address which lingers in my mind, "Millions there are who take him as a personal treasure. He had something they would like to see spread everywhere over the earth. We can't find words to say exactly what it was, but he had it. It's there in the light and shadow of his personality." Some-

Sermon Nine

CREATION BY EXPLOSION

BISHOP GERALD KENNEDY, PH.D., D.D., LL.D., LITT.D., L.H.D., H.H.D.

Resident Bishop of the Los Angeles Area, The Methodist Church, Los Angeles, California, and President of the Council of Bishops of The Methodist Church

This dramatic sermon takes its background from Amos. It is a good example of Bishop's Kennedy's fine preaching ability.

Born in Michigan in 1907, Gerald Kennedy studied at the College of the Pacific and the Pacific School of Religion, then took his Ph.D. at Hartford Theological Seminary in 1934. He was ordained a Methodist minister in 1932 and began his ministry as pastor of First Congregational Church, Collinsville, Connecticut, 1932-36. He was appointed to Calvary Methodist Church, San Jose, California, in 1936, and to First Methodist Church, Palo Alto, in 1940. He was Acting Professor of Religion at the Pacific School of Religion from 1936 to 1940.

His talent for public leadership was first evident when he became pastor of St. Paul Methodist Church in Lincoln, Nebraska, in 1942. There his preaching, influence in university circles, and participation in community work made him one of the important men in the city and state. In 1948 he was elected a Bishop of the Methodist Church and was Bishop of the Portland Area until in 1952 he became Bishop of the Los Angeles Area. This area includes Southern California, Arizona and the Hawaiian Islands. He has been President of the Council of Bishops of the Methodist Church since 1958.

Bishop Kennedy has preached in many parts of the world and has traveled for the Methodist Church visiting world wide mission fields. He has given the Beecher Lectures on Preaching at Yale and the Auburn Lectures at Union. He tries to make administration second to his preaching, yet he is an able executive. He has established a new theological seminary in Los Angeles and has directed his ministers in the building of many new churches.

He is a trustee of the Pacific School of Religion, Southern California School of

Theology, the College of the Pacific, and California Western University. His books include: *His Word Through Preaching, The Lion and the Lamb, Go Inquire of the Lord, God's Good News, I Believe, The Methodist Way of Life, The Reader's Notebook, The Second Reader's Notebook, The Christian and His America, I Believe.*

Bishop Kennedy has received ten honorary doctorates, including the D.D. from Pacific School of Religion, Redlands University, and Bucknell University, the LL.D. from the College of Puget Sound; the Litt.D. from Nebraska Wesleyan University, and the H.H.D., from Bradley University.

CREATION BY EXPLOSION

Woe to you who desire the day of the Lord!
Why would you have the day of the Lord?
It is darkness, and not light . . .

Amos 5:18

Harlow Shapley, emeritus professor of astronomy at Harvard University, is one of the world's great astronomers. He pointed out that one of the main scientific problems in the creation of the universe was how enough heat had been generated to form the heavier elements which are necessary for life. We can understand the hydrogen-into-helium process for the sun has heat enough for that action and we have learned to do it ourselves. But even a temperature of over ten million degrees would not carry the process farther.

In 1054, Oriental astronomers noted the appearance of a dazzling new light in the sky which for a few weeks, was visible in the daytime. Gradually it faded, but now, centuries later, a light is still visible in the same position. Under examination with the instruments of modern astronomy, it proved to be expanding at such a regular rate that it was possible to estimate the time of its origin. This Crab Nebula is the product of the explosion in 1054 which actually happened four thousand years before, as it took forty centuries for the light to reach the earth. Such an explosion was what the astrophysicists were seeking, for here was heat enough to produce the heavier elements. Which is to say, God explodes stars to produce the materials for His creation.

As I thought of this, it seemed to me that while creation by explosion may be a startling idea to us, it would not have been so to Amos in the eighth century B.C. He came into a society that robbed the poor and exploited the weak but was smug, prosperous, complacent. It looked forward confidently to continual success until the Day of the Lord came when Israel would be crowned conqueror over its enemies and established as ruler of the world. But Amos reversed the whole idea. It would be, he cried, an explosive destruction. It would be, "as if a man fled from a lion, and a bear met him; or went into the house and leaned with his hand against the wall and a serpent bit him. Is not the day of the Lord darkness, and not light, and gloom with no brightness in it?" (Amos 5:19-20)

Today we are as the generation to whom Amos addressed his warnings. Our silly little ideas of a God who exists to vindicate our ways and guarantee our victories are just as unrealistic. We need to see again that His Day is darkness and not light, judgment and not approbation, explosion and not ease. Professor Shapley along with Amos shakes us from our complacency and a world of make-believe, by bringing us face to face with the God who creates by explosion.

<h1 style="text-align:center">I</h1>

Now let us look at this first in the light of the Bible.

When I was a seminary student, the Bible was a great embarrassment to my generation. We were brought up on the theory of a gradual evolution that was practically inevitable. It seemed to us that the world and man were evolving toward higher goals and the process was to be understood scientifically. We tried to fit the Bible into this theory and it was difficult, for it was often sudden, abrupt, explosive and personal. We emphasized anything in the Scriptures which bolstered up our theory, which took considerable doing, as you would understand.

In 1938, Dr. Harry Emerson Fosdick published his *Guide to Understanding the Bible*. It traced the development of great ideas through the Bible and quoted Paul Elmer More's observation that one of the permanent contributions of the higher criticism was "the discovery of the evolutionary character of the Bible." This is still a fine book but it reflects the spirit of that time and neglects the Bible's breaks, crises and decisive moments of creation.

Paul was a problem for us in those days because his tempestuous genius did not fit our picture of the gradualness of Christian experience. His conversion was too violent, and his whole interpretation of God's action in Jesus Christ was not smooth enough to suit us. No wonder some scholars condemned the Apostle to the Gentiles as having led us astray and urged us to get back to the simple teachings of Jesus.

But the Bible is full of explosions, and its story is of mighty acts, sudden visions, dramatic moments. I had said something uncomplimentary about one of the reactionary groups of super-patriots and a lady wrote to me and said, "A Christian is one who if he cannot say something nice about people, never says anything." It is a pity that Amos and the Prophets had not heard about that idea! For they said things about the rich, the successful and the self-appointed guardians of orthodoxy that even in Elizabethan English sound far from nice. They seemed to think that God would destroy the pleasant patterns their people cherished and out of the wreckage He would create something new and better.

Israel never understood her history as smooth and gradual. At the Feast of First Fruits the people were to speak these words in the ritual: "A wandering Aramean was my father; and he went down into Egypt and sojourned there, few in number; and there he became a nation, great, mighty, and populous. And the Egyptians treated us harshly, and afflicted us, and laid upon us hard bondage. Then we cried to the Lord the God of our fathers, and the Lord heard our voice, and our affliction, our toil and our oppression; and the Lord brought us out of Egypt with a mighty hand and an outstretched arm, with great terror, with signs and wonders; and he brought us into this place and gave us this land, a land flowing with milk and honey." (Deuteronomy 26:5-9)

The Crucifixion was not only a stumbling block and foolishness to Paul's generation. It was to mine. For the great moment was defeat and torture of the Son of God. It was a shattering of every reasonable, logical idea of the way God would work. The new Kingdom was born out of an explosion. Even the missionaries in the Book of Acts were regarded as those who were turning the world upside down. Read Acts again and see how a wild, uncontrollable power of the Holy Spirit was set loose in the lives of those early Christians. We may make the Church a good safe and sound institution, but this is not what it was in the New Testament.

The Revelation has been a problem for all except the sects which foolishly make it a mechanical foretelling of history. We feel ill at ease with its terrible imagery and its awful visions. I can remember how my professors tried to explain it all in scholarly, prosaic terms, but it never quite came off. The apocalyptists had an insight into the nature of things which we cannot tame or ignore. God is not the abstract, gentle influence which never varies. He is the Creator, the Exploder, the All-Terrible.

More than twenty years ago there was a story about a strange fish that had been caught off the coast of Africa. The strangest thing about it was that such creatures were supposed to have been extinct for more than fifty million years. But there it was on the deck and, according to the report in

Time, it bit the captain. So it has been sometimes with the Bible. We have thought its ideas were long outdated and extinct. But suddenly we are in a situation where it comes to life and bites our complacency. Its explosive nature erupts and our tame ideas of God and the world are shattered by it.

II

In the second place, we might take a look at this idea in relation to history.

The view of history as a record of inevitable progress is pretty much discredited. But because this generation has nothing much to put in its place, we still assume that somehow history is on our side and after another crisis or two, things will settle down. Normal life seems to us to be secure life. Wars are abnormalities and crises are what we must avoid at all cost. We dedicate our efforts to keep things from exploding and we make the assumption that sitting on the lid, is statesmanship. This gives us tyrants and exploiters as allies too often, but if we can postpone a revolution or prevent one, then we feel that our diplomacy has worked and our foreign policy is a success.

History, however, when taken seriously, is far from a smooth flowing stream. The American historian Charles Beard when asked to sum up what he had learned from his long study of history, replied with four propositions:

1. Whom the gods would destroy, they first make mad.
2. The mills of god grind slowly, but they grind exceeding fine.
3. The bee fertilizes the flower it robs.
4. When it is dark enough, you can see the stars.

These observations suggest explosions rather than continuous, gradual progress.

Some years ago Thornton Wilder wrote *The Skin of Our Teeth*. I remember the play because the drama department at the University of Nebraska was producing it and the professor of drama asked me to discuss it with the cast. He said the students did not get what the main point was and he hoped I could make it clear. The play was a philosophy of history and it showed what a near thing our survival has been. Mankind has advanced by great moments of discovery and always we have escaped by "the skin of our teeth." To the students, this was so radical an idea that they needed help in interpreting the drama.

One of the great creative periods in history was the hundred years from the middle of the fifteenth to the middle of the sixteenth centuries called the Renaissance. It was a period of intellectual and artistic ferment with a great outburst of creative energy. We might take Michelangelo as a representative genius of the period and then note that Irving Stone called his biography *The Agony and the Ecstasy*. Fired by masterpieces of the past, the Renaissance men had a creative, dramatic and apocalyptic quality. Compared with such a period, the eighteenth century, sometimes known as the Age of Reason, seems to be marked with complacency. The great periods of history are explosive.

When I was a boy, I read about the American Revolution and 1776 seemed like a wonderful year to have lived. Surely there was no dull existence then! I read about the French Revolution with its overthrow of the ancient regime and its brave promise of liberty, fraternity, equality. But it has come to me that I live in the midst of a revolution bigger and more crucial than either of those. For our revolution is world-wide and does not involve merely colonies or a nation, but continents. And an upheaval is not so much fun to live in as it is to read about. It is frightening and dangerous, and so many of us cry for a quieter time when men felt an assurance about the future. But from what the past indicates, this must be another of God's creative periods and the explosions all about us are the sure signs of His presence.

When Emily Brontë was about eight years old, her clergyman father took her for a walk out across the moors from their little village of Haworth. He tried to tell her of the wonders of creation and growth and asked, "What is here which was not here a hundred years ago?" And Emily answered, "Me." It was a good answer. God is always bringing new forces into His world and upsetting the old. Not for us the sad French proverb that the more it changes the more it is the same. Every new person is a new possibility for a new creative act of God.

III

In the third place, we may look at God's explosions in society.

For those who are comfortably situated, the good society is the stable society. Such are the reactionary ones who see every change as subversive and cling to the established order as if it were sacred. They long for a day when the strata of society has become petrified and everyone knows and accepts his place. Their religion is a system of divine decrees bidding every man to be content with the state in which it has pleased God to place him.

I was in Africa just before the Congo received its independence. So many of the old timers could not believe what was happening. To them Africa was a continent rightfully being ruled by colonial powers. Of course the native peoples must be treated kindly, but it was clear to them that the natural resources were to be exploited by Europeans. Most of them were not willing to go to the South African extremes, but it was plain that for them a society was on the right path if no radical changes were being contemplated.

The adoption of reactionary tactics to prevent change is ruinous. Witness Hitler's Germany which in the name of anti-communism plunged Europe into a war that gave the communists half of Europe. Let the United States stop dreaming of going back to a past day by resisting all pressures for growth and change. Samuel Dill said in his *Roman Society in the Last Century of the Western Empire:* "The Roman Empire did not fall because of the disruptive influence of Christianity, or because of sheer moral weakness, but because of an intellectual complacency that froze the lifeblood."

There was a period when it seemed to me that the Middle Ages represented the high point of Christianity. Under the influence of Henry Adams, I was impressed by the unity of Christendom and the way the Church entered into all of life. But I have changed my mind. The Middle Ages was a period of terrible suffering too, and there was disease of bodies and control of minds. Too much of life had been frozen into rigid patterns and there were too many indications of the human spirit under the bondage of yesterday. I take my stand on the proposition that the Church was nearer its best in the revolt of the Reformation. If the old forms would not yield to reform, then it was better to break the old forms and create new ones. Why should the Church think itself exempt from God's creative explosions?

Democracy which is talked about so abstractly and sentimentally, is a dangerous experiment and full of terrible possibilities. When the Bastille fell on July 14, 1789, King Louis XVI said, "Why this is a revolt!" But the Duke bringing him the news replied, "No, Sire. It is a revolution." Democracy is an explosion. A little later at the Battle of Valmy, Goethe observed the ragged recruits of the French Republic withstand the attack of the professional Prussian veterans and wrote in his diary, "From this place and this day, dates a new epoch in the history of the world, and you will be able to say, 'I was there!'" When we talk about democracy we are not talking about some harmless, safe little thing. It is one of the most upsetting and terrifying experiments in all history.

Today we are in the throes of trying to establish racial equality in this country. We have professed it for a hundred years, yet I hear men say that we must go slower and we are doing ourselves much harm by pushing forward against the set customs of our people. But I do not know of any social changes that have come without the pressure and sacrifice of concerned people. The Freedom Riders are being jailed for doing only what the Constitution says is their right. The young Negroes and whites who receive the blows and suffer the insults are regarded by many as "troublemakers." But they are the kind of trouble that has been in the forefront of every advance man has taken toward freedom. The set customs do not give way until there is an explosion.

I have seen pictures of Negro children subjected to the screaming hatred of adults and when people can do that, they are sick people. Do not talk to me about such behavior as a legitimate attempt to protect a way of life. The best word for that situation was spoken by Jesus: "Whoever receives one such child in my name receives me; but whoever causes one of these little ones who believe in me to sin, it would be better for him to have a great millstone fastened round his neck and to be drowned in the depth of the sea." (Matthew 18:5-6)

Our sin is nowhere more apparent than in our stubborn resistance to brotherhood and justice until God cracks our recalcitrance.

Two men were on a houseboat tied to the dock. In the night it broke loose and drifted out to sea. In the morning one of them came on deck and in panic saw no land. "Joe," he yelled, "get up quick. We ain't here no more." And so it seems to those who resist change. Their safety is gone and they are terrified by being cut adrift on an unfamiliar sea. But God would rather have us saved than safe.

IV

Finally, this idea of creation by explosion has a real meaning for us as persons. This is an idea that goes contrary to the modern attitude toward religion and character.

Popular preaching today is concerned with personal tensions and problems. The main drive is toward solving a man's inner conflicts and worries, which is important. How to solve individual troubles and how to cure insomnia seem to be the main themes of our message. It is as if our God had become primarily a divine sleeping pill or tranquilizer. We seldom suggest that men should come to church and get stirred up for the battle, but they should come to get so soothed that they forget there is a battle.

Whether cause or effect, our addiction to psychology is a sign of the times. At the first sign of unhappiness, we must now seek a psychiatrist or psychologist to analyze why we feel the way we do. That gentleman is supposed to give us names for our feelings and assure us so that we are not to blame for them. We must be rid of our guilt and adjust ourselves to conditions about us and thus resolve the conflict. We spend so much time having our complexes analyzed, defined and massaged that we have time for little else.

The messages coming from our pulpits are little, squeaking words of cheer. Gone are the thunderings from Sinai and the call to heroic living. One seldom hears the awful authority of a "thus saith the Lord." We have the strange idea that our religion ought to keep us from getting involved in the terrible issues of today. In the *Peanuts* comic strip, there was a baseball game being played and Lucy was in the outfield. A ball dropped beside her but she made no move to catch it. Charlie Brown the manager came rushing out in anger to ask why she had not caught the ball. He pointed out that she did not even have to take a step, but simply hold out her glove. And Lucy answered simply, "I was having my quiet time." I have nothing against quiet times but there is a time and place for them. A life that is all quiet times is for sloths but not men.

Is this the life God gives to men in the Bible? Remember Hosea whose personal tragedy was the loss of a wife he loved. He found her at last, now a common prostitute, and brought her home. Out of this devastating tragedy, he learned the love of God and wrote a message the world cannot forget or escape. Isaiah in the year of the king's death and the consequent end of his hope, saw the Lord in majesty and holiness.

The great moments of inspiration come to us so often like explosions. That fine poet and strange genius Emily Dickinson said this about poetry: "If I read a book and it makes my whole body so cold no fire can ever warm me, I know that is poetry. If I feel physically as if the top of my head were taken off, I know that is poetry. These are the only ways I know it. Is there any other way?" Not in a retreat from life and responsibility do we find inspiration, but in the midst of the battle. For in those moments, the fire of creation touches us as if a star had exploded and we saw a new world.

Strangely enough, sometimes these great experiences happen in the midst of illness. I have known more than one man whose great contribution came out of a cruel sickness which crushed him down into weakness. God has a way of interrupting the even tenor of things and out of the consequent disturbances, He often brings a new vision and creates a new man. Our fathers were more aware of this than we are, and the Christian story

71

from Paul onward is of men shattered out of their complacency and born again.

I can bear witness to this in my own poor life. I would not take any romantic view of suffering and disappointment, and defeats are wormwood and gall to the spirit. Failure is bitter and hard to forget. But when God has exploded a man's self-confidence and his pride, then out of the wreck he may find the new truths and the divine pattern. In our own lives we may find similar clues to God's creative way, as the astronomer found them in the explosion of a star.

There was a period in Martin Luther's life when he was forced into retirement. In order to stay alive and continue the fight, he had to hide and stay quiet. But the idleness robbed him of his courage. "Would that we might live no longer," he wrote to his friend Melancthon. "Our God has deserted us." But a little later when he could come out of hiding and throw himself into the center of the struggle again, his courage came back and he wrote that mighty hymn of the Reformation: "A mighty fortress is our God, a bulwark never failing." Not in hiding but in battle is our place. For God would create out of the poor stuff we offer him, new creatures, a new heaven and a new earth. And the method he uses is often an explosion. Consider this in a day like ours, and rejoice.

Sermon Ten

THE STRUGGLE FOR MEN'S MINDS

REVEREND WILLIAM M. ELLIOTT, JR., PH.D., D.D., L.H.D.

Minister, Highland Park Presbyterian Church, Dallas, Texas

Born in Charlestown, Indiana, Dr. Elliott is the son of a Presbyterian minister. He attended high school in Clovis, New Mexico. He graduated from Park College, received his B.D. from Louisville Presbyterian Theological Seminary, and a Ph.D. from the University of Edinburgh in 1938. Davidson College conferred the honorary D.D. and Park College the honorary L.H.D. upon him. He was ordained a Presbyterian minister in 1930, was instructor in Homiletics and Church History at Louisville Presbyterian Seminary in 1929-1930. He became pastor of Fifth Avenue Presbyterian Church in Knoxville, 1930-1935; pastor of Druid Hills Presbyterian Church, Atlanta, 1935-1944, and has been pastor of Highland Park Presbyterian Church, Dallas, since 1944.

He is the author of: *Coming to Terms with Life, For the Living of These Days, Lift High That Banner, Two Sons.* He has preached on the radio for the National Council of Churches and *The Presbyterian Hour* and has been special preacher at conferences at Montreat, N. C., Massannata Springs, Virginia and at Chautauqua, New York. He is popular as a speaker at the University of Georgia, Washington and Lee, Duke, Agnes Scott College, Vanderbilt, Southern Methodist University, Texas A. and M. and other colleges and seminaries. He has made two trips to the Far East for the Board of World Missions of the Presbyterian Church and in 1946-47 spent four and a half months surveying mission work in China, Japan, Korea. In 1957 he made a second trip to the Far East to attend conferences in Japan, Korea, Taiwan. He was Moderator of the General Assembly of the Presbyterian Church, U. S., 1957-1958, and is chairman of the Board of World Missions of the Presbyterian Church.

THE STRUGGLE FOR MEN'S MINDS

These are fateful days. They are days in which you and I are witnessing—indeed are a part of—a vast human struggle. It is without doubt the most widespread and the most significant struggle the world has ever known. Upon its outcome will rest the fate of civilization, if not of the human race.

The struggle to which I refer is not physical except superficially, but mental and spiritual. It is a contest for men's minds. Whichever side conquers in the realm of thought wins in the end, regardless of who conquers now in outer space.

The free world then, cannot defeat communism by force of arms alone, nor even primarily, for communism is not a nation. It is not an army. It makes use of military power to frighten people into submission and to enforce its will, but it is not an army. Communism is a system of ideas—an ideology, a philosophy of history. It is a way of looking at man, at things, and at the world. Wrote Dorothy L. Sayers in 1949: "Christendom and heathendom now stand face to face as they have not done in Europe since the days of Charlemagne. . . . The people who say that this is a war of economics or of power-politics, are only dabbling about on the surface of things. . . . At bottom it is a violent and irreconcilable quarrel about the nature of God and the nature of man and the ultimate nature of the universe; it is a war of dogma." [1] Our so-called "cold war" then, is a war of ideas—"a war of dogma." Some words which St. Paul addressed to the Christians in Ephesus in the first century accurately describe the nature of the struggle in which we are now engaged. "We wrestle," he says, "not against flesh and blood, but against principalities, against powers, against the rulers of the darkness of this world, against spiritual wickedness in high places" (Ephesians 6:12).

Now these intangible forces which live in the minds of people cannot and will not be destroyed by missiles. Guns can stop armies but not movements. Ideas will not fall before atomic weapons. Said Abraham Lincoln: "You can't shoot sense or religion into a man any more than you can beat daylight into the cellar with a club." We need to get that clear, for millions of Americans are over-simplifying our problems and are putting entirely too much confidence in military and nuclear might as the final solution to all that we despise and fear.

---

[1] *Creed or Chaos?* (New York: Harcourt, Brace & Co., 1949), p. 25.

74

The only way ultimately to defeat communism, or any other false philosophy, is with the power of another and better ideology. We must overcome error with truth; we must overcome evil with good. No nation will fall a victim of communism which is spiritually right, morally sound, and socially just! As John A. Hutton said to his fellow Britishers during the dark days of the London blitz: "No nation dies that is fit to live."

So, in the crucial struggle now going on in the world, our weapons must be largely mental and spiritual if we are to win. Invading military forces can be detected by radar and halted by superior weapons, but military victory alone will not suffice. It may postpone our destruction, but it will not save us in the end. In this warfare of the spirit we must use spiritual weapons. We must resort to what St. Paul called, "The whole armour of God."

Then it matters, and matters terribly, what men believe and think. To say that it does not matter particularly what one believes is sheer nonsense. There never was a more superficial, untrue statement. The individual who contends that it is of no consequence what a man believes just so he is conscientious, is, to use an expression of Studdert-Kennedy's, talking straight through the middle of his Sunday hat! It *does* matter what goes on in men's minds. Thought patterns are crucial. It was never more clear than it is right now that the most important thing about any man is his creed, whether it be political, economic, social or religious.

What do you think brought on World War II? Well, a good many things, but primarily certain accepted ways of thinking and believing. Nazism, fascism and Shintoism were basically philosophies which had captured the minds of the people of Germany, Italy, and Japan and impelled them to do what they did. Military aggression was simply the implementation of these national ideologies which had won the allegiance and devotion of the masses.

Then one magnificent way to combat atheistic communism in this country and around the world is to deepen and strengthen the convictions of people in Christian beliefs and in the democratic concept of life. And the supreme way to do this is to teach, teach, teach!—in season and out of season, line upon line, precept upon precept—intelligently, consistently, vigorously, enthusiastically.

Do I mean indoctrinate? Precisely that. I am not afraid of the word. If people are not indoctrinated with the Christian faith and philosophy of life, they will be indoctrinated with something else; that is sure. We must invade men's minds with the principles of democracy, but more especially with the spiritual bases of democracy.

75

The Christian religion then, is not an elective in life's curriculum. It is not some decorative fringe. It is not a pleasant pastime for people who have nothing much to do, and are trying to fill up their time. Christianity is not some psychological crutch for pious introverts to lean upon. It is the trellis upon which democracy climbs. Said T. S. Eliot, the English poet: "Western civilization rests upon Christianity as a house rests upon its foundations." It was our religion which inspired such documents as the Declaration of Independence and the Bill of Rights. Without a strong commitment to the Christian faith, the various freedoms we talk about are idle pipe dreams. We cannot have these golden eggs without the goose that lays them. Mr. John Foster Dulles was speaking sober truth when he said: "Our institutions of freedom will not survive unless they are constantly replenished by the faith that gave them birth." [2]

When we relax our hold on Christianity, we ensure the corruption and impotence of democracy. "Communism," writes Dr. Charles L. King of Houston, "will increase in this country only as our hold on the fundamental conception of the Christian religion decreases. If the people of these United States conclude that a personal God does not exist, and therefore man is not the son of God, that all of those God-given rights we speak of are to be subordinated to the interests of a particular class, all the king's horses and men cannot keep out Communism . . . Once the American people conclude that the New Testament teaching of the infinite worth of human personality is exaggerated, all the measures Congress can pass cannot save our way of life." That, my friends, is the gospel truth!

Our own nation is still Christian on the surface, but underneath the foundations are beginning to crumble. Witness the dominance of materialism. We Americans are not seeking first the kingdom of God and His righteousness; we are seeking first the almighty dollar and the creature comforts it can buy. Increasingly we are establishing a sensate culture in this country, and if that is not fertile soil for communism, I do not know what is.

Witness also our increasing wave of moral depravity. Witness our crime record which Mr. J. Edgar Hoover keeps telling us is growing worse instead of better. Witness our alcoholism, our sharp decline in truthfulness and personal integrity, our preoccupation with sex, and our relaxed standards of modesty and decency. And the dismaying feature of all this is that

---

[2] Address at 150th anniversary of his home church, the First Presbyterian Church of Watertown, N. Y., October 11, 1953.

multitudes of church-related people are actually helping along this tidal wave of depravity by their own moral indifference and shabby practices.

The situation which I have been describing is not unrelated to the growing spiritual illiteracy in our so-called Christian nation. The ignorance of this present generation in spiritual matters is both shameful and appalling. Millions of adults and young people know little or nothing of the simplest and most rudimentary facts of the Christian faith, and that goes for many who hold membership in our churches. Multitudes of parents possess scarcely any such knowledge themselves, and seem to desire none for their children. Our contemporary society is living largely on the moral and spiritual reserves of a former generation. These reserves are running out, and unless they are put back through the faithful indoctrination of our children and young people, we may witness in our time the almost complete de-Christianization of America.

So we must teach. We must teach the historic facts of our faith. We must teach its principles, its injunctions, its precepts, its dogmas, and most of all, its Person. And we must gird up our loins and go about this task as if we meant business. We seem to be desperately in earnest about almost everything else except this one all-important matter. We have just been toying with this job of spiritual indoctrination, and it is our only hope.

Most of the things to which we give our major thought and time are trivial in comparison with mastering and communicating Christian truth. What I am pleading for in this sermon is infinitely more important than economic affluence, or political power, or social prestige, or the Miss America pageant, or placing first in the Olympic Games. It would be tragic if we became so preoccupied with other things, even military preparedness, that we had no time or disposition to step up our teaching offensive. And this is not the business of religious professionals alone; it is the business of every Amercan Christian, regardless of his business or profession.

Then let the Church do a better job of teaching. We must admit that the average Sunday school—the teaching arm of the Church—is actually doing a fair-to-middling, if not an inferior job, and I will tell you why: it is handicapped by poor physical equipment, haphazard planning, visionless leadership, and indifferent teaching. I hope and believe that our own Sunday School here at Highland Park is above the average in equipment, planning, leadership, and teaching skill. But are we all that we ought to be? Are we getting the job done? Are children and young people going out of our departments and classes thoroughly informed on the basic tenets of historic Christianity? Are we turning out a generation of informed and zealous Christians? Well, are we?

I beg you Church School teachers to teach religion! You have very little time at your disposal on Sunday mornings, so I implore you: do not waste it! Make every minute count. A noted educator says that by way of experiment he asked boys from time to time what they studied in their Sunday school classes. One class had spent the time studying soil conservation. Another class had spent the greater part of the time during the autumn season discussing Saturday's football game. There is nothing wrong with either soil conservation or football, but under no circumstances should our class time be used up in a discussion of such matters. I agree that Christianity should touch redemptively every phase of life, and it is right that we should bring our faith down where people live. But if we are not careful, we will find ourselves talking about everything under the sun except the Christian faith itself. It has been wisely said that it is not the church's business to do everything; it is the church's business to do that without which nothing else is worth doing.

And let the home do a better job of teaching. The home is the supreme nursery of religion. It is God's first and holiest school. "And these words, which I command thee this day, shall be in thine heart: and thou shalt teach them diligently unto thy children, and shalt talk of them *when thou sittest in thine house*" (Deuteronomy 6:6, 7).

Christian nurture is primarily a task for the home. It is only secondarily a task for any other institution. It irks me to hear some parents criticize the Church School for not doing a better job, when they themselves are making no serious effort at home. The Church School cannot do the job alone; it was never intended that it should, and it is futile for parents to expect it. The Church School does not get the children and young people often enough, regularly enough or long enough. The average child attends Sunday school spasmodically. He is often tardy, and is usually indifferent, listless, and unprepared. When you stop to think about it, it really is amazing how much the Church School accomplishes considering the difficulties under which it has to work!

We parents then, must get down to business both in our teaching at home, and in our cooperation with the Church School. Let us take religious education at least as seriously as we take secular education. We would not dream of letting our children and young people skip day school, or be habitually tardy and unprepared. Such a situation would give us great concern. But does it concern us when these same children and young people miss spiritual instruction and worship in the Lord's house? What has happened to our sense of values? Have we forgotten how to put first things first? Does intellectuality mean more to us than Christian character? Let

78

us then see to it that our Church School has the best physical equipment available, and let us assist its officers and teachers by our prayers, our regular attendance as a family, and by any possible service that we can render. Our own Church School is in constant need of trained teaching personnel. Will you offer yourself for this great service?

We must teach others as we have been taught, and better. And our teaching ministry must be world wide. The missionary enterprise was never so sorely needed as it is now, but so many Christians are indifferent and the adversaries are powerful. The communists are also out to win the world, and they mean business. They have flung the challenge of the "hard sell" right in our teeth. Through skilful and relentless propaganda, they are convincing the masses in other lands that colonialism and Christianity are synonymous, and that exploitation and missions are one endeavor. They offer men a stone instead of bread, and then goad them into hurling it with hate-filled invectives against those who choose the Christian way.

If we Christians expect to compete with these determined fanatics, if we hope to conquer the world for our Lord, then we must be as sacrificially committed to our cause as they are to theirs. No half measures, no pink tea program, no watered-down gospel will win. We must go "all out." No price is too great to pay in the struggle for men's minds.

The days are crucial. The task is clear. We'd better mean business, for it may be later than we think. We ask our military personnel to be willing to die for democracy abroad. Is it too much to ask that the rest of us *live* for it at home?

Sermon Eleven

THE LONG WAY HOME

REVEREND GENE E. BARTLETT, D.D.

A Minister of the American Baptist Church and President of Colgate Rochester Divinity School, Rochester, New York

Gene Bartlett has served pastorates of the Baptist Church at Hilton, New York; of Calvary Baptist Church, Syracuse, New York, 1937-1942; First Baptist Church, Columbia, Missouri, 1942-1947; First Baptist Church, Evanston, Illinois, 1947-1953; and of First Baptist Church, Los Angeles, 1953-1960. He has held several important lectureships, such as "Preacher of the Quarter" at Garrett Biblical Institute; convocation preacher, Cole Lectures, Divinity School of Vanderbilt University; Lyman Beecher Lecturer on preaching, Yale University, 1961. He has taught homiletics at Garrett Biblical Institute and Southern California School of Theology, and conducted seminars on preaching sponsored by American Association of Theological Schools in Berkeley, Chicago, St. Paul, and Dallas.

Dr. Bartlett is the author of *The News in Religion;* the chapter on "The Role of Preaching" in *The Church and Mental Health,* articles in *Christian Century, Current Religious Thought, Pastoral Psychology,* and other magazines and journals. His Beecher Lectures were published under the title *The Audacity of Preaching.* He studied at Denison University, took his B.D. at Colgate Rochester Divinity School in 1935, and received the honorary D.D. from Denison University in 1952 and from Kalamazoo College in 1961. He has traveled extensively in Europe, went to Europe with the Sherwood Eddy Seminar in 1952, and in the Fall of 1954 visited Air Force Bases in Japan and Korea on a preaching mission.

This sermon was preached in The Riverside Church, New York City, June 18, 1961.

THE LONG WAY HOME

It is related that one day when G. K. Chesterton was packing his bags in his London apartment a friend came in and asked where he was going. Chesterton surprisingly replied that he was on his way to London. Somewhat taken back by this answer, the other countered that it might be in order to remind Chesterton that he already was in London. To this however, the essayist replied with a characteristic twist, "No," he said, "that's where you're wrong. I no longer see London. Familiarity has closed my eyes. The real meaning of travel is to come home again and see it as though for the first time. So I really *am* on my way to London though I'll go by Paris, Rome, and Dresden."

Good point! But it runs into matters deeper than travel. Most of us will concur that it was in some such way that we came home to some things which mean most to us, not to be sure, by chosen journeys only, but often by compelled journeys. Why do we so often take the long way home? For we do, returning only after much wandering to the abiding realities of living. That's true, for example, of trust. In the childhood years there seems to be a trust so natural that it will be placed somewhere or in someone almost spontaneously, to be confirmed or tragically, on occasion, to be betrayed. In a sense at the beginning of life we do not need to learn trust; God seems to have given it to us as one of the natural gifts. But the day comes when trust, if it is to be ours in maturity, must be found again often after we have travelled the long way through uncertainty or despair or fear. The trust of maturity is not a natural endowment, but an achievement, a home to which we come after taking the long way around.

The same seems to true of joy. At the beginning of life, given half a chance, joy is an unlearned response. But not so in the later years when one sees the whole of life through the eyes of maturity, its adversity as well as its beauty, its anxiety as well as its assurance, its sordidness as well as its splendor. Beethoven's "Hymn to Joy" was born out of anguish, glorious testimony that he had come home again after taking a very long and dark way around.

Perhaps this is one reason we are brought again and again with certain inevitability to the story which remains the most classic parable Jesus gave us, that of the prodigal son. We walk with him so often, taking our prodigal journey in an imperative search for fulfillment. No single description of the way that leads to fulfillment quite matches the simple moving word, "And he arose and came to his father." It seems presumptious to look at the story again. Yet even

> Those who know it best
> Seem hungering and thirsting to hear it like the rest.

All of it is so familiar: the younger son who asked his father for his inheritance, who took it to a far country and spent it all in a great spendthrift fling, who found himself in want, abandoned, ashamed and despairing, but who came to himself and went back home only to discover there a surprising truth too good not to be true. Yes, it's a presumption to walk with him once more, yet the urge to fulfillment is in us and it is a word so deeply needed in our culture in which many of us seem ready, through either despair or sheer lassitude, to take up permanent residence in some far country.

So our personal fulfillment often takes us the way the prodigal walked. We can see in his unfolding experience the assurances of God at work in every life making for that fulfillment for which we hunger.

I

Our story, like his, begins with the rightful claim, "I want my share." The language of the story is simple but stately. "The younger son said, 'Father, give me that portion of the goods which is mine.'" This you see, was asking no more than his due. The father had made a provision for each son, so he only wanted what his father had already reserved for him.

This awakening of want is a time of great significance in any life, an indispensable preface to our fulfillment. Even in economics it is said that there are two kinds of poverty, the lack of goods for the higher wants on the one hand and the lack of wants for the higher goods, on the other. The awareness of a new want often may be clearest evidence of God's dealing with us. Most of us add whole dimensions to our lives by those moments of awakening. We discover music and know that it will claim us all our lives. Or we see a life of faithful service and know that all our years we must seek to walk a similar way. Or we meet another person, and love comes, so that all of life is different because of it. Or perhaps we see a need and feel its claim upon us until we know there is no peace until we throw ourselves into that need. All of these are the ways of awakening, the times when in some way a work begins in us and a man says, "I want my share." And it is a rightful demand. It well may be God's working in us, calling out the re-

83

sponse that we might begin to ask of Him, as He already is ready to give, to seek as He already is seeking.

There is evidence enough and more that this is true. It has been many years since a young man newly arrived on the campus of Haverford College sat down in the study of Rufus Jones and began with the surprising affirmation, "I am going to make my life a miracle." It was a student's response to the invitations to life he sensed on every side in his first experiences on a campus. Looking back we can see that in a sense Thomas Kelly's life was a miracle, though not exactly as he expected. Well acquainted with struggle through most of the years, he has left us an enduring "testament of devotion," the distilled experience of a man who, after years of struggle, learned the meaning of centering down in God. It seems evident that God indeed was beginning his work in him on the day when in his own words Thomas Kelly said, "I want my share."

Perhaps one ministry of the hour of worship is to remind us that, like those legacies about which we occasionally read that are waiting for someone to claim them, there are surely spiritual inheritances waiting for our wanting of them. This is a constant part of the Biblical understanding of life, the reminder that God's provision is prior to our asking. Certainly there are reserves of strength which wait for our praying. Yet they may not be claimed today, for we will not pray. But the time may come when, awakened by some circumstance of life, we plead for strength and will lay hold upon those reserves. Those first Christians, caught up in the experience which produced the New Testament, spoke often of joy, love, and peace. We may be sure that such gifts have not been withdrawn but wait for that day when we know our need, take up our claim, and move at last into the possession of that which God has provided. So it is a part of His work in us when, seeing for a moment the full potential and dimension of life, the life made whole and enriched by God's gifts, we begin the journey to fulfillment with the plea, "I want my share."

II

Then comes so often that strange turn seen in the prodigal. What is it that makes us say next, "I want my way"? The story again is simple yet eloquent. "Shortly after, the younger son took his inheritance and went into a far country." Here we stand before a deep enigma. We have our theories and our myths and our systems, but it's still a mystery. There's some turn in the human heart that sends us out to a far country. Here is the source of so much of the misery and here is the description of so much of the tragedy that marks human life. When all our explanations which are not reasons have been heard, we know within us that we are following a prodigal way we have chosen, yes often chosen, to the far country.

Undoubtedly one reason Jesus spoke so bluntly to the religion of His time was that it so often covered a basic disobedience beneath an outward faithfulness. He knew so well the subtlety and subterfuge by which we insist upon our own way at the very time when we are claiming that our devotion is to God. He knew so well that self-righteousness is not really righteousness at all, but a front behind which men try to use God rather than serve Him, insist upon their way while calling it His will, and seek the far country at the very time they call it home. John Henry Newman, whose hymn has spoken to each generation, made precisely that confession about himself. Though in the writing of the hymn he was praying, "Lead, kindly Light," he had to add,

> I was not ever thus, nor prayed that Thou
> Shouldst lead me on;
> I loved to choose and see my path; but now
> Lead Thou me on.
> I loved the garish day, and spite of fears,
> Pride ruled my will; remember not past years.

This may give us some key to understanding that truth about Jesus so much in contrast to our common judgment, namely, the way in which he reserved his most vigorous word of rebuke for precisely the people we honor most in our culture: the moral, the intellectual, the wealthy, the religious leaders. Though Jesus spoke a word of rebuke to them, we may be sure it was love which spoke. If on the one hand, He withheld a word of condemnation from those already broken by life, it was love that withheld that word. But if, on the other hand, He spoke a word of judgment it was also love that spoke. And surely his sternness must have been His way of breaking the shell in order that the grace of God might get through to the rebellious center of many a life outwardly so self-sufficient.

Many of us have discovered that the most difficult word in our experience is not "forgive," as some who have been wronged might suppose. Nor is it "brother" though it brings conflict and often anguish, as we well know today. But there is another word, so difficult that even Jesus suffered agony with it in the time of his greatest testing. That word is "nevertheless." "Nevertheless, not my will but thine be done." Some who have come to worship today find themselves confronted with this demanding word. At some point where you have been going along able to say, "I want my way," the showdown has come. Now there must be added, "nevertheless, not my

85

will but thine be done." And there can be pain in it. For that same drive that sent the prodigal to the far country is in us, deep within us, mystery but reality.

III

What follows is stark and simple. For the next word was, "I want." The story itself is almost as direct as that, "He began to be in want." Unlike the younger son, however, we come to know our emptiness in the very midst of plenty. We do not have husks, we often have the best. Yet who can estimate the spiritual questioning brought out in our time by the experience of having what you want only to discover that there is no fulfillment in it? Our emptiness is not when we are deprived, but when we have arrived. This is our tragedy, yes, and the opening for the gospel in our generation. The poverty of those who have been deprived of the goods of life seems understandable, a quite logical failure of supply and demand. But the poverty which comes in the midst of plenty, the emptiness that is felt when life is supposed to be full, the letdown when we have climbed the highest— ah, that is the time when the very meaning of life seems threatened.

A contemporary, thoroughly immersed in modern ways, highly successful in his field, came to this painful realization in a recent writing, "Pages From My Life." Sergei Eisenstein, forced to review his life in the middle years, looked back to see how he had lived it. He said he had lived it "at a gallop" like a "man forever changing trains," and went on to add:

> And suddenly I realized something terrible.
> That none of it has been retained. Nothing grasped.
> My lips have only touched the cup of life, never draining it.
> I have sunk my teeth into life, never savored it.
> While ascending I was thinking how to descend.
> Opening a suitcase I was already thinking of repacking.

Most of us have known such times. They are the modern counterpart of Jeremiah's description of his own time, "My people have gone from mountain to hill; they have forgotten their resting place." And the word we must use for it is old and Biblical and sometimes alien in our culture—judgment. Only the immature still think of judgment as something that happens *to* us; we know it may happen *in* us. We each know that often judgment is most real when it is marked by what does *not* happen. It may be life at dead level—descriptive words! It is life without savor, the vain repetition, momentum without meaning. It is increasing satiation and decreasing satisfaction. It is vain striving after an illusory self-sufficiency supposed to be the sophisticated way, but in fact the most naive of expectations in God's

86

world. It is being caught in that increasing absorption propelled by a belief that if we had just a little more power, a little more status, a little more achievement we at last would feel safe and whole and fulfilled! To all of which one sometimes must respond in the words of the old hymn, "O, the needless pain we bear!"

Hugh Latimer is remembered in the Christian story as a martyr whose life and death illumined a darkened age. But there was a time when something else was disclosed in him. Once when he preached at Cambridge he impressed the whole community by the intellectual grasp of his subject. But as he came down from the pulpit he was met at the foot of the stairs by a member of the Cambridge community, another scholar known as Little Bilney. "Father Latimer," said Bilney, "may I confess my soul to thee?" So they went together to a little room beneath the pulpit where Bilney told of his days of search, his hunger, and his need. He told how he was finding it at last in that faith which Luther later was to describe as one in which a man "throws himself upon God in life and in death." But as he spoke Latimer's eyes filled with tears and he in turn confessed his hunger and his search. So both men started the long way home, an awakening which began with the confession so old, so constant, "I want."

IV

And the end of it? That's the purpose of the whole story—to tell the end! All this we have known, but it is a word which makes the end remarkable news. It was the discovery, "I am wanted." The words have poetry in them now. "While he was yet at a distance his father saw him and had compassion and ran and embraced him." A few words, a simple story—and tremendous news never to be withdrawn. That's real news, "I am wanted."

But what difference does that really make? What has it to do with fulfillment of life? Consider a simple picture. One morning as I left our home to walk to my study one of our sons, hearing the door close, remembered that he had something to ask me. So down the stairs he ran, through the house, out the door, and down the street. As I was about to turn the corner I heard him call and turned to see him. You can imagine the look on his face: strain, uncertainty, anxiety as to whether I had heard and would turn. That evening, however, as I was returning home he was playing in front of the house and I saw him first. So I called him by name. Hearing me he turned and a second time that day ran toward me. It was the same boy, the same street, the same father. But one thing was vastly different—the look on his face. For this time it was not anxiety and strain. It was certainty and rec-

87

ognition and response. One thing had made it so. I had first called him. For a moment the picture can be useful, for this in part is the meaning of the Biblical word, "He has first loved us." We may differ in our ways of saying it, but something wondrous has been said, and the significance of it cuts deep into our time, offering the hope of that personal fulfillment we seek.

When is a life fulfilled? Surely it is when the essential relations have been established, those loving relations which mean acceptance and trust and joy. But this is both our despair and our release—our despair because we can not achieve that first relation with God, yet must receive it, our release when we stand before that tremendous word which He has spoken to us before we come toward him. He has seen us while we are at a distance and in compassion has come to us. It is the word that, as Abelard put it, God has already reached out in Christ that "He might illumine the world with his wisdom and excite it to the love of Himself." News indeed, tremendous news!

When that is found one has come the long way home. It is the kind of wholeness we see in lives centered down in God. Walter Rauschenbusch, known to most of us as the prophetic voice which stirred the conscience of the Christian church, is best remembered by those who knew him for the depth and simplicity of his own soul. In a book there was found this note written to a close friend in 1918 when he knew that death was near. Does it not speak to us of a kind of fulfillment, an at-homeness which is the greatest gift we receive? He said: "I leave my love to those of my friends whose souls have not grown dark against me. I forgive the others and hate no man. For my many errors and weaknesses I hope to be forgiven by my fellows. I have long prayed God not to let me be stranded in a lonesome and useless life and this is the meaning of my present illness. I shall take it as a loving mercy of God toward his servant. Since 1914 the world is full of hate, and I cannot expect to be happy again in my lifetime. I had hoped to write several books which are on my mind, but doubtless others can do the work better. The only pang is to part with my loved ones, and no longer be able to stand by and smooth the way. For the rest I go gladly though I have carried a heavy handicap for thirty years and worked hard. W. R. March 31, 1918."

Has the world become too hectic, too involved, too sophisticated to find such grounding?

V

At the last this word becomes a deeply personal, even intimate, matter. It addresses each of us at the point of his own want, in the search for fulfillment. Like a mirror, such a word enables us to see ourselves as we are, yet at the same time, reflects a new light of hope which illumines our situation. We do not set out deliberately to take the long way home. But again and again, we look at the prodigal and say, "It's true. We are that way." Then there is that further hope. We look at the word of a waiting, seeking God, and say, "I shall trust that He indeed is like that."

At that point we know why the story ends, "And they began to be merry."

Sermon Twelve

THE CHALLENGE OF THE CROSS
TO SOCIETY

REVEREND ERNEST GORDON, T.D., LL.D.

*Dean of the Chapel, Princeton University, and a
Minister of the Presbyterian Church, Princeton,
N. J.*

Although "The Challenge of the Cross to Society" was preached at the Princeton University Chapel and was therefore directed primarily at an academic audience, it has a message for all men.

All of Dr. Gordon's sermons bear witness to his wide experience with life and death and suffering. During World War II he was a Captain in the Argyll and Sutherland Highlanders, was wounded in Malaya, and on the downfall of Singapore made his way to Sumatra. Here he helped fifteen hundred men, women, nursing sisters, wounded soldiers, and children make their way to freedom. When the Japanese arrived, he escaped again in a sailboat with eight others, but after twenty-four days on the Indian Ocean, he was recaptured by the Japanese Navy.

For three and a half years he was forced to work on the infamous "Railway of Death" between Thailand and Burma. During this time he helped to organize and taught in "The Jungle University," which stimulated morale, and in addition, he served as lay minister to his fellow prisoners of war. After the war he was ordained at Paisley Abbey, where he served three years as deputy minister. For a year he was Chaplain to Presbyterian students at Princeton, and he was appointed Dean of the Chapel in July, 1955.

Ernest Gordon did his undergraduate work at St. Andrews University in Scotland before the outbreak of war in 1939. Later he completed his theological studies at Edinburgh University, Hartford Theological Seminary, and at Glasgow University. He is the author of *A Living Faith for Today* and *The High Way by the River Kwai,* and has conducted Religious Emphasis Week on various university campuses. He is the Founder and first President of the Church Service Society of the U.S.A.

THE CHALLENGE OF THE CROSS TO SOCIETY

The particular claims that Christianity makes are an offense to many reasonable citizens of our Western civilization. The average man—if there is such a person—is religious, there is no question about that. Statistics in profusion proclaim this as a fact, but there is a vast difference between the vague generalities of religiosity and the specific doctrines of Christianity. The reasons are obvious. The acids of modernity have eaten deeply into the soul of the West, so that the faculty of faith has almost been destroyed. We have been conditioned to disbelieve—to deny the insights of faith. There is a concentration of belief in the supremacy of reason over faith, of a naturalistic over a biblical cosmology, of determinism over personal freedom, of materialistic over spiritual values, all this being part of our inheritance from the Renaissance and its enlightenment.

This is not an hysterical outburst in condemnation of everything within our civilization, but a quiet appraisal of the situation as it exists. We are living on the fringe benefits of Christianity. Its ethics has been abstracted from its theology and secularized, and its emphasis on brotherhood has been separated from its emphasis on divine fatherhood. We uphold the dignity of man—or at least we think we do—but deny him the very source of his uniqueness and dignity. We are not at all unlike the Corinthians to whom St. Paul wrote, "For consider, what have the philosopher, the writer and the critic of this world to show for all their wisdom? Has not God made the wisdom of this world look foolish? For it was after the world in its wisdom had failed to know God, that he in his wisdom chose to save all who would believe by the 'simplemindedness' of the Gospel message. For the Jews ask for miraculous proofs and the Greeks an intellectual panacea, but we preach Christ crucified—a stumbling block to the Jews and sheer nonsense to the Gentiles."

Like the Corinthians we are willing to gamble (what is left to gamble and that is not much) on the wisdom of this world—the wisdom of our pride of intellect—the wisdom that denies the sovereignty of God—the wisdom that forecasts greater inventions than the A-bomb.

The offense of Christianity is not only its doctrines, but the One who came that there might be a message to teach—the One who is not only God's messenger but God's message; the Son who became so involved in the common life and the common ventures of men that He ended His days on a criminal's cross.

There is something embarrassing about the death of an innocent man; we know that such a thing should not happen. In the case of Jesus, however, it is doubly embarrassing because He was condemned for blasphemy— for claiming to be equal with God His father—and as Albert Schweitzer has demonstrated in his thesis for his M.D. degree, He was not insane. He was rationally aware of the claims He made. No matter how you may regard this, it was God's man who was executed. Someone or some group was responsible for His death. We cannot very well blame the Romans, for Pilate, the mouthpiece of Rome, did his best to have Jesus released. We cannot blame the ignorant masses, for they liked Jesus. We can only blame the clergy and the scholars, the Church and the University, for they were the ones, who by guile contrived the whole vile business. They knew better, of course they did, but they deliberately chose evil. This is where we touch the raw nerve of the whole matter; they knew what was right but they didn't do it.

We like to think that knowledge saves, that the man of knowledge is the good man, the philosopher-aristocrat who is guided by his knowledge into the virtuous life. This sort of thing is stated in countless commencement addresses given throughout the country. I wonder, however, if it is as simple as that?

What is the difference, for example, between an ignorant rogue and an educated one, except that the latter is more dangerous? The former may steal a ride on a freight train and be sent to jail; the latter, however, will probably steal the railroad, if it is worth stealing, and become a college trustee.

In the anti-utopian novels of Aldous Huxley and George Orwell, the new type of controller or dictator is shown as one who is intelligent and well educated, yet who deliberately renounces the obvious conclusions of his knowledge in order to guarantee the greatest happiness of the greatest number. He is the Grand Inquisitor, of Dostoevski's prophecy, who deprives men of their freedom for their own good, who burns men's bodies for the good of their souls, or vice versa. Our universities are probably loaded with embryo Grand Inquisitors. At the end of the Second World War, Professor John MacMurray reminded our generation that one of the scandals of our time was that our universities were producing men who were intellectual giants but moral pygmies. The university, the repository of knowledge, like the individual, may gain the world at the cost of its soul.

This business about knowing the good and therefore doing it is essentially the same kind of argument as that put forth by Augustine and Pelagius. The latter said, "I can be good if I so will," to which Augustine replied, "I could be good if I would; but I won't," and went on to point out that the evidence of human experience is that we cannot move our wills;—our wills may move mountains, but they cannot move themselves. The will is diseased, and cannot cure itself; it just does not possess the power. The answer of Augustine and of Christianity is that God in Christ grants us a new dynamic, namely, grace, and it is this dynamic that changes our wills so that they become more like His own. Self-will, that is, will turned in upon itself, is essentially enslaved, irrational, and destructive. We may know, but we cannot do. Like St. Paul we may well say, "I do not understand my own actions. For I do not what I want, but I do the very thing I hate. . . . For I do not do the good I want, but the evil I do not want is what I do." Or doesn't this apply to us? Perhaps Christianity is right after all when it tells us that it takes more than knowledge to change men and women, and therefore society.

"What has this to do," you may say, "with the death of Jesus?" Namely this, that our self-will, which is in opposition to God, causes Him to take action in order that we may be released from its bondage. Moved by love, God sends His son to take His place as a man with men. You may interpret this in a wide variety of ways so long as you realize that the divine life—God's life—was lived out in the man Jesus. To the first disciples it seemed as though He was the moment in time and space when God burst upon the world. It was an explosion significantly greater than that of the A-bomb over Hiroshima, for it had this difference that it released creative power upon the earth—the power of God's love. The task of Jesus was to set men free, and to release them from the demonic forces at work in society—and there are plenty of them—seven deadly virtues and all. We know it is wrong to enslave the colored people by economic, political, and social means, yet we do it. We know that destruction by war or any other means is wrong, yet we destroy not only on battlefields, but on the roads, by capital punishment, and by countless other means. Have you ever thought of the vast number of people who are dead before they are put into their coffins—of those who are being destroyed by the fiendish ideologies of our times—of those who are being suffocated by the miasmic fogs of our materialistic society?

Jesus lived as a lover of life and men. In thinking of Him you don't need to begin with His deity, but with His humanity; and that, Christianity declares, is perfect. Clear away the mass of verbiage that has been written

94

about Him, both for and against Him, and see Him for yourself—that is why the Gospels were written.

He is the proper man, the true man, the responsible man who responds wholeheartedly to the doing of His Father's will on earth. His life is an answer to the ultimate question of human existence. As an answer, however, it is in the form of a paradox: for by living according to the divine imperative, He must die. This is the sentence of men pronounced against their King—the sentence of men enslaved by their own destructive wills. Jesus was the one truly free man, the one who was love incarnate, yet His death sentence was pronounced by the first act of self-willed rebellion on the part of man.

He knew this, no question about it; that is why He told his fractious disciples, "For the son of man has not come to be served but to serve, and to give his life to set many others free." To be a true man He could not take shelter behind prestige or artificial dignity; His place wasn't with the enforcers and the reinforcers of enslavement; instead He became a rebel for man against oppression. Because of this He had no alternative but to walk the *Via Dolorosa* to the cross. As He did so he viewed His imminent death as an at-one-ment by which mankind would be exempted from the sentence of final destruction. Steadfastly, therefore, He set his face to go to Jerusalem to encounter His enemies in their own headquarters. Because He was free He accepted the burden of man's irresponsibility, and because He was love He bore the burden of the world's hate and rejection. So completely did He identify Himself with mankind that He took its place at the point where logic breaks down, at the point where the human will is no longer operative, at the cross where the vertical plane of grace crosses the horizontal plane of human despair.

"The cross is both God's view of man, and man's view of God."

This is what we are really like, we are those who destroy the innocent, the humble, the faithful, the righteous, the free, the loving. "We don't do any such thing," you may say. "We are far too nice." Don't we? Do we not take care of ourselves first without thought of our neighbor? Is it not usually me and mine rather than thee and thine? We take from life, and by the very taking lose it so that what we are is marked by a minus sign. When God meets us in the fullness of His love we don't want Him, because His demands are too high—and so we shout, "Away with Him, let Him be crucified, and with Him anyone who doesn't contribute to the prestige of ourselves and our selfish ways."

It is only as we see God, in His mercy, taking our place, standing up for us where we have fallen down, that we see ourselves as we really are in all

95

our poverty and nakedness. The love the crucified Christ released upon the world is not the love of man, but the love of God for man. God is the lover—man is the beloved. This, by the way, is quite in contrast to MacLeish's thesis in his play *J.B.*, where J. B. is made greater than God because he can love whereas God is nothing but a destroyer. Archibald MacLeish, I think, got hold not only of the wrong God, but the wrong man.

We are created by love, for love, to love; and the one commandment given us by God is, "Thou shalt love." Yes, but how? Only by love can God's law be obeyed, yet love is not ours to command. We know we should love; but we don't. Love isn't the work of our hands, it is given to us as the gift of grace, that is, it is the result of God's gracious presence with us. "We love, because He first loved us."

God in Christ suffered for our sake—took our place in the depths of human despair—and led, and is leading, mankind out of the abyss of nothingness into the authentic experience of life—the life of love, the life of grace.

Christ and Him crucified is an offense to the civilization of the twentieth century, yet it is because of the offense that we are challenged. We are clever, and may be becoming increasingly so; but is it a diabolical cleverness, the cleverness of the most advanced I.B.M. machine? If so, what have we gained? Without love, love that is patient, kind, creative, self-sacrificing, we are nothing, nothing at all, nothing but a fanfare of trumpets and the clashing of cymbals. Without the love of God as the guiding power of our destiny, our intellectual excellence may become nothing but the means of our destruction. Thinking doesn't take place in a vacuum, it must have the power of love behind it to make it heroic and free. When it has, then it can initiate action which will be for the healing and restoring of mankind. That is why we are commanded to love God with all our mind.

Despite the conclusion about me some of you may have come to, I am not a complete pessimist. Within our Western civilization we have put all our emphasis upon accumulation—accumulation of power, of wealth, and of knowledge, and we have sought security by means of such hoarding. We have still to learn from the crucified Christ that there is no security that way. He laid down His Life—the just for the unjust—but He took it up again full of the glory and power of divine love, at His resurrection. Instead of hoarding, He gave away; He held on to nothing, yet gained everything. He lost His life only to find it again, not only for Himself but for all men, that they might indeed be His friends, His brothers.

We are at an end of an era and another one is beginning. I am optimistic enough to believe that the people of the world will still learn from the crucified Christ and be redeemed, restored, recreated by the simple mind-edness of the gospel message. As Christians we take our stand with the colored people in the South, and in South Africa; with the poor of India and China; with the lonely and unloved in Russia and Yugoslavia—and with our forgotten neighbor—not to take but to give, not to hate but to love, not to enslave but to free, not to seek our own glory but the glory that is God's in the other. This is not easy; it is hard, with the hardness that our Lord bore on the Cross!

Sermon Thirteen

FOR THE LIVING OF THIS HOUR

THE VERY REVEREND JOHN C. LEFFLER, D.D.

Dean of St. Mark's Cathedral, Seattle, Washington

Dr. Leffler was born in North Ridge, New York, 1900, attended high school in Buffalo, Wesleyan University, and the Church Divinity School of the Pacific. He was ordained a Deacon in 1928, by Bishop Brent, and ordained a priest by Bishop Ferris in 1929. From 1922 to 1927 he was a Methodist minister; from 1927 to 1929 he was assistant at St. Paul's Church, Rochester, New York. In 1929 he became Rector of St. John's Church, Ross, California, where he remained until 1940. During the last three years of his stay in Ross he was instructor in homiletics at the Church Divinity School of the Pacific. His next position was as Rector of St. Luke's Church, San Francisco, and in 1951 he was called to St. Mark's Cathedral, Seattle.

FOR THE LIVING OF THIS HOUR

Grant us wisdom; grant us courage
For the living of these days.

The great hymn from which these words are taken, might have been written especially for this very hour.

When Dr. Fosdick wrote these words in the quiet of his summer retreat on the Maine coast in 1930, the Great Depression had just begun. No one had given a thought to Hitler, and the League of Nations had the full support of every power, including Russia. Yet with a prescience which only a great prophet possesses, this noted preacher of the first half of the twentieth century seems to have caught in his poetry the constantly recurring prayer of believing men in all the years of violence since that peaceful summer of 1930.

This prayer for wisdom and courage must be our prayer today. In a way and to a magnitude never dreamed of thirty years ago "the hosts of evil 'round us scorn our Christ, assail His ways." Fears never known by preceding generations have us in their tight grip. The madness which breeds war denies the divine destiny of mankind. Our pride, ever fearful as pride must be of losing face, our reckless indulgence in epicurean pleasure as an escape from the grim realities of our days, these attitudes have made us richer in things and poorer in soul than any generation in history. These are our days, this the time, and this the condition in which, more than ever before, we need so desperately the wisdom and courage for which we have just prayed.

The dilemma America faces is the age-old dilemma the Christian has faced since our Lord hung on the Cross and rose from the grave. It is a dilemma of means more than ends. We want peace for ourselves and the world, but how do we get it? We cherish the liberty of free men for ourselves and the world, but how do we attain it and keep it without running the risk of losing it in the process? We love our country and her welfare, even as Peter and Paul loved the Roman Empire, but when does our citizenship as Americans leave off and our professed loyalty to the Kingdom of God begin? We are rightly concerned lest our great land fail in the challenge of these times and know that she must be strong and unflinching in

100

the midst of hostile forces, but what kind of strength shall we pray for and strive after?

These, you might say, are political problems which must be determined by the President and his staff. Quite so, but at heart they are not political at all but deeply involved with the moral and spiritual problems of being a Christian in our age and time. The dilemmas are the same; and in the solution of them I dare to believe the thoughtful Christian has not only a big stake, but a clear duty.

On first thought, one might be tempted to reach the cynical conclusion that, while the gospel may be applicable in a limited way to man's individual life, it is completely impracticable in the affairs of nations. This is the real gist of many of the suggestions being made by editorialists, columnists, and commentators. When we are told that our foreign policy must be shaped along the lines of subversion, bluff, and cynical realism employed by our enemies and applauded by some of our half-hearted friends, what else are we doing but admitting that the ruthless, cynical, and underhanded methods of those who scorn Christ and assail His ways are the only methods which work in the real world of our times?

But wisdom would bid us pause before we reach that conclusion. The flaw in such thinking is the assumption that our relations with the world since World War II have been motivated by Christian ideals; when as a matter of fact they have not. It is just barely possible that the reason for the failure of our foreign policy is this: since Western man from the time of the Emperor Constantine has made Christianity the official religion of the West, he has indulged in moralistic lectures to his enemies and friends which sound nicely pious and Christian, but in other ways he has compromised those moral ideas just as cynically as any one. Much of our foreign aid has been an attempt to buy friends and increase our own trade. While we have paid lip-service to freedom and independence, our economic imperialism, particularly in Latin America, has controlled the copper of Chile, the oil of Venezuela, and the sugar of Cuba. We have been friendly with some of the most ruthless dictators. Much of the present tragedy in Cuba goes back to our support of the repressive Batista who, teamed up with American capital, kept that island impoverished, diseased, and ripe for communism. In all the sorry story of the cold war—of brinksmanship and containment and massive retaliation and the missile race— we have at times belied our professions of innocence and high morality. Therefore, I cannot attribute our failure to the impracticable nature of Christian deeds, but to our compromise with them. Never since Constantine has any world power taken those ideals seriously and in this fact lies

101

the essential tragedy of Western man, who, in this age of world-wide re
lution, finds himself on the defensive at every point—not because he
Christian, but because he is only half-Christian.

Of course, it is neither my place nor my objective to suggest a new
eign policy. I must trust our President and his advisors to do that. But a
Christian and loyal American it is my place to suggest some thoughts
this dilemma.

In the first place, as a Christian I must recognize the revolutionary nat
of the present and continuing struggle and the reasons for it; I must g
thought as to how Christian men of good-will can take over that revoluti
and keep it from destroying all the values I cherish.

I must care even more than the communist, and for better reasons, t
the black and yellow races struggle for freedom from exploitation; it is
identical struggle my forefathers engaged in nearly two centuries ago; a
I must care enough to help them find this freedom.

I must be concerned that vast millions of earth's people are living
poverty, disease, and ignorance—the easy prey of those who for selfish
sons promise them relief.

I must not be afraid of that word "subversion" and must remember t
the very Christianity I now enjoy openly itself began as an undercover a
secret movement, and, in fact, has become one again in many sections
the world. I must remember that the most revolutionary ideology in hist
is not communism or fascism but the gospel of Christ, which, getting at
roots of man's individual life, must always issue in his passionate devoti
to the ideal of the Kingdom of God.

In all this I must pray for the realism of Christ who neither undere
mated the power of evil, nor was defeated by it; nor allowed it to force h
into employing evil means for good ends. Part of that realism is the rec
nition that men are sinners; that all earthly powers are under judgme
and that no one more than the idealist can be taken in by rationalizati
and compromise, often confusing means and ends. I must be ready to
the highest motives defeated by baser ones for a time, even as Christ w
to His cross; but I must not forget that in the long run truth is more pow
ful than falsehood, love than hatred, and that it is not by might nor
power but by God's spirit that the victory is won. Every time a man o
nation puts his trust in chariots or horses, as the psalmist says, or in tai
and atomic missiles as we must say, he tends in the end to come a cropp
Always there is someone else who builds bigger ones or more of them.

Frankly, I wonder if the good God may not be using our present pli
to strip us of our robe of pride and clothe us with some much-needed

102

tional humility before it is too late. "Pride goeth before a fall" is just about the truest observation ever made—true of men and true of nations.

But it is in humiliation that the character of man stands forth. It takes infinitely more courage to pick one's self up and go on after a fall than it does to ride confidently to victory. And it is the evidence of this courage in our gifted young President that gives me heart. I am not ready to give up my belief that there is a Christian solution to the dilemma of our times. If there is not, I must still go on believing with the psalmist in Israel's dilemma that "the earth is the Lord's and all that is therein"; "that He sitteth between the cherubim; be the earth never so unquiet."

Sermon Fourteen

THE RIGHT TO BE CALLED CHRISTIANS

REVEREND G. HAROLD ROBERTS
Minister, First Christian Church,
Atchison, Kansas

G. Harold Roberts has been the minister of First Christian Church in Atchison for fourteen years. During his career as a minister he has been president of the Christian Ministers' Institutes of Missouri, Iowa, and Kansas, and president of the Kansas State Convention of Christian Churches. He is a contributor to his denominational publications, *The Christian, The World Call, The Secret Place* and has served on various committees of his denomination at state and national levels.

He is a charter member of the Mark Twain Association of America and has had several articles on Mark Twain published in *The Twainian*.

THE RIGHT TO BE CALLED CHRISTIANS

> . . . and in Antioch the disciples were for the
> first time called Christians. . . .
>
> Acts 11:26

We have reason to believe that when the disciples were first called Christians they were called so derisively. They were looked down upon. They lacked social prestige. They were strange in their beliefs and peculiar in their conduct. They belonged to a new and upstart movement, lacking social approval. How natural it was that such people should be scorned.

Such scorn did not last long. It was soon discovered that these followers of Christ were remarkable people. They manifested great courage. They were utterly sincere. They were dedicated disciples of Him whom they acknowledged Lord. Their lives revealed deep humility. It was clearly the supreme purpose of their lives to be worthy to bear the name of the Christ to whom they gave joyous and complete allegiance. Little wonder that scorn of them gave way to admiration. Dedicated lives have ever disclosed a conviction that others have been quick to perceive and honor.

How did these Antioch Christians become worthy to bear His name? Is there anything in their achievement to teach and inspire us as present-day Christians? Can we, by emulation of these early Christians, come to great worthiness? I believe that they have much to offer us.

First of all, the Antioch disciples knew the value of surrender. They submitted themselves to the will of God as they knew it in Christ their Lord. They learned the value of submissiveness. They found power and poise in dedication. They were not afraid of the demands of discipline. They discovered that obedience brought freedom. They were eager to make their witness for the Christ who was all in all to them. There could be no equivocation in their loyalty. They took seriously Christ's declaration that he was the way, the truth, and the life. They entrusted their lives completely to Him. They lived by faith.

Man reaches highest wisdom and power as he learns to submit. By submission he conquers pride and vanity. He lets himself be used by the Almighty. It is when the world swaggers in its conceit, and ruthlessness is matched with ruthlessness and suspicion with suspicion, that civilization faces its gravest dangers. One would think that we had learned our lesson from catastrophic wars and failure to achieve a peace which is peace.

106

Strange—isn't it?—how often man unfits himself to face the crises of human experience because he will not surrender his life to God. He will try one desperation remedy after another, and embrace this nostrum and that, when what is needed is a deep penitential submission which brings him to the throne of God to receive the mercy, the pardon, and the power he needs to stand up to life. Pride gets us into trouble and keeps us there. It is a tyrannous master.

Can man do better when he tries to stand alone than when he tries to stand up to life in the power of God? It is the Christian's conviction that man needs God. In himself, man has no sufficient wisdom. In himself, he has no sufficient strength. Giving the thorough-going humanist credit for refusing to snivel and show the white feather in the presence of life's ills, the Christian yet believes that the humanist is to be pitied. He misses so much that he might have! The humanist neglects the great wisdom and spiritual power that God is ready to vouchsafe to those who are willing to accept his gifts. The humanist walks a lonely road, the while God is willing to walk with him. He refuses fellowship with a loving God. He refuses divine guidance. He denies hospitality to the highest. He impoverishes himself.

Nowadays the humanist is subdued. Modern war, with its barbarity and threat of total destruction of civilization, has sobered us to the point where humanism seems terribly superficial and inadequate as a way of salvation. Once in awhile a Julian Huxley will speak boldly in espousal of humanism but he is not likely to convince many that he has a message to be taken seriously. The "pep talks" of the humanists to the effect that "we just have ourselves but let's be brave" do not impress a troubled society. Less and less in the kind of world in which we live are we inclined to believe that man can go it alone. Rather, we are becoming more and more confirmed in the theists' affirmation that man must be guided and sustained by the spirit of God if he is to come to mastery of life. "Our wills are ours, O Lord, to make them Thine."

Furthermore, the disciples at Antioch were worthy to bear the name of Christ because they knew the strength of union. For them it could not be rich against poor, white against black, liberal against conservative. They must needs stand together. They were bound together by the indissoluble ties of Christly affection—unity of the spirit in the bonds of peace. They loved one another. Their loyalties were deep and true. They were willing to bear one another's burden. They achieved great democracy in the recognition of their essential brotherhood in Christ, knowing that they would be called upon to prove their brotherliness under severe testing. They

107

would keep fellowship, let the world do its worst. And the world often did just that to them—its worst, only to discover that they were not to be vanquished!

Modern Christians must learn to get along together. We must close up the ranks as we march forward. We must stress our agreements and not our differences. We must magnify the great doctrines and traditions we hold in common. We must talk in terms of one Lord, one faith, one baptism. We must realize that the Holy Spirit is eager to lead all Christians in discernment of God's will. Ours is a feeble voice in the forum of the world's life if we cannot speak as united followers of Christ.

Here we are engaged in a fight to the death against secularism, against war, against greed, against racism, against dehumanizing and depersonalizing forces in modern life, against scientific inventiveness which has given us giant powers for which we have not yet achieved moral controls, against nationalism which men make a kind of religion. As Christians we must unite to present Christ's claims upon our world. We must declare concertedly the mighty acts of God. Let the ecumenical church, like a mighty army, move forward. We can win the day but we had better hurry!

The disciples at Antioch proved their worthiness to wear the name of Christ because they achieved identity with him. They sought for that mind and spirit which were in Christ Jesus, their Lord. They lived distinctively. They walked under the sign of the cross, they maintained the spiritual glow, they bore on their bodies the marks of Christ. They gave a clear testimony. Theirs was a positive witness.

To live the life is the greatest argument any age can offer for the claims of Christ. It is the indisputable logic of Christianity. It is the unassailable truth. It is the steady light that shines in the midst of the world's darkness. It is the word of God that comes alive. It is what the world wants most of us who profess to be Christians. It is the answer to doubt and longing.

Does not modern Christianity err grievously in its failure to be distinctive? We make too many compromises, we lower our banners too often, we do not act from Christian motives. It is often impossible to tell a professing Christian from one who does not profess Christ. The Wordsworthian lament is certainly true for Christians, "the world is too much with us!" We have lost a great deal of ground by our inability to live in the world but not to be of the world. We have forfeited respect for our failure to achieve unmistakable Christian identity. One recalls Samuel Butler's withering indictment: "The average Christian would be equally amazed at hearing his religion doubted or seeing it practiced."

The time has come for us to achieve identity with Christ. We must act from Christian motives. We must make Christianity dynamic and revolutionizing in its confrontation of the issues of life. We must discern the will of God and do it. We must stop playing at religion. We must seek first the kingdom of God and His righteousness. We must stop letting lesser loyalties tell us what to believe and how to act.

To illustrate: I recall a congregation that rejected participation in behalf of its minister in the newly established pension fund of its denomination. A year later the same congregation unanimously voted to participate. Why the change of heart? One would like to answer that the gospel as preached in the church led to the change: but the truth of the matter is that it was brought about by the fact that both major political parties had placed planks in their platforms advocating pensions, old age assistance and concern for security in twilight years. Too often it is thus. The church lets its decisions be made elsewhere. Too often it is true that the church is the last to challenge conscience.

The one important thing is to believe and act as Christians should believe and act. We must act from Christian motives. We must act, for instance, not as Democrat or Republican, employer or employee, but as Christians who seek to make Christ ruler of all the relationships of life. We must seek to spiritualize the concepts by which men live. Only thus can we conquer the giant evils of our day that threaten to down us.

We will have to pay a big price for such identity. We will have to give up ease and complacency. We will have to learn the deeper meanings of discipline and denial. We will have to learn what it means to sacrifice. We will have to dare the world's contumely. We will have to suffer for earnest convictions. Only thus can we be true to Christ's expectation of us. Only thus can there be renascence of first-century Christianity's devotion and power. Only thus can we achieve "the total penetration of our total culture by the total gospel" (the phrase is Elton Trueblood's), and only thus can we today earn the right to be called Christians.

When I was a high school lad I had the privilege of hearing William Jennings Bryan speak. The eloquent Commoner spoke more about religion than politics and made impassioned plea for utter commitment to Christ. He spoke of the courage of the early Christians. He described their death before wild beasts in the Roman arena. They went to death with songs of faith on their lips and indomitable courage in their hearts and many of the Romans who had come to taunt left asking themselves these questions: "What is that can enter the lives of people and make them die as these Christians die? Is it not that a higher power inspires and sustains them?"

Archibald MacLeish once castigated authors who refuse to take a stand charging that they become, thereby, indifferent to values, careless as to significance, and refugees from consequences.

The same, unfortunately, can be said of many of us who claim to be Christians. Our commitment to spiritual values is so shallow that we show little concern when such values are placed on trial before the judgment bar of a secular and pagan society. We lack awareness of the significance of Christ's lordship and let superficial loyalties rule our lives. When things have gone morally wrong in our world because of our poor discipleship we have refused to repent and have retreated from consequences.

This is the more tragic when one ponders the fact that Christianity has uniquely what our world needs. Our world needs commitment to truths that are universal. In such commitment lies the conquest of provincialism and nationalism. In it lies the conquest of racial egotisms and chauvinistic loyalties. Man has come into a new day when he cannot afford to be petty. He cannot afford to hate other men and make war against them. Christianity speaks, as can nothing else, of universals. God is the God of all peoples. Christ is saviour of all. Human personality is infinitely and eternally precious in the sight of God. Life can be abundant and it can be glorious. Man can know the way of salvation.

It is high time for Christians to achieve their true identity and give their true witness. The supreme tribute to present-day Christians will come when the world characterizes them as it did first-century Christians—"eager to turn the world upside down!"

> We have not known Thee as we ought,
> Nor learned Thy wisdom, grace, and power;
> The things of earth have filled our thought,
> And trifles of the passing hour.
> Lord, give us light Thy truth to see,
> And make us wise in knowing Thee.
>
> We have not loved Thee as we ought,
> Nor cared that we are loved by Thee;
> Thy presence we have coldly sought,
> And feebly longed Thy face to see.
> Lord, give a pure and loving heart
> To feel and own the Love Thou art.

Sermon Fifteen

THE DISPLACED CHRIST AND OUR DISORDERED WORLD

REVEREND CARL F. H. HENRY, TH.D., PH.D.

A Minister of the American Baptist Church, Professor of Theology and Christian Philosophy at Fuller Theological Seminary, Pasadena, California, and Editor of Christianity Today, Washington, D. C.

Dr. Henry was formerly chairman of the Department of Philosophy of Religion at Northern Baptist Theological Seminary in Chicago. He has served as Visiting Professor of Theology at Wheaton College, Gordon Divinity School, and at Winona Lake Summer School of Theology. Dr. Henry studied at Wheaton College, took his Th.D. at Northern Baptist Seminary and his Ph.D. from Boston University. He also did graduate research at New College in Edinburgh, Scotland. He is now Professor of Theology and Christian Philosophy at Fuller Theological Seminary, Pasadena, California, and is Editor of *Christianity Today*.

Among his books are *Remaking the Modern World, The Protestant Dilemma, Notes on the Doctrine of God, Fifty Years of Protestant Theology, The Drift of Western Thought, Christian Personal Ethics,* and *Successful Church Publicity.* Evangelical Books recently distributed the compilation *Contemporary Evangelical Thought,* of which he was general editor and author of the chapter on "Religion and Science." Formerly a Long Island newspaperman, he once edited *The Smithtown Star* and *The Port Jefferson Times-Echo,* both Long Island weeklies, and has served as suburban correspondent for the *New York Herald Tribune, The New York Times, Standard News Association,* and the *Chicago Tribune.* From 1945 to 1952 he was literary editor of *United Evangelical Action* and he is a frequent contributor to other religious publications.

He was acting dean of Fuller Theological Seminary when it began in 1947. In 1951 he gave the W. B. Riley Lectures at Northwestern Schools; in 1952, he presented a course of lectures at Central Baptist Seminary, Toronto; and in 1957, he gave the Wilkinson Lectures at Northern Baptist Seminary.

In 1952 he was one of four Americans who accompanied a "flying seminar" of sixty-five students to Europe and the Near East under the sponsorship of Winona Lake School of Theology. His book, *Glimpses of a Sacred Land*, came from observations made on that trip.

This sermon was delivered at the Third Annual Convention of the American Association of Evangelical Students at Evangel College, Springfield, Missouri.

THE DISPLACED CHRIST AND
OUR DISORDERED WORLD

We live in a world almost fatally divided against itself—a world hopelessly disunited from God and tragically unaware that Jesus Christ is the lost center of human life and existence. The times are out of joint because Jesus Christ is out of place—that is our theme; our subject, "The Displaced Christ in a Disordered World."

Whoever visits those massive United Nations quarters in New York must at the same time face the hard fact of our divided world and its disunited nations. Whoever takes part in ecumenical conclaves stressing "the unity of the Church" is repeatedly reminded of the divisions of Christendom (Eastern Orthodox, Roman Catholic, Protestant—both inclusive and exclusive). Whoever participates in the secular dialogues and seminars of the day soon senses the discordant community tensions that now increasingly vex our pluralistic society. We live in a time of international, national, and domestic discord.

Beneath these many divisions lurks another—a division that is fundamental to all others. Not only is society at odds with itself, but homes and families are divided on the great issues of life. This is an age of divided minds. There is a lack of intellectual integration in the face of the divergent claims impinging on the souls of men. There is a deep cleft in the conscience of the West regarding the Christian religion, its inherited religion. There is halfheartedness in the matter of ultimate commitment to the Christian world-life view.

Multitudes of men and women, of course, still celebrate Christmas and Easter; they proudly claim a connection with some branch of the Church; and they give with some measure of generosity, if not of sacrifice, to what they consider "Christian causes." But Jesus Christ is not on this basis really their Lord. No longer is the Bible for most men "the final rule of faith

112

and practice," that is, the authoritative source of their religious conceptions and moral convictions.

This revolt against the Christian outlook has been gaining momentum since A.D. 1600. The rise of modern philosophy meant the substitution of speculative ideas for the biblical revelation of God and His will for man. In the first stage of this exchange, biblical theism gave way to philosophical or speculative theism among the intellectuals, who sought more and more to promote theories of God and man outside the premises of human sinfulness and divine redemption. A century ago this revolt swept toward its climax: evolutionary explanations challenged the Christian doctrine of creation as well as of redemption. The consequences of evolutionary naturalism were not fully apparent until our twentieth century. They were the decline of the democracies which were trusting the wants of the majority rather than seeking the will of God, Nazi Socialism and its concentration camps and gas chambers in the land of Luther, the rise of communism into a world force that breaths slaughter against all gods but the absolute state. The fruits of evolutionary naturalism are seen also in the wilderness of American life—in our lost sense of national purpose and in our gold-greedy and sex-saturated society. Ours is a declining culture sagging out of orbit, a civilization sinking like a meteor in the night, a generation that has lost its reason for being.

I

Once it was not so. In her finest hour the West knew Jesus Christ as the true center of human life and existence. That immovable conviction lifted the Western world above paganism and made her a bearer of life and hope to distant lands in darkness and despair. Probably no passage states this message of the centrality of Jesus Christ as comprehensively as the prologue to John's Gospel, which cuts squarely across our modern indecision of mind and heart by announcing the same challenge that once swept the ancient mind and shaped a new mind in its place.

Once the West knew that the multiple man-made gods have met their match in the supreme revelation of monotheism, knew that Jesus Christ has swept away all competitors and triumphed over them. Once the West knew that God in Christ is the key to intellectual integration, to the integration of all life's experiences. Once the West knew that Jesus Christ is the true and right answer to the dilemmas posed by the world religions, by the movements of history, by the world of nature, and by man's troubled moral conscience.

113

1. Once the West knew that Jesus Christ, the eternal Logos incarnate, unravels the enigma posed by the fact of the many world religions. He alone is the ultimate Word; He alone among the founders of religions is God come in the flesh; He alone personally redeems all who put their trust in Him.

He is the ultimate Word. For He is forever with God in eternity past and in the eternities to come. Who can escort man into the presence of the Father but He who said, "I am the way . . . no man cometh unto the Father but by me" (John 14:6)? "In the beginning was the Word, and the Word was with God," or, as *The New English Bible* has it, "The Word dwelt with God" (John 1:1).

Yet more, He is Himself God, God come in the flesh. "And the Word was God" (John 1:1)—"what God was, the Word was" (*The New English Bible*). And in His coming, God has shown His face; indeed, has poured His fullness into human flesh in the supreme and final guarantee that God is as the prophets declared—personal, righteous, merciful, and sovereign. "And the Word became flesh and dwelt among us (and we beheld his glory). . . ." "For in him dwelleth all the fulness of the Godhead bodily" (John 1:14; Colossians 2:9). So Christianity towered above all other religions—it knew the eternal Logos incarnate, Jesus of Nazareth.

More than this, the ultimate Word, the incarnate Word, is also the redemptive Word. Jesus Christ personally redeems fallen man. "Behold the Lamb of God, that taketh away the sin of the world" (John 1:29). "We beheld his glory . . . full of grace and truth. . . . The law was given by Moses, but grace and truth came by Jesus Christ" (John 1:14, 17). Once the West knew that Jesus Christ is the superlative answer to the world religions; that He towers above their pathetic contradictions, that He unmasks them as the human gropings of fallen men who are now brought face to face with the ultimate Word, the incarnate Word, the redemptive Word, in Jesus of Nazareth.

2. Once the West knew that Jesus Christ, the eternal Logos incarnate, supplies the real answer also to the enigma posed by the universe. The space-time universe is no blind, unthinking process empty of ultimate meaning. Things are not the ultimate reality, but have been fashioned by the Logos, their Creator. "All things were made by him; and without him was not anything made that was made" (John 1:3). ("Through him all things came to be; no single thing was created without him," *The New English Bible*.) The Marxists are therefore dead wrong, as is every evolutionary, naturalistic speculation that things or stuff came first, and that mind and values are a late emergent of transient significance. It is a commentary—

114

wide as the heavens, intricate as the atom—on the Living God. It mirrors the infinite mind and will of its Creator and Preserver; it is, in fact, a mirror of His glory and is intended to drive us not only to our laboratories but also to our knees. "The heavens declare the glory of God; and the firmament showeth his handiwork" (Psalm 19:1). "For all that may be known of God by men lies plain before their eyes; indeed God himself has disclosed it to them. His invisible attributes, that is to say his everlasting power and deity, have been visible, ever since the world began, to the eye of reason, in the things he has made" (Rom. 1:19-20, *The New English Bible*). "The world was made by him" (John 1:10). Once Western man knew this majestic truth, and recognized Jesus Christ, the incarnate Creator-Preserver of all things, as the key to the universe.

3. In its finest hour the West knew more. In Jesus Christ, the incarnate Logos, it found light on the enigmas of ethics and the widespread confusion over the good life. The Genesis creation account reminds us again and again of God's eye to "the good" in the beginnings of life, and then pointedly records God's "very good" when man at last is made in the divine image. The Logos is more than the agent of man's creation; He is the light of man's life. "That was the true Light, which lighteth every man coming into the world" (John 1:9). "In him was life, and the life was the light of men" (John 1:4). So human life is to be specially understood, not through the lower life of the beasts, but through the light of the Logos. Even in sin and shame that light ferrets us out. "The light shines on in the dark, and the darkness has never quenched it" (John 1:5, *The New English Bible*). The light, fractured by our fallen consciences, nonetheless hails us still before the judgment throne of God, and opens a causeway to the Redeemer: "Behold the Lamb of God, that taketh away the sin of the world" (John 1:29). He is Himself the Light of the world; He baptizes with the Holy Ghost, sanctifying His followers, restoring them, repairing the broken image of God. Once the Western world knew that the God of incarnation and the God of creation is the God of sanctification too—that the answer to the moral enigma is Jesus Christ, who stands also as the key to the universe and the world religions.

4. Nor dare we stop here, alive as is our generation to historical events. Once the West knew that the center and climax of history belong to Jesus Christ, the eternal Logos incarnate. History is no accumulation of meaningless fragments, no series of recurring cycles. The whole of it—all human decision and action—stands related to the Logos with eternal consequences.

Human history is now fallen history; so it has been since the Garden of Eden became a resort for Adam's rendezvous with Satan. "The light shin-

115

eth in the darkness" (John 1:5). You cannot understand history if you think it is a trail of glory or a paeon of divinity; philosophies and religions that make that mistake must try to lie sin and evil and death out of existence. You can understand history only under the hand of God's judgment and in the light of the incarnation of God in Christ.

"Now is the judgment [crisis] of this world; now shall the prince of this world be cast out" (John 12:31). All the other "crises of our time" (Laos, Cuba, East Germany) are really sub-crises. The incarnation is the decisive center of human history; and sacred history is the realm in which God is working out man's destiny. There are two orders of humanity; all who reject Him are exposed forever to God's wrath, whereas the "sons of God" (John 1:12) reign forever with the Son of Man. He who has stepped into history from His home in the eternities will supply history's climax as well; beyond the incarnation and resurrection stand the second advent and the final judgment of the race.

Once the West knew all this—that Jesus Christ is the key to the nature of the world and man, the key to our moral predicament and to the religious quest, the key to the whole sweep of historical events. In her finest hour, the West recognized that Jesus Christ is Saviour and Lord, and in this commitment found the rational and ethical integration of all of life's experiences. The theologian, the scientist, the moral philosopher and the historian traveled the same road; they referred the yearnings of the soul, the secrets of nature, the proddings of conscience, and the pattern of history to one and the same principle, indeed, to the person of Jesus of Nazareth. Western culture found its unity and its elevation from paganism in the recognition of the eternal Logos become incarnate—the key to the universe, to man, to nature and to history.

II

To multitudes of modern men all this now sounds strange and foreign. The world today is engaged in a search for a center of unity other than Jesus Christ. We live in a century in revolt against the Christian heritage and biblical traditions. The whole world seems now to be caught in the cross-current of three cultural forces competing to displace and to replace the Christian claim upon human thought and decision. Each of these cultural movements assumes that Christianity has collapsed, and that instead it is now destined to fill the role once supplied by Christianity as the integrator of man's thought and life.

1. One of these cultural forces is *scientism*. Who can doubt the signifi-

116

cant contributions of modern science? It has revolutionized the material side of our living. Not only in the realm of scientific theory, but in respect to its practical applications, we are indebted around the clock to changes that now occur so swiftly we can hardly orient ourselves to them in a single life-span.

But modern science has intensified rather than relieved the ethical and spiritual crisis of the West. The pretension of many of its champions that science alone can save us has made of scientism a false god, worshipped on the premise that science alone is qualified to mediate between the old and new elements in our culture. So the notion has grown that science "saves us" by delivering us from any reliance on the supernatural, and by trusting only in the experimental method and verification by sense experience. Unchanging truths and fixed values now go by the board; the meaning of life is never finally established but is subject to constant revision.

But social scientists are in hopeless disagreement today over what and who man is, and over what social organization best meets human needs. There is widening recognition that experimental methods (so useful in the physical and biological sciences) cannot be applied to the social sciences. Experimental science leaves man without abiding norms, without a true center of reference, and thereby enlarges the danger that every age and every person will establish a realistic and arbitrary measure of life.

Scientism has advanced the cause of secularism. It has intensified the agonizing convulsions of our age by stripping civilization of conscience and by materializing the spirit and soul of man. Instead of its long-promised rejuvenation of Western culture, through its professed and pretended omnicompetence, scientism has deprived mankind or moral ultimates while providing the implements for the destruction of modern civilization and for erasing all civilized existence from the face of the earth.

That is why there is today a decline of popular faith in science—one of the great cultural forces which many modern men trusted absolutely to restore the broken meaning of human life. Instead of fulfilling that promise, scientism stands unmasked as a pretender, and already it is beginning to enlarge the spirit of pessimism abroad in the world.

2. Another cultural force which seeks to fill the vacuum in modern life is *political democracy*. This is a comprehensive search for a workable organization of modern life on the basis of individual rights and liberties.

We in the United States know how much our people have owed to the spirit of 1776, with its repudiation of tyranny and its emphasis on human rights and the individual man's dignity as a person.

But the political upheavals in the Western world make it clear that modern conceptions of human freedom and political democracy have inadvertently enlarged the moral crisis and have even deepened the discords of our century. The emphasis on rights to the neglect of human *duties* has encouraged the majority to regard the right as whatever the majority wishes—in other words, men have lost the sense of *absolute right,* and in its place are learning to live with what seems statistically or numerically right. This emphasis on rights without duties, on rights as a distillation of popular opinion, soon dignifies license and deteriorates to anarchy; thus it prepares the way for a strong man on a horse, that is, for a dictator who relies on power to cement a crumbling nation.

If you wish to gauge how far our Anglo-Saxon political morality has deteriorated, contrast the U.N. Declaration of Human Rights with the U. S. Declaration of Independence. The U.N. Declaration is preoccupied with human rights; it neglects an emphasis on human responsibilities; it says nothing about a divine source and divine sanction of man's freedoms and duties. The Declaration of Independence, on the other hand, is not content to speak only of human equality; it declares that all men are *created* equal, and that they are *endowed by their Creator* with inalienable rights. When human rights are detached from the will of God, they are swiftly attached to the whim of the state—or of the superstate—and political democracy is on the skids.

The loss of the will of God as a live consideration has contributed to the deterioration of the democracies, and thus to a decline of popular faith in democratic ideals. Walter Lippmann has reminded us that faith in the democracies has been on the wane since the first World War. Instead of fulfilling its promise of a new era of human hope, political democracy as a cultural force is likewise beginning to enlarge the spirit of pessimism abroad in the world.

3. The third major force seeking to reinterpret the whole of life and culture today is *communism.* It seeks to revolutionize society—the family, education, economics, politics, culture—within the totalitarian premise that the state is absolute and that every phase of man's life exists for the sake of the state.

Whoever feels a throb of sympathy for impoverished masses will sense something of the appeal communism gives through its promise of a new world order. So much poverty and suffering have stalked the world. A comprehensive proposal guaranteeing utopia is sure to enlist the interest both of the underprivileged and of utopian moralists, especially if it relies on something more automatic than voluntary spiritual dedication and something less commanding than supernatural regeneration to achieve its goal.

But it is increasingly evident that communism has exploited the great vacuums in modern life to advance and achieve state absolutism. It has perfected a crisis technique for overthrowing the existing order and for promoting totalitarian world revolution. Those repressed multitudes which have subsisted under the communist flag for a generation know its hollow pretensions to honor the dignity of man; its pernicious distortion of the truth into whatever is serviceable to the rulers; its blatant rejection of absolute morality. The fate of modern Hungary, where blood bath and tyrannical terror suppressed the clamor of the mobs for elemental human freedoms, symbolizes the ruthlessness of communism and its indifference to individual dignity.

It is therefore not surprising that at long last some quarters show evidence—even if Red power is still far from spent—of a decline of faith in the communist ideology. Instead of a fulfillment of fond hope for tomorrow, those caught in the stern grip of a communist fate are tempted to skepticism as propaganda for social justice gives way to the realities of totalitarian injustices. Communism succeeds in correlating and integrating the human enterprise only through the power of the sword, not because of the inherent power of dialectical materialism as a world-and-life view.

These then are the cultural forces to which the West has looked in its fruitless search for a modern alternative to the Christian integration of life and experience: scientism, political democracy, and communism. They compete with each other for the souls of men, but instead of fulfilling a pledge of bright hope, each contributes to the culture crisis of the West. Unless confronted and challenged, one and all will hurl us at last over the precipice of a civilization in utter collapse.

III

The Christian evangel must exhibit Jesus Christ afresh as the only true and changeless center of abundant life and enduring culture.

The special urgency of Christian integration of life and experience now arises from the fact that the recent modern alternatives have tended to become openly anti-Christ in spirit. Science, human liberty, and the concern for social justice were all preserved from demonic expressions when sheltered by the lordship of Christ. But in our century the naturalistic thesis has proved most aggressive and influential in the reigning philosophies of science, of history, of politics, of economics. The modern philosophy of science revolted against miracle, then scorned the supernaturalness of Jesus Christ. The modern philosophy of history became so enamored of evolu-

119

tionary expectations concerning the future that it refused to locate the central historical event in the past, particularly the incarnation of Jesus Christ. The modern philosophy of politics snubbed the fixed will of God as a significant criterion in political decision and action. The modern philosophy of economics no longer connected economic freedom with its biblical motifs, and soon became enamored instead with secular and collectivistic theories. All these philosophies lost touch with the eternal order, and gave direction to the interpretation of human affairs from an essentially secular standpoint: modern science is *ignorant* of the supernatural; political democracy is *indifferent* to the supernatural; communism is *intolerant* of the supernatural. This hostility to the Living God incorporated wittingly or unwittingly by the cultural dynamisms of our century has created a new and terrible vacuum. World-wide in its implication and in its indecisions, this vacuum raises anew for the fast-fading twentieth century the problem of morality and the good life, the problem of the inherent nature of the universe, and the problem of the meaning of history.

Over against the superficial religiosity and speculative philosophy now crowding into this vacuum, evangelical Christianity with its cohort of modern disciples of Jesus Christ has a special obligation to proclaim the eternal Logos become flesh as normative for all our aspirations and ideals. Surely men who are strangers to the Gospel of Christ cannot be expected to herald the good news. You and I know that Jesus Christ offers this world its one and only hope of a truly coherent perspective of life and experience.

We know too, of course, that the faith and witness of the early Christians were set aflame by something more than a revealed philosophy of reality. In all simplicity they knew what seems again and again to escape the brilliant modern mind; they knew what our modern world, with all its sham sophistication, needs to recover once again.

They knew the Living God, beside whom there is no other, and they worshipped Him!

They knew the will of God, in the form of divinely revealed commandments and precepts, and they yielded themselves in moral obedience.

They knew a perfect morality lived in the flesh by Jesus Christ, and they longed for restoration to the divine image as man's holy destiny to come!

They knew the forgiveness of their sins, purchased by the Redeemer, and they looked with thanksgiving to the blood of the cross!

They knew that Jesus of Nazareth had conquered death and had brought immortality to light by His triumphant resurrection!

They knew the gift of the Holy Spirit, providing a moral dynamic that staggered the pagan world!

120

They knew that the ascended Christ heard their prayers, and in their tribulations they knew that from the shadows of eternity He was keeping watch over His own!

They knew they were commissioned for a special task of evangelizing a lost world, and that "neither is there salvation in any other" (Acts 4:12)!

They had the prospect of a blessed immortality, an eternity in the Father's house and in reunion with their crucified and living Lord!

Now, what do the beleaguered multitudes of our twentieth century need more than this? These were the spiritual treasures that shaped a spirit higher than that of Greece or Rome and brought newness of life to the Western world while the Orient sank deeper in its pagan mires. What do *you* need, more than these great realities? Tell me—if your heart beats to the pulse of history, if you have a feeling for eternal destiny?

Find Jesus Christ as your Redeemer from sin, as the saving Lord of your personal destiny, and you discover Him at the same time to be much more. He is the answer to the problem of the world religions and cults; He is the key to the enigma of the universe; He is the central figure of human history; He is the perfect guide through the labyrinth of ethics. Our heritage and our destiny are both meshed to these great Christian realities. The One who alone can bring order into our tangled lives supplies also the one enduring prospect for uniting our divided world.

Sermon Sixteen

STAR OUT OF ORBIT

REVEREND DAVID HAXTON CARSWELL READ, D.D.

Minister, Madison Avenue Presbyterian Church, New York, New York

Every Christmas Dr. Read gives a fantasy as his Christmas sermon. This fantasy was given on Christmas Day in Madison Avenue Church to a congregation that has come to expect and to love these special Christmas messages.

Dr. Read was born on January 2, 1910, at Cupar, Fife, Scotland. He attended Daniel Stewart's College in Edinburgh, and studied at the University of Edinburgh from 1928 to 1932, then at Montpellier, Strasbourg, and Paris (in 1932 and 1933), and at Marburg in 1934. He took his theological degree at New College, Edinburgh, and was ordained and installed at Coldstream West, Church of Scotland, in 1936. From 1939 to 1945 he was chaplain to the Forces of the British Army, and was a prisoner of war from June, 1940, to April, 1945.

From 1939 to 1949 he was minister of Greenbank Church, Edinburgh. He was the first chaplain to the University of Edinburgh, in 1949, and was appointed chaplain to Her Majesty the Queen in Scotland in 1952. When Madison Avenue Presbyterian Church in New York City sought a minister to succeed Dr. George Buttrick, Dr. Read was called, in January, 1956. He received the honorary D.D. from Edinburgh University in July, 1956.

He was Warrack Lecturer on Preaching at the University of Glasgow in 1950-51, Old Saint Andrew's Memorial Lecturer on Worship in Toronto in 1954, and George Shepard Lecturer on Preaching at Bangor Theological Seminary in 1959; he has led University Christian Missions in Scotland, Australia, Canada, and the United States. He has also had much experience in the field of radio and television.

Dr. Read has written *The Spirit of Life, Prisoners' Quest* (a collection of lectures given in prisoner of war camp), *Call It a Day, The Communication of the Gospel,* and *The Christian Faith.* He has also published articles in *The Scottish Journal of Theology, The Atlantic Monthly, The Expository Times,* and many other religious and secular journals.

123

STAR OUT OF ORBIT

Once upon an eternity, in the darkest corner of outer space, there was a little star—so small that, when he looked through the wrong end of a telescope he couldn't see the Earth. They were very busy out there in his department, for it was an expanding universe where Nothing was becoming Something all the time and the little star found it all very puzzling. The years were flying past him so quickly that he gave up trying to count them after the third billion, and just floated gently on listening to the gentle humming of new born stars getting into orbit and the occasional crackling sound as Possibilities exploded into Probabilities and then undulated away into nothingness. It was only after he had got used to the calendar of space that he realized that the reason he couldn't see the Earth was that it had not yet come into existence.

Then, one fine Light-year, the little star got bored. The universe was as beautiful as ever, but it seemed to him that it was a cold and mathematical beauty. It was all arithmetic and algebra and geometry up there, and the other stars seemed perfectly content swinging around in their orbits and figuring out how fast the universe was expanding around them. There were numbers lying about everywhere; square roots were always being extracted, and decimals repeating all over the place. The little star began to wish that something else would happen than these perfect patterns and just more and more Space-Time. It was all so exact, so rhythmic, and so dull. Might there not be something more interesting somewhere, some time, in this universe that came spinning out of the mind of God?

He pondered this for a few billion years. Then one day, just when he was feeling relatively exhausted (everything was relative up there and that made it worse), and thoroughly sick of his orbit, he caught a Rumor. It came floating past on a cloud of star-dust and he was just able to grab it as it passed. It was just a tiny whisper of a Rumor but it was enough to make him jump and send a little shiver along his orbit.

This was the story as it came to the little star that day. It seemed that once upon a Space-Time a certain constellation had gone waltzing off into a corner of the universe, and there one of its smaller stars had streaked away on its own with a cluster of tiny planets in orbit around him. So far the Rumor told of nothing new. This kind of thing was always happening and it was just as mathematical as everything else. The exciting part was

124

still to come. On one of these tiny planets that were going round the new star a new experiment was being made. It was called Life.

Rumor didn't know if this experiment was going on anywhere else but it was happening on that planet. "They call it Earth," said Rumor, "and it's so small you could balance it on a decimal point." "Size isn't everything," said the little star, "look at these exploding atoms—you can't even see them." "Well, there it is," said Rumor, "there's Life on Earth, and next time I pass I'll tell you more about it."

The little star waited impatiently for a couple of billion years till Rumor came again. He kept thinking about Earth and the new experiment. This was what he had been looking for—anything to get out of the rut. He sang over and over again the only song he knew:

> "Twinkle, twinkle little star,
> How twinkle-twinkle bored you are,
> Always in your orbit loop,
> Spinning like a hula-hoop."

Then, one century, Rumor arrived breathless, and rode three times round the orbit before he could tell the whole story. It was a tale of Life— of green grass pushing up through the stones, of trees spreading out their leaves and dropping all kinds of luscious fruit to the ground, of flowers weaving patterns of color, and great, dark, shaggy things moving in the depth of the sea. And he told of scaly fish of a million different kinds darting about the waters; and of snakes and lizards that crawled across the land, of birds that swooped among the trees, and of all kinds of animals, fast and slow, furry and sleek, that ran or swam or climbed or burrowed in the ground. He told about the hippopotamus, and the little star liked that best. "If only," he thought, "there was a hippopotamus up here, just one hippopotamus amongst all this mathematical perfection.

Then a thought struck him. "Is anyone enjoying this Life? I suppose God is enjoying it or he wouldn't have made it, but is there anyone else?" "That," said Rumor, "is the most wonderful thing of all. There are beings down there, human beings they're called, and God has made them differently from everything else. They don't have only eyes and ears and legs, they have minds to think about all these things, souls to wonder and absorb and enjoy, and spirits to share it all with the God who made them. Best of all, they can love."

"Love," said the little star, "What is that?" "Love," said Rumor, "is what God is. And it's love he wants more than anything else. Love is what makes things; love is what keeps things going; love is beauty and goodness and other people's happiness. Love is the shining orbit of God."

"I don't altogether understand," said the little star, "but it seems that Life must be very exciting and that these human beings must be the happiest creatures in the universe."

"Don't you believe it," said a great deep voice beside them, "that's only Rumor." And there was an angel, with the tiniest orbit the little star had ever seen circling round his head.

"Don't you know," said the angel in a voice that tinkled like broken star-dust, "don't you know that when God makes someone able to love he makes them free. If they were not free they could not love; for love is freedom. When God sets a star in orbit it just obeys. All this expanding universe is just obedience. But when God sets a man and woman in motion and bids them love him, and love one another, they can obey or disobey. They can love—or not love. He lets them choose."

"Do you mean," said the little star, trying to follow all this, "that they have chosen not to obey and therefore they are not happy?"

"Well," said the angel, "there's been a lot of trouble—things you wouldn't understand, like hate, and fear, and sickness, and murder, and crime, and war. But God has gone on loving them. He's never forced them, but has been like a light shining in the darkness and that light of men has never gone out."

"Can anything more be done," said the little star, "to help these poor men and women, to get them on to the right way, to show them how to love?"

"Nothing more," said the angel, "they know the way, don't they? Who can stop them so long as they are free to go wrong?"

And the little star was very sad and wished and wished that he could help. A few thousand years flashed past and then suddenly the universe began to thrill with a new and wonderful music. There were angels everywhere and Rumor darted from constellation to constellation in an ecstasy of astonishment. From the deepest vaults of the heavens that lapped around the edges of the universe came a Voice that trembled through space and echoed against eternity: "When the fullness of time was come God sent forth his Son, born of a woman." There was a rush of angel wings past our little star and he heard a chorus sliding down to earth on a moonbeam of purest love: "Glory to God in the highest and on earth peace to men of goodwill."

The little star tugged frantically at his orbit. One, two, three—and he was away, chasing the angels through space to see what it was that God had now given to men. "It's a King," said an angel as he flashed past, "a King for the world of men, a King to lead them in the way of love."

126

The little star was delighted to be out of orbit. Now something was happening. He was no longer bored. He wanted to see this Earth where there was Life. He wanted to see the grass and the trees, and the animals and the birds. He wanted to see the hippopotamus. He wanted to see men and women, these creatures who could love. And most of all he wanted to see this King—God's King—who was going to make them love. How was he going to do it? Would he show them more of God's power? teach them the secrets of the atom? dazzle them with the knowledge of the stars?

As he grew near the earth he paused. There was the little round ball and somewhere on it were these little specks called men and women. How would he find the King? He circled a few thousand times looking for a brilliant light and listening for a tremendous peal of thunder. But nothing much seemed to be happening. Then it occurred to him that God might have warned some of these men that his King was coming. So he came very close and began to look carefully across the continents and islands. It occurred to him that he'd better find the wisest men on earth—even wise enough to know about God and his King.

After a long search he found them. Three wise men were travelling across a desert, making for a little land on the edge of a great sea. So he swooped down very near and wherever they went he went too. In fact it looked almost as though they were following him. And then, one day, as the darkness began to roll over this part of the earth, the wise men stopped and stabled their camels. With slow and deliberate steps they passed a small hotel and went into the stable yard. The little star drew near as he possibly could without burning anyone and stared and stared. A wooden door creaked open and he was just able to send a little shaft of his light inside. It fell on a heap of straw, and on the straw lay a woman—and beside her a new-born child. And the wise men were bowed down to the ground, for they had found their King.

And the little star remembered what the angel said. "Love is free; you cannot force love." There was God's answer to the needs of his human family—the gift of perfect love. And he had entrusted his Son to this world of men. There could be no force, no thunder and lightning, no nuclear flash. "Here is Love; I'll let them choose," said God.

The little star climbed back to his orbit satisfied. Everything was now clearer, happier, more interesting. Even the orbits seemed less dull. For he had shared for a moment in the vision of Life, and had beheld the Love that is God.

The story would end here, except for something that happened to the little star on his way back to his orbit. It takes a longish time to make that

Sermon Seventeen

THE UNITY OF CHRISTIAN CHURCHES

His Eminence Archbishop Iakovos, D.D., L.H.D.

Archbishop of the Greek (Orthodox) Archdiocese of North and South America, New York, New York

Archbishop Iakovos (Demetrios A. Coucouzis) was born July 29, 1911, on the Turkish Island of Imbros. He graduated with high honors from the Theological School of Halki of the Ecumenical Patriarchate in Istanbul in 1934, was ordained a Deacon that same year, and served as Archdeacon to the Metropolitan of Derkon from 1934 to 1939. In that year he came to the United States and served as Archdeacon of the Greek Archdiocese and as Professor of the Archdiocese Theological School, then located in Pomfret, Connecticut.

He was ordained a Priest in Boston on June 14, 1940, and served in this capacity at Hartford, Connecticut, 1940-1941, was Preacher at Holy Trinity Cathedral, New York City, in 1941-1942, and later in 1942 served for a brief period in St. Louis, Missouri. In 1942 he was appointed Dean of the Cathedral of the Annunciation in Boston, where he remained until 1954. For a brief period in 1954, prior to his selection as a Bishop, he served as Director of the Holy Cross Orthodox Theological School in Brookline, Massachusetts. While in Boston he studied at Harvard Divinity School.

In 1954 Archbishop Iakovos was elected Bishop of Melita (Malta) and was assigned to the Archdiocese of Central and Western Europe. The following year he was appointed Representative of the Ecumenical Patriarchate at the World Council of Churches headquarters in Geneva, and a year later he was elected a Metropolitan. Then in 1959 the Holy Synod of the Ecumenical Patriarchate elected him Archbishop of North and South America, to succeed the late Archbishop Michael.

As the Representative of the Ecumenical Patriarchate in the World Council of Churches, Archbishop Iakovos, then known as Metropolitan James, traveled extensively throughout the world and attended many ecclesiastical councils. He also visited the United States on several occasions and delivered lectures at Harvard, Boston University, and other institutions. He is the author of several books. The Archbishop is an American citizen, has close ties with Protestant and Episcopal groups in the United States, especially within the World Council of Churches and the National Council of Churches.

The Greek Archdiocese, which is under the jurisdiction of the ancient Ecumenical Patriarchate of Constantinople now headed by Patriarch Athenagoras I, has 1,150,000 communicants and 375 churches in the United States. It is the headquarters of the Greek Orthodox Church, which is the largest of many Eastern Orthodox bodies in America. Archbishop Iakovos was elected a President of the World Council of Churches in August, 1959. He received the honorary D.D. from Boston University, 1960; the D.H.L. from Franklin and Marshall College, 1961.

THE UNITY OF CHRISTIAN CHURCHES

There is a subject which I consider of ageless importance—one which is easier to talk about, than to understand. The subject to which I refer is that perplexing but compelling question of Church unity.

As you are all surely aware, this question has become a topic of popular concern. The approach to it, however, has been either purely academic or grossly one-sided; whereas it can only be approached with sincerity and humility. Under no circumstance should we encourage others or allow ourselves to become involved in "unity-deliberations," for the sake of simply talking about unity, or arousing public interest in it. No responsible clergyman of any faith would discuss or consider the subject of Church unity, without recognizing the danger of its being taken lightly, or of giving the impression that his sole concern is to be talked about, or quoted by romanticists and sentimental ecumenists. I say this because I am afraid that careless discussions or disputes over this critically important subject can only result in making our *dis*-unity more apparent and more detrimental.

The Greek Orthodox Church—the mother of all Slavic Churches, and sister of the ancient Churches of Antioch, Jerusalem, Alexandria, and Rome, mourns over the continued existence of *dis*-unity, caused only by *human vanity*. We find the seeds of this disunity even in Apostolic times. St. Paul voiced his dismay in the following soul-shaking and caustic manner: "It hath been declared unto me of you, my brethren, by them which are of the house of Chloe, that there are contentions among you. Now this I say that every one of you saith, I am of Paul; and I of Apollos; and I of Cephas; and I of Christ. Is Christ divided? Was Paul crucified for you? Or were you baptized in the name of Paul?" (I Corinthians 1:11-13)

The book of Revelation, on the other hand, informs us of the deeds of the Nicolaitanes (Revelation 2:6), a sect within the bosom of the primitive Church, attributed to a Nicholas the proselyte from Antioch. (Acts 6:5) It is not a secret that the early Church went through turmoils and tribulations, caused to a great degree from within, rather than from without. It was assumed, however, that with the passing of the time, Christians would become both mature and wise, and more conscious of their sacred duty to remain united with Christ. Therefore, indignation and disillusionment on the part of true Christians, is wholly justified today, faced as we are with the most perilous antichristian forces, the world has ever known. Our division and disunity is welcome fuel for this unholy fire, by which these forces mean to consume and destroy all which remains alive and blooming in the hearts of men.

The Holy Scriptures refer to cardinal and mortal sins; but I find no cardinal or mortal sin greater than our disunity—an act of treason and betrayal of Christ, and of our very soul. If we must be tortured by remorses, the greatest of all should be that we failed Christ in a most lamentable way.

The very proof of our disunity is the fact that we like to talk about unity as if unity were something not in existence or to be discovered. But the unity of the Church already exists; for this is the Church: the very body of Christ; Christ Himself is the Church. And Christ is the same, yesterday, today and forever. So is also the Church: one and the same, yesterday, today and forever.

If in our days we talk about Churches and not about one Church, it is because we have lost sight of the true conception of the Church. And we must rediscover the meaning of the Church before we talk about unity. We must also define the exact meaning of the word unity, before talking about Church unity, or unity between Churches.

Let us examine first what do we mean by "Unity," and "Church Unity"; Do we mean a conventional, an agreed-upon Church union, or do we mean an organic, an all-absorbing and assimilating merger and union? After we answer this question, let us consider the word "Church." The Church, as we said a moment ago, is the very Body of Christ. We are the members of this body. The moment the Church is perversely conceived as an institution or organization, it loses all meaning for us and becomes simply a community, large or small, headed by an elected man and governed by its members. As a result we would talk and think as parishes, as communities, as institutions and religious organizations; and we attempt to approach the problem of unity from the very limited and narrow field of vision, which

131

may be Orthodox, Roman, or Protestant, but which is, in each instance, unrealistic, slanderous, sectarian and false. We would then fail to think of ourselves as "fellow-citizens with the saints and of the household of God." We would avoid truly identifying ourselves as members of the Church, "established upon the foundation of the Apostles and Prophets, Jesus Christ Himself being the chief corner-stone; in whom all the building, fitly framed together, groweth unto a holy temple of the Lord; in whom we also are builded together for an habitation of God through the Spirit." (Ephesians 2:20-22)

If we actually recognized this, we would not be worried about unity, for it would become more than obvious that Christ is our bond of unity, or, as St. Paul says, "Christ is our peace, who hath made both one, and hath broken down the middle wall of partition between us." (Eph. 2:14, 15)

It is apparent, therefore, that instead of talking of Church unity we should talk about unity or reunion with Christ, for it is in Him that we, as Christians, "live and move and have our being." (Acts 17:28)

Unfortunately, however, Christians and Christian Churches all over the world, even today, fail to realize their duty to Christ; they function as institutions, rich and powerful, bent on increasing their influence and their numbers. Instead of stretching their arms to embrace each other, they do everything to widen the distance between them; either by vain and meaningless proselytizing activities among the members of another Church, or by making careless pronouncements, thus killing even the faintest hope which may exist for a Christian rapprochement.

These same Churches, however, talk about Church unity, while remaining immobile themselves, and expecting others to move in their direction to meet and unite with them.

If Christian Churches are really concerned with the restoration of long-disrupted unity and the oneness of the Church, they must give more convincing proof of their intentions. They must decisively begin to move, one towards the other. This is the only way that they can eventually return all to Christ and to His one and only Church. The Orthodox, for instance, must realize that it is high time that they cease advertising their "ecumenical-mindedness" and their democratic type of Church administration, and get busy meeting their brethren. Roman Catholic Christians should stop talking about those Christians who do not belong to their jurisdiction, of separated or schismatic brethren, for they know too well that their share of guilt is equally great for the existing separation and division between Churches and Christians. Protestant Episcopal and Protestant friends in general should re-examine their missionary theology and re-evaluate their

132

ecumenical direction, for it is only through such revision and re-evaluation that they may hope to recapture the true meaning of Christ's great commission. If we are Christians, we should never fail His last prayer, that we all be one, in the manner in which He and His Father are One.

We live in the year 1961; one-thousand-nine-hundred-and sixty-one years after Christ's birth, and yet we do not seem to realize how grave is our responsibility to attest to our professed faith in Christ.

Our age is called the space age. And rightfully so. We are about to explore and conquer space. Yet there is another space, an unexplored and vast space—of far more imminent concern—separating Christian hearts, that must be conquered for Christ's and for our own sake. We owe it to Christ, and to ourselves. The whole world, Christians and non-Christians, is waiting for this great day that God has made for us and from which we are still far away.

Unity is too sacred a word to be taken irreverently or lightly. It is as sacred as prayer. And it is as dangerous as prayer. Prayer and unity are not empty words; both are a kind of commitment; a serious commitment to God. When we pray to God and call Him our Father, we must act as His children; otherwise we are committing a double sin and evoking the wrath of God upon us. So it is with unity. Only those united with Christ, and only those willing to live "unity" are entitled to talk about it.

I believe that unity is not a commodity; and that it is not—it cannot be—a conventional unity. It must be an organic unity with Christ; an act of faith and loyalty to Him. Christ is not the God of Christians; He is the God of the world. All these, therefore, who confess Christ as God and Saviour should see that there is only one path for them to follow: the beautiful and noble path of Christ, climaxed in unity and love.

But what of the path that our professed Christianity follows today? Take a good look at it for yourself. Instead of having a Christianity preoccupied with the spiritual and moral uplifting of man in general, we have a shameless and boisterous ungodliness trying to raise man through space, and to the stars. Instead of having a Christianity working vigilantly for the elimination of social evil, moral delinquency, crime and corruption, we have an organized atheistic communism making unchallenged strides in the direction of bringing about order through enforced discipline and police law.

Instead of having a united Christianity, busy, dedicated to serving human want and distress, we have a state-supported welfare to come to the aid and assistance of all those in need.

All these unquestionable realities are not enough to shake up our conscience or to bring us back to our senses, so that we may see our inadequa-

133

cies and inability to cope with the situation. We are all to be lamented over our self-admiration, the overdose of narcism that keeps us numbed and that leads us into self-righteousness and spiritual bankruptcy.

But we still want to talk about Christian Unity. And we do little more to bring it reality. We would do better if we started to talk about the possibility of bettering our inter-church relations and the purposefulness of adopting a new policy of united Christian action and stand, on all important local, national, or international problem.

We all shed tears over present-day immorality and low ethical standards. We even prophesize the end of the world and are content to shake our finger from the pulpit, and point out the source of the ills of our times. We grumble and growl over the small omissions of Divine Law, while we ourselves omit "the weightier matters of the law, judgment, mercy and faith." (Matthew 23:23) As far as our relation to Christ is concerned we act no differently than the women that stood afar off, beholding the Crucifixion and the Lord's death. When are we going to become true to ourselves and true to Christ? When are we going to brave the obstacles, the hindrances and the difficulties and accept the challenge presented to us by our divided and confused world today?

I do not believe that we must avoid discussing unity; I believe that it must be discussed with a committed Christian mind and heart. I should emphasize, however, that Unity begins and ends with Christ, the cornerstone and the head of the Church. Endless theological discussions have never contributed to the healing of the wounds, which we, the divided Christians, inflicted on the oneness of the Church. At this point, I cannot but with a great deal of pain recall the awesome scene described by St. John in his gospel: "Then the soldiers, when they had crucified Jesus, took his garments, and made four parts, to every soldier a part; and also his coat: now the coat was without seam, woven from the top throughout. They said therefore among themselves; let us not rend it, but cast lots for it, whose it shall be: that the scripture might be fulfilled, which saith: they parted my raiments among them and for my vesture they did cast lots. These things therefore the soldiers did." (John 19:23-24)

How familiar this picture is; How often it is relived in our inter-church relations! Like the soldiers, we take Jesus' garment and make it in parts—to every Church, a part. But unlike the soldiers, we have tried to rend the seamless robe of the Lord, and then we cast "arguments" and "pseudo-documents" to prove that ours is the Christ, and ours is the Church.

The lenten season provides us with more than illustrations, demonstrating the duty of Christians towards Christ and the Church. The robe of

134

Christ is without seam and so is the Church. The robe of Christ belongs to Him and to no one else. The robe of Christ is woven from the top throughout. It is our obligation to respect it and to keep this robe stainless, without blemish or wrinkle or any such thing.

What, therefore, shall we do? How should we understand unity? How shall we act from now on about it?

I will try to answer these three questions and thus conclude my talk with you on Church unity.

1. We must repent and ask the compassion and the forgiveness of our Lord, because we have tried to make Him our possession—instead of making ourselves possessed by Him.

2. We must understand unity as an organic unity between man and Christ and try, therefore, to incorporate ourselves into the life and body of Jesus. He is the vine and we are the branches. If a man abide not in Him, he is cast forth as a branch, and is withered. (John 15:5) It is only this unity that can lead into Church unity.

3. If we are truly concerned with unity, we must learn to love it; it is the most difficult art; to be compassionate, understanding, tolerant, brotherly. We have much to gain from such an approach to unity. Unity can result from such an attitude. Humility, obedience and prayer are the only elements that can enhance Church relations. Living together and praying together without any walls of partition raised, either by racial or religious prejudices, is the only way that can lead surely to unity, for unity in its last analysis is the work of God, not of man.

Unity will, by no means, sever our relations with our own particular tradition; on the contrary, it can fortify our common tradition, which emanates from the Holy Spirit.

Let us, therefore, pray and live with the image of an united Church, sheltered under the saving Cross and guided by its Founder, our Lord and Saviour Jesus Christ.

Sermon Eighteen

PRIESTHOOD NOT PRIESTCRAFT: THE MISSION OF THE CHURCH

REVEREND WILLIAM HENRY LAZARETH, PH.D.

A *Minister of the United Lutheran Church in Amer-ica, and Associate Professor of Systematic Theology at Lutheran Theological Seminary, Philadelphia, Penn-sylvania*

Born in New York, William Lazareth studied at Princeton and the Phila-delphia Lutheran Seminary, and took his Ph.D. at Columbia. He then spent time as a Samuel Trexler Fellow at Tuebingen University in Germany and at the University of Lund in Sweden. He is the author of *Luther on the Christian Home, A Theology of Politics*, and *Man: In Whose Image*; he had reviews and articles in *Christian Century, Lutheran World, Lutheran Quarterly, The Lutheran, Interpretation, Luther Life* and is a contributor to *Life In Community, Every Tribe and Tongue*.

In 1948 he was a ULCA Youth Delegate to the World Council of Churches in Amsterdam. Between 1949 and 1950 he was Area Director of the Lutheran World Deferation Refugee Service, Wuerttemberg-Baden, Germany; Chief In-terpreter, Lutheran World Federation Assembly, Minneapolis, Minnesota, 1957; ULCA Representative, Department of Church and Economic Life, National Council of Churches. He was ordained a clergyman in 1956.

This sermon which was delivered to a Joint Assembly of the Divisions of Home and Foreign Missions of the National Council of Churches at Atlantic City, New Jersey, shows that distinctions between real faith and mere forms is needed in our day.

PRIESTHOOD NOT PRIESTCRAFT

Our ultimate purpose in meeting together today should be stated simply and boldly. We are here to reaffirm our faith in Christ as the Head of the Church, and in the Church as the Body of Christ. In every healthy organism the head and the body are inseparable. So too here. Where Christ is, there is the Church; where the Church is, there is Christ. This conviction lies at the heart of our Christian faith.

But first we would do well to clear the air of any "ecclesiastical activism" which may have found its way into this service of worship by way of our anxious and over-busy souls. Activity—for the Gospel's sake—is of God; activism—for its own sake—is of the devil. We begin, therefore, with the humble confession that it is only as Christ reaches downward in grace that his Church is empowered to reach inward in faith and outward in love. The Church's hope lies neither in its own faith nor its own love, but solely in its gracious Lord. Apart from Christ we have no mission, because apart from Christ we are no mission.

Probably nowhere in Holy Scripture is this truth more vividly portrayed for us than in the ninth chapter of the book of Hebrews. Here we are given a colorful description of Christ as the High Priest of God's New Israel and of the Church as the royal priesthood of all his believers.

The words in testimony to Christ as the true High Priest of the New Israel are clear and unequivocal: "But when Christ appeared as a high priest of the good things that have come . . . he entered once for all into the Holy Place, taking not the blood of goats and calves but his own blood, thus securing an eternal redemption." (11, 12)

The writer has in mind, of course, the dramatic parallel between the work of Christ on the cross of Calvary and the work of the Jewish High Priest in the temple of Jerusalem. To the mind of a pious Jew, no more striking or reverent analogy could be used.

May I quickly recall for you the peculiar function of the High Priest in the Jewish religion. Every year on the tenth day of the seventh month, the Day of Atonement was celebrated as the most sacred day of the Jewish year. On this one day of the year alone, the High Priest himself took the fresh blood of the sacrificial animals through the temple curtain which separated the "Holy Place" from the most sacred "Holy of Holies" behind.

Once inside this inner sanctuary, he stood where no other mortal was permitted to enter. There he renewed Israel's covenant with God by sprinkling the sacrificial blood upon the "throne of Jehovah." This was the Mercy Seat which covered the venerated Ark of the Covenant. We are told that this contained the most treasured relics of the Jewish faith, "the golden urn of manna, the rod of Aaron that budded, and the two tablets of the covenant."

Following this most holy of ceremonies, the High Priest reappeared and chose another unblemished goat. This time, instead of slaughtering it, he placed both hands upon its head and confessed over it all the sins and iniquities of the children of Israel. Then the animal was led out into the wilderness where it was driven over a precipice as an innocent "scapegoat" for the guilt of the community.

The rationale behind this twofold priestly action was simple and direct. First, the blood-offering in the Holy of Holies was meant to cover the sins committed unwittingly in the worship at the temple. At the same time, the transference of guilt from the people to the scapegoat was supposed to take care of the conscious commission of real sins in everyday life.

When the writer of Hebrews calls Jesus Christ Israel's true High Priest, he therefore calls up in the minds of his readers all the rich imagery of Jewish religion. Yet he no sooner draws the parallel when he feels constrained to point out three underlying differences which far outweigh the superficial surface similarities.

In the first place, he says that Christ "entered once for all into the Holy Place" whereas the efficacy of the Jewish High Priest's action lasted only annually. The decisive difference, of course, is derived from the unique person of Christ. He has already been identified in the epistle as "the divine Son of God who reflects his glory by bearing the very stamp of his nature." God is himself at work in the mighty acts of Christ.

As the Lord of history, Christ's birth, death, and resurrection have a once-for-all power about them which knows no limitations of time or place. Everything points forward to the cross in B.C. and everything points backward to it in A.D. This is the first great difference. The Jewish High Priest acted annually on behalf of man; Christ acted once-for-all on behalf of God.

The second contrast is even more striking. While the Jewish High Priest offered the blood of undefiled goats and calves, the writer proclaims that "Christ offered himself without blemish to God." Long before, the Isaiah of the Exile had prophesied that God's Suffering Servant "would be put to grief when he makes himself an offering for sin." Here is one who is himself the priest and the victim, the noble offerer and the ignoble offering.

139

Jesus Christ is miraculously the High Priest, the bloody sacrifice, and the innocent scapegoat all in one!

For mark well that he offered himself "without blemish" to God. The sinless Son of God comes forth totally unexpectedly and completely undeservedly as a divine self-oblation. His cross is a free gift of grace to all who believe on his Name. The contrast could hardly be drawn more sharply. The Jewish High Priest was acting sacrificially to placate an angry God; Christ was acting sacramentally to reveal a God of mercy and forgiveness.

If both the actors and the sacrifices were diametrically opposed, so were the saving benefits. The action of the Jewish High Priest could at best atone for unwitting liturgical mistakes. Real sins had to be transferred to a scapegoat and then driven out of sight into the wilderness. The action of Christ, on the other hand, is said to have "secured an eternal redemption."

Here is an atonement which is effected by one who "in every respect has been tempted as we, and yet is without sin." Here is the action of a God whose righteousness demands that he take man's sin very seriously, and yet one whose love constrains him to take the punishment for that sin on his own shoulders. Here is an innocent scapegoat who deserves only praise, honor, and glory. Yet solely for our sake, he voluntarily assumes scorn, suffering, and death. In this third important way, the difference is portrayed for us in bold relief. The Jewish High Priest could do no more than make a man ceremonially pure in the temple; Christ offers men the saving righteousness of God himself.

Here we have arrived at the very heart of the Gospel. This is the *kerygma*, the good news of a forgiving and merciful God who has reconciled the world unto himself. The Church's confession of faith is grounded in this once-for-all atonement of the sinless Son of God for the eternal redemption of mankind. This is the primary reason we are here!

*   *   *

Now on the basis of this gracious action of God, the writer of Hebrews goes on at once to develop the faithful and loving reaction of man. This gets painfully close to home. In fact, it bites right into the core of our fellowship together today. "For if sprinkling with the blood of goats and bulls . . . sanctifies for the purification of the flesh, how much more shall the blood of Christ . . . purify your conscience from dead works to serve the living God." (13, 14)

This is God's call for us to serve him in the priesthood of all believers under the leadership of the New Israel's true High Priest, Jesus, the Christ.

We are told that the blood of Christ must purify our consciences from "dead works." Dead works are those faithless and loveless little deeds by which we try to trick God and fool our neighbors, but only deceive ourselves. In fact, when modern biblical scholarship digs a little below the surface of these very verses, we discover a startling example of what ecclesiastical "dead works" are really like.

For all that the author of Hebrews depends upon in his description of the temple is derived directly from the prescriptions of the ancient book of Leviticus. In point of actual historical fact, however, the Holy of Holies in the post-exilic temple was empty. Empty! All the sacred contents were lost during the Jews' Babylonian captivity. From the days of Ezra and Nehemiah through Caiaphas and Annas, there was no Mercy Seat, no Ark, no manna, no rod, no Decalogue. When the Jewish High Priest slipped from the sight of the people behind the temple curtain, he splattered his blood-offering into dark and empty space. This—amidst all the ceremonial pomp and circumstance—was the most sacred event of the Jewish year!

It is highly significant, therefore, that the very first result which St. Matthew records after "Jesus yielded up his spirit" is that "the earth shook . . . and the curtain of the temple was torn in two." This is the Bible's way of saying, "To Hell with all your religion!" Yes, to blazes with all man's faith in what he has done for God rather than in what God has done for him!

This is meant to be the finish of all priestly "hocus-pocus" deceiving the gullible laity. The one true Mediator has come who has "torn in two" all kinds of attempts—especially professional churchmen's attempts—to separate God from his beloved people. The Creator of heaven and earth is too big to be "boxed up" in men's "Holy of Holies." Jesus Christ has revealed the living God whose Spirit inhabits not dead places and things, but the hearts of his believers. "You are temples of the Holy Spirit," declared St. Paul to the early Christians.

The results are as earth-shattering as they are revolutionary. If religion is essentially man's quest for God and revelation is essentially God's quest for man, Jesus Christ marks the end of all human religion. To be a Christian priest, very simply, is to accept and pass on what God gives—and, as a God of love, he always begins by giving himself. Since God accepts us just as we are, in grace, we must likewise accept others just as they are, in faith and in love.

The pious hypocrisy underlying the elaborate sacrificial system in the Jewish temple should give us some real concern today about our own "dead works." May I remind you that a congregation or a church convention is often a particularly tempting place to re-introduce religion into Christianity. Here we can get involved in all kinds of religious "dead works" in our own annual rite of oiling the ecclesiastical machinery:

1) *parliamentary dead works*—in which your political knowledge of *Robert's Rules of Order* becomes more important than your pastoral knowledge of the Sermon on the Mount;

2) *budgetary dead works*—in which your financial knowledge of amortization becomes more important than your theological knowledge of the pearl of great price; and

3) *statistical dead works*—perhaps the most blasphemous of all today—in which men who go around peddling Jesus like soap and analyze their annual reports as if they were stockholders in Procter and Gamble.

Brothers in Christ, we have been called "to serve the living God" as faithful priests and not as successful salesmen. The "St." before the names of the apostles stands for "saint" and not "statistician." Indeed, it is only because they were saints and not statisticians that they were able to look upon a 5 ft. 10 in., 165-pound, bloodstained Jew hanging on a cross—and call it a divine victory, rather than a human defeat. I sometimes wonder what Jesus' annual congregational report would have looked like if he had made one out on Good Friday afternoon. Certainly there would be little there to justify his "promotion" to a growing suburb of Jerusalem, to say nothing of Pittsburgh or New Delhi!

In the presence of Almighty God, I urge you to be faithful to the High Priest whom you worship and be loving in the royal priesthood which you represent. A living faith in Christ is always active in loving service to our neighbors. For God's sake, therefore, let's have as little religion here as possible.

Sermon Nineteen

THAT ALL MAY BE ONE

REVEREND LISTON POPE, PH.D., D.D., S.T.D., L.H.D.

*A Minister of the Congregational Church, and Dean of the
Yale Divinity School, Gilbert Stark Professor of Social Ethics,
and Fellow of Saybrook College in Yale University, New Haven,
Connecticut*

Dr. Pope was ordained a Congregational minister in 1935 and held two pastorates before joining the distinguished Yale Divinity School faculty. He served as associate pastor of Wesley Memorial Church, High Point, North Carolina, 1932-1935, and pastor of Humphrey Street Congregational Church, New Haven, 1935-1938. At present he is Dean of the Divinity School and Gilbert L. Stark Professor of Social Ethics and Fellow of Saybrook College.

A native of North Carolina, he has been a resident of New Haven since 1935. He studied at Duke University, took his Ph.D. at Yale. Boston University, Duke, Bucknell, Bradley, Rollins, Grinnell, Geneva University, and Coe College conferred the honorary doctorate upon him. He is the author of *Millhands and Preachers, The Kingdom Beyond Caste,* editor of *Labor's Relation to Church and Community,* and was editor of *Social Action Magazine,* 1944-1948. He is a trustee of Vassar College and of the important Phelps-Stokes Fund. In 1949, he was a Rosenwald Fellow and Phelps-Stokes Visitor to Africa. He was chairman of the pace-setting Congregational Council for Social Action, 1950-1952. He is on the editorial board of *Christianity and Crisis.*

THAT ALL MAY BE ONE

Almost from the beginning the history of Christendom has been marred by division and schism. Jesus Himself feared that the unity and love He sought for his disciples might be broken; in the Garden of Gethsemane, just before his betrayal, He prayed again and again that His followers might all be one, that the world might believe His mission from God. His prayer has not been fully granted. To be sure, observers commented on the love the early Christians had for each other, and there can be no doubt that a new community of an extraordinary kind existed among those first followers of Christ. For a time they had all things in common. But there were early disputes also, between Peter and Paul, and within the new congregations—so that Paul had to remind one of them rather severely that one Christian was not of Paul and another of Apollos, but that all were one in Christ.

Through the centuries the differences and schisms have multiplied, with Eastern Orthodox and Roman Catholic breaking apart, with Protestants leaving the Roman Church and in turn splitting into hundreds of denominations. Inspired by their Master's command to teach all nations, Christians have carried His Gospel to the ends of the earth. But they have not succeeded in answering the prayer that was on His lips just before He died for them all, that they all might be one. To the contrary, the Church, the Body of Christ, has been rent asunder.

One condition today is not only that of division into three major communions: Orthodox, Roman, and Protestant. Protestant and Orthodox Christians are still further subdivided, so confusingly that only experts can trace the lines of division. In the United States alone we have sixty-four separate Protestant bodies with more than fifty thousand members each, and there are an additional one hundred and fifty smaller denominations. A well-known promise of Jesus should be rephrased to read, "Where two or three are gathered together in my name, there shall immediately be division among them." Christianity discovered fission long before the science of atomic physics was born.

The net results of all this fragmentation are difficult to calculate from a purely practical point of view. Certainly the growth of the churches has not been prevented, at least so far as the United States is concerned; church membership here is at an all-time high, having increased about fifty per cent in the last fifteen years. About five per cent of the population were church members in colonial days; there are slightly more than sixty per cent now. It may be that a certain amount of competition between the churches is a good thing from an institutional standpoint.

Further, it may be desirable, for the purification of religion and the preservation of democracy, to have available a range of choice in religious beliefs and practices, as well as a choice between political parties and freedom in other fields. If we had only one church, it would probably become oppressive and our freedom of religion would be limited or lost. Our American forebears recognized this danger when they wrote the First Amendment to the Constitution, prohibiting the establishment of a state church and guaranteeing religious liberty.

On the other hand, there are practical disadvantages arising from all this subdivision. For example, the influence of the churches on public affairs is weakened by the absence of united effort. An American historian concluded recently that the Roman Catholic Church, with about half as many members as the Protestant churches, has had more influence on public issues in the United States since 1940 than all the Protestant churches combined—and there is considerable evidence that this is true. Let it be remembered that half of the Roman Catholic congregations were still foreign language groups only one generation ago; within a single generation a church characterized by unity above all else has become a powerful force in American life.

Consider also the confusion in our witness when we go to the mission field. New Christians in Asia and Africa have confessed a great deal of bewilderment over our Western divisions, and they have tended to discard them as rapidly as possible when control over the younger churches came into their own hands. It never made much sense to try to establish a Southern Presbyterian Church or a Southern Methodist Church in Northern China; the Chinese have never been greatly interested in the slavery issue in the United States in the 1840's when the Southern churches split away from national bodies. And Bishop Henry Knox Sherrill tells of the effort years ago to translate the words, "Protestant Episcopal Church," into Chinese; when a stranger to the effort translated the Chinese characters back into English, he came up with the title, "The Church of Kicking Overseers." His version was better than he knew, but confusing all the same. A comparable confusion of tongues has caused many in the Western world to turn away from the churches, and even to scoff at the pretension of a saving Gospel proclaimed by a divided church.

Whatever the practical and prudential considerations may be, the neces-

145

sity for Christian unity goes much deeper. A Church divided in spirit is a church unfaithful to her Lord, who clearly prayed that all His followers should be one. Talk of the love of Christ is a blasphemy unless we love all his followers, despite all our differences of nation and race and denomination. Talk of the Christian love of neighbor is a mockery in the ears of the world unless we demonstrate it in our own household of faith. How can the Church be the Bride of Christ if she is many brides? How can she be a gathered flock if she be scattered? How can she be the Body of Christ if she is broken and sacrificed by hands other than His own?

In simple fidelity to our Lord, Christians and Churches must seek unity among themselves. We must express that unity not only in our hearts and in personal relationships but also in our institutional life. Unity of spirit is the essence of the matter, but unity of faith and of worship and of work are also necessary. Above all, a new awareness of the true nature of the Christian church, universal in outreach, rising above all barriers of race and nation and creed, is essential before visible unity can ever appear. It is little use to tamper with denominational machinery unless the bonds of unity have already been forged by devotion to a Church above all our Churches. A new kind of churchmanship must always precede unity, as well as its consequence.

Happily, the tides toward unity have been running powerfully in this century. In the last fifty years there have been many world conferences of Protestants, and they led at last to the organization in 1948 of the World Council of Churches, the emergency of which is regarded by many as the most significant religious event since the Reformation in the sixteenth century. In this Council nearly all of the Protestant religious bodies in the world and most of the ancient Eastern Orthodox Churches come together for common worship and work, and for exploration of further ways toward unity. This mutual endeavor is only in its infancy and many problems remain. It has not yet been possible, for example, to have a single communion service in which all could participate. Common communion probably lies at the beginning of true unity rather than at the end; it signalizes common acceptance of the precious gift of Christ, rather than being a goal to be worked for by the efforts of men. But the movement toward unity is no longer a vague hope: it is a thrilling fact.

Nor has the movement been restricted to the top level. It has also manifested itself in national councils of Churches, and in greater mutuality among the various bodies of a single confession (as in the emergence of the Lutheran World Federation, the Anglican world conferences, and comparable bodies). Further, there have been more mergers and reunions of

146

denominations in the last 50 years than in the previous four hundred years, with some sixty-five church bodies joining in twenty unions since 1910, and with more than a dozen considering similar action at the present time. Slowly but surely the movement grows, and this new unity is already a powerful force in a divided world. Now there are stirrings of an effort to reexamine the alienation between the Roman Catholic Church and other Christian bodies—stirrings only, but whispers that may one day lead to words of reconciliation. A New Reformation, a reformation leading to unity rather than schism, is underway. It is the great new religious fact of our time. Its progress will be impeded, and it may continue to be slow, but it will not rest until a broken Christendom is whole again.

I am not suggesting that we are moving toward uniformity or toward one single church for all Christians. Any such outcome would be undesirable, and discussion of it at the present time is as premature as discussion of one world government. If our movement toward unity is founded on the one basis that can give it power, that of fidelity to Christ and His leading, we shall be shown the way and the ultimate outcome is in His Hands. When men consider that they alone are the architects of unity, and that by their own unaided efforts they can build an edifice to explore the ramparts of heaven, the Tower of Babel is the result and God scatters such men in confusion. True unity begins with God's design, not man's visionary schemes. And the final pattern of our unity is beyond our view. Perhaps at the moment we can use only metaphors to express the nature of our hopes—the metaphors of the vine and the branches, or the sheep and the shepherd, or any metaphor so long as Christ is the center. Or we might refer to the church bells that call worshippers on Sunday morning; they ring in a cacophony rather than a symphony, but the time will come when they will make one music, each with its own part.

Doubtless all this discussion of statistics and church organizations and "one far-off divine event" seems rather remote to many of you. But unity in Christ, like peace among the nations, begins in the hearts and minds of individual persons. It will become manifest only as you and I, separately and together, reveal it in our lives. This requires that our own faith be deepened, not diluted. True unity will never come from a lowest common denominator of conviction; to minimize the importance of a particular confession of faith is to betray the deeper quest for knowledge of Christ. Christ is beyond all creeds, but we follow Him and know Him as Savior only when we can say from the depths of our own souls, "I believe: help thou my unbelief."

At the same time, personal convictions must be submitted, sincerely and in a spirit of concord, to enlargement and purification in relation to all fellow Christians of all confessions and creeds. The old Chinese often refer to their religion as "my miserable faith," and before the glory of Christ each of us should be equally humble. We need to be willing to have our own precious preferences and traditions and convictions brought into a larger design if Christ so requires. Professor John Baillie tells of a Scotsman who watched the processions marching to a church to consummate a union of two churches in Scotland; the old man shook his head and muttered, "It is no just . . . it is no right . . . but it is the will of God." Let us trust that the old man joined the processions, and that we shall follow in his train. But not in his train, for it is Christ whom we would follow, remembering always that He prayed, just before the cross, that all may be one. As we become faithful answers to his prayer, the true nature of his church will shine through and beyond all the rites and creeds of our devising, and we shall be one.

Sermon Twenty

LIFT UP YOUR HEARTS

Reverend Robert E. Cushman, D.D., Ph.D.

*Dean of Duke University Divinity School and Professor
of Systematic Theology, Durham, North Carolina, and
a Minister of the Methodist Church*

Robert E. Cushman was born in Fall River, Massachusetts, the son of Maud E. Cushman and the late Bishop Ralph S. Cushman. He was educated in the public schools of Rochester, New York, and graduated from Wesleyan University in 1936. He completed his studies for the Bachelor of Divinity Degree at Yale Divinity School, 1940, and received his Ph.D. degree from that institution in 1942.

Dr. Cushman was minister of the South Meriden Church, South Meriden, Connecticut, 1936-1940. He was for a short time pastor of the Park Methodist Church, Hamilton, New York, before returning to Yale as instructor in Systematic Theology. From 1943-1945 he was Professor of Religion and Director of Religious Activities at the University of Oregon, and went to Duke as Associate Professor of Systematic Theology, becoming Professor in 1948. He was elected to the deanship in 1958.

Dean Cushman was Methodist delegate to the Third World Conference on Faith and Order, Lund, Sweden, in 1952. Instrumental in the inauguration of the Commission on Ecumenical Consultation of the Methodist Church, he has continued a member. He has served on the North American Commission on Worship of the World Council of Churches. He is a member of the North Carolina Conference of the Methodist Church and of its Board of Education.

Dean Cushman is an author of numerous articles published in learned journals and the author of a volume entitled *Therapeia: Plato's Conception of Philosophy*. Dr. Cushman is presently Director of the Wesley Works Editorial Project, sponsored by four American universities. He is a frequent lecturer and preacher, both within and without the University.

LIFT UP YOUR HEARTS

Easter day has come and gone; and, today we find ourselves in the afterglow of the great event. Yet every Sunday is the Lord's Day, a celebration of Easter. And it has been so from the early days of the Christian church. Christian worship is, centrally, a celebration of praise and thanksgiving—a time of rejoicing in the resurrection of our Lord.

For this reason the New Testament is full of doxologies. These doxologies reflect the joyous and triumphant note of early Christian worship. This note of triumph is echoed in the peerless words of St. Paul to the Corinthians: "The sting of death is sin; and the power of sin is the law, but thanks be to God who giveth us the victory through our Lord Jesus Christ." And the Petrine epistle takes up the refrain: "Blessed be the God and Father of our Lord Jesus Christ, who according to his great mercy, begat us again unto a living hope by the resurrection of Jesus Christ from the dead, unto an inheritance incorruptible . . . that fadeth not away."

I do not think we should allow Easter to slip away, to become lost amidst the insistent and encompassing concerns of our common days without searching further into its meaning; for, at Easter we are confronted by the truly momentous event in our history—the event which has for nearly two thousand years given the controlling perspective, the depth dimension to the life of Western man.

I

It is an event which can only be referred to the wisdom and the power of God. And this was what the early Christians were always asserting: that their faith, as St. Paul declared, stood "not in the wisdom of men, but in the power of God." (I Corinthians 2:5)

Therefore, "Blessed be the God and Father of our Lord Jesus Christ, who according to his great mercy begat us again unto a living hope. . . ." This it was that, from the beginning, was the substance of the doxological message of the early Christians. Their faith was not in what was possible according to some general view of the nature of things. Their confidence rested upon what God had done. God had acted redemptively in the ministry of Christ, victoriously in the sacrificial death of Christ, and triumphantly and reassuringly in the resurrection of Christ; and of these things

150

they were witnesses. In this unexampled and mysterious configuration of events God had shown his hand decisively. In this fragment of man's own history, God had manifested his purpose. It was the purpose to rescue a self-destroying human existence from moral defeat, and spiritual stultification, and directionlessness.

Is it not fitting, therefore, that the *Sursum Corda* should be among the most ancient words of Christian common worship? The priest cries out to the assembled congregation, "Lift up your hearts!"; and, out of hearts rejoicing in hope, the people shout back with one accord, "We lift them up unto the Lord!" This is the thanksgiving, the *eucharistia*, which is called forth by the event of Easter. And it is Easter, with its manifest triumph of the power of righteousness over the power of sin and death which casts its light back upon Advent and Christmas: the people that sat in darkness had seen a great light, upon these dwelling under the shadow of death the light had shined. The eternal recurrence, the endless cycle of life and death, was broken through. Direction was given to human existence. It gained dimension in depth, and an open end toward God. And men's feet were guided into the way of peace. It was now true for them, as John the evangelist declared, that Christ was "the way, the truth and life"; he was "the resurrection and the life." (John 11:25)

II

These things at least suggest, if they do not spell out, the kind of hope that long ago burst upon the world and literally revolutionized its structure and man's conception of his own destiny. But what about us? Do we pause long enough in the headlong rush of our daily existence, our preoccupation with the things that lie at hand, to ask ourselves what our world would look like if this hope had never been given? Now, then, suppose it were just not there and never had been—that this were a world immersed in care and unrelieved by hope, a world that knew no acceptance of death in obedience to God and no resurrection as God's responding vindication of that obedience!

Obviously we would not be gathered here to celebrate the Lord's Day. And this *here*, these aspiring arches, that embody the Christian hope in chiseled stone, and others like them, would never have been. The world of men, we may suppose, would still be here—still anxious, still tired of itself, and burdened with the weight of its own baffled existence. The stoic might still be winning adherents to the life of world-transcending apathy. The oriental religions might by now have convinced the most of mankind that

151

existence is without goodness and illusory and, certainly, the ever-recurring apostles of hedonism would be at their old-time game: "gather ye rosebuds while ye may."

Yes, if the Easter perspective upon human life and destiny had never been given, we may suppose that the world of men (however vastly different its history) would still be here—still restlessly questing and, doubtless, still just as reluctant to receive God's answer as it is now to receive and accept the one that has been given. And that answer is the perfect obedience of Christ's Cross and God's decisive vindication of that obedience in the Resurrection. Is it possible that, out of pride, men are unwilling to receive any answer to the riddle of existence they do not contrive for themselves? And, in the event, can they have any ultimate hope at all? Man is no "match" for the ultimate.

So it behooves us to consider the possibility that an answer has been given and received and that its visible sign is the unbroken and continuous line of Christian history, and Christian faith, and Christian witness. To tell the truth, it is almost impossible for us, who are—whether we will or not—inheritors of the Christian view of life and the world, it is virtually impossible for us to divest ourselves of our religious and intellectual inheritance and so to view the world devoid of the gospel. Yet it was out of such a world —a world devoid of the gospel—that the first Christians were born, born into another world. It was a "new birth," a birth into a world of expanded horizons, a world suddenly glorified. As the rending of the clouds lets the light of heaven shine through, so the world of human existence was illuminated and given meaning as light was shed upon it by the ministry and resurrection of Christ. The veil of the temple was rent, and God's purpose was no longer hidden in inscrutable darkness. The Sun of righteousness had arisen with healing in his wings. And for those of us who share in this Christian perspective, the doxology of Peter is the suitable word of praise and thanksgiving: "Blessed be the God and Father of our Lord Jesus Christ, who begat us again unto a living hope by the resurrection of Christ from the dead, unto an inheritance incorruptible . . ."

III

But, now, you will be asking, what is the special nature of this hope? And it will have to be answered that it takes the whole of the New Testament to tell it and the apostolic fathers, and, indeed, the whole of Church history; and, in the final analysis, you yourself must declare it. The Petrine doxology does venture to frame it in a word. The content of the hope is

152

called an "inheritance incorruptible." But, in order to grasp what is meant, this inheritance has to be contrasted with its opposites—an inheritance corruptible. This is the fundamental, the deep-going contrast, that finds expression in all serious efforts to uncover the crisis in human life from the opening chapters of Genesis to Melville's *Moby Dick* or Dostoievsky's *Crime and Punishment.* It stands disclosed equally in the tragedies of Sophocles.

There is such a thing as an "inheritance corruptible!" And St. Paul may be honored in the thesis that "the wages of sin is death," but the free gift of God, to those who are not too arrogant to receive it, is eternal life. This is what the doxology exults in as the Christian knows himself to be begotten to "a living hope," "an inheritance incorruptible. . . . that fadeth not away."

But I do not know that the pure joy of this inheritance can be really grasped by an age that estimates the goods of life in terms of the satisfaction of unlimited desire—conveniences, Cadillacs, and dual exhausts—or in terms of "better things for better living through chemistry." An inheritance incorruptible is not likely to touch deeply those of us who are mainly engrossed in the pursuit of goals purveyed to us by a culture that revels in the unexamined life and glories in "standard brands."

So we are apt to acquire the "inheritance corruptible." It is not often in any generation, especially in prospering times, that men are brought to raise, with sustained seriousness, the question: What, after all, is the meaning of this round of days, this human existence? Either we are prone to assume we have the answer in the cliches of our time or else we resolutely evade the ultimate question. For a long while now we have been inclined to assay only the questions we can answer, or think we can by a certain kind of method; and we call our answers science. And we have had some real comforts from them. But it is a brave man who can really face the question, and stay with it, of where does life come out? Such a man is a brave man or else one at bay and under the constraint of necessity—a man like Macbeth, faced with the dreadful outcome of his violent experiment in self-determination, who, in his frustration, spits out his vituperative answer about life's meaning: "It is full of sound and fury, signifying nothing." He had made it so. It is an inheritance corruptible!

But for most, however, it is seemingly possible to postpone confronting the ultimate question of life's meaning with any seriousness until the shadows of life's little day begin to close about us and we can no longer dismiss the fact that "all flesh is grass and as the flower of the field so it flourisheth and the wind passeth over it, and it is gone." Then, it is no longer possible

153

to defer the question of life's meaning: Is all the world a stage and all the men and women only players who have their exits and their entrances? If so, what is the plot? Is it a farce, a comedy or a tragedy? And who is the plotter? In the hour of man's extremity—whether it is in the expectation of death or in the certainty that he has irremediably botched and disfigured the canvas of his life—the ultimate question confronts him in its stark inescapability and all the palliatives of the herd and all the pseudo-securities of graceful living become as nothing.

IV

The Christian answer to the ultimate question about the drama of life and of human history is given in the startling pronouncement: "He is not here; he is risen!" And this is echoed in all the doxologies of the New Testament that find, in the display of God's sovereign power, the only ultimate answer to the ultimate question, and man's hope. "Blessed be God . . . who according to his great mercy begat us again unto a living hope . . . unto an inheritance incorruptible."

If we marvel at the vibrant, unfaltering, and exultant faith of the ancient Church, then we should remember that the resurrection was, to them, not only an objective deed of God. It was also something in which men participated, so that it was to them the source of a transformation of life—a transition from an inheritance corruptible to one incorruptible. The resurrection meant death to sin, a new life. According to St. Paul its fruits were: "love, joy, peace, longsuffering, kindness, goodness, faithfulness, meekness, self-control"; and, in these fruits of the Spirit, the Church possessed already an earnest intimation of the resurrection life. As fellow-sufferers with Christ, Christians were united to the undying life of God. For them the Resurrection was not just a spectacle to behold but the hand of God extended to man in his extremity, a hand which they grasped.

And then too we should remember that the world was still God's world. It was in His keeping. In it He was not deprived of His sovereignty. The creation was God's creature and subservient to his purpose. The so-called laws of nature had not been codified by men to contest God's sovereignty. An order of the world there was, but it was God's order and at God's disposal, and, thus, subject to His purpose of redemption. And the first Christians not only shared the resurrection life; they discerned in the matchless ministry of Jesus, perfected in his death and glorified in his Resurrection, the divine pattern which gave its meaning to the riddle of human existence. In this fragment of history, the Christ-history, the meaning of all history

154

suddenly came into focus. It was disclosed decisively, in God's vindication of the perfect obedience of the Cross. And Jesus himself had prepared their understanding, for he had taught them that he who would save his life shall lose it, but he who loses it for God's sake shall find it. This our Lord had done: He had placed life back into the hands of Him who gave it and with whom there can be no losing it. And this is our opportunity also.

Where there is death to sin, to all that is contrary to God, there is union with God; and where there is union with God, there is life everlasting. Therefore, lift up your hearts!

Sermon Twenty-one

CHRIST IS ALIVE!

REVEREND CHALMERS COE

*Minister, First Congregational
Church, Columbus, Ohio*

Born December 31, 1922, in Boston, Mr. Coe lived in Waterbury, Connecticut, and Oak Park, Illinois. He took his A.B. at Yale in 1943, his B.D. at Yale also, in 1945. He was minister of the Congregational Church in East Hampton, Connecticut, from 1945 to 1948; of the First Church in Amherst, Massachusetts, from 1948 to 1954; and of Mount Vernon Church in Boston from 1954 to 1956. He was at Hartford Theological Seminary from 1956 until he was called to Columbus.

CHRIST IS ALIVE!

". . . Jesus himself stood among them. But they were startled and frightened, and supposed that they saw a spirit."

Luke 24:36-37

"Tell me a ghost story," says a child. And with a groan of slight impatience you pull the shades against the remnants of the day, turn the lights out everywhere, and lie down on the bed frantically trying to think of a new plot. I told one recently about a short, stocky ghost name Jacqueline, whose foot-blisters caused her to walk gingerly down the street and made her friends laugh spitefully. And children do love such tales, want to have them as "scarey" as possible, and delightedly remind you of the story you told last week which to your amazement you have entirely forgotten. Part

157

of the reason for their enthusiasm lying, of course, in the fact that none of us any longer believes in ghosts; not even children do, at least with half their minds. So that when the story is over they snuggle contentedly in bed and sigh with happiness as you tiptoe out; and you can hear them chuckling briefly before their eyes close and sleep comes.

But it was different once. We modern folk cannot possibly imagine how ridden with evil spirits were the minds of most of our ancestors. Sumner reminds us baldly that, according to reliable estimates, one hundred thousand persons have been killed as witches in a single European country. A ghastly record, which we fail to match only because we happen to live later. And the Jews of our Lord's day, who for the most part had no developed understanding of eternal life, did believe this much: that the shades of the dead inhabited a gloomy underworld, ill-defined but certainly undesirable, far from the vision of God or the pleasant society of other men. A ghost, a spirit, a shade: why, the suspected presence of any one of them could make a man's teeth chatter and his eyes bulge with terror. God was God only of the living.

That accounts in part for the violent reaction of the disciples to whatever it was they saw. The ghost of Jesus, they were sure, was standing before their very eyes. What evil thing was He about to do, He Who throughout His earthly life had tried to do nothing but good? What solemn and terrifying portent was He bearing to them?

Well, we do not have that dread of Jesus Christ. And, as I say, ghosts no longer have the power to frighten men. But in other ways we treat Him as though He were one; act, even in church, as though only the shade of a noble man were beckoning to us across the distant centuries, wistfully reminding us of the truths we have forgotten. When in fact, and if the Christian claim is valid, He is infinitely more than that, and does far more. The disciples, after their initial mistake, were quickly convinced of it. And what I want to do is to explore what happened in that room of eleven men to change their minds.

I

For one thing, He assured them of His life. When R. W. Dale, the great Congregational minister of a hundred years ago, was sitting in his study one Holy Week preparing the Easter sermon, he was in a black mood. Like so many of us parsons, he didn't know where to begin, or what to say; and the rigors of the Lenten schedule had evidently robbed him of his power to think. Then, unaccountably, the thought struck him: "Why, Jesus is alive, as alive as I am and in this very room with me! Jesus Christ is alive!" And that, he knew, was what he had to tell the congregation: not merely that they had a chance of surviving into an after-life, and not merely that the flowers bloom in the spring; but rather that the same Lord Who had once swept mightily over the arid hills and wooded valleys of Palestine was, in a different sense, still living. And so, for Dale, the sermon wrote itself.

I wish we all had his conviction. But we do not. Even the most impeccable churchmen among us behave for all the world as though Jesus Christ were non-existent, are not so much intellectual as practical atheists; speak of Him respectfully enough at morning worship, decorously repeating the old phrases about God's "inestimable love in the redemption of the world by our Lord Jesus Christ," and then blithely forget all about Him in the tug and tumult of daily living. "What's real?" we ask. And the answer, for all practical purposes, is clear. Lawn mowers are real—and we'll have to be thinking of them soon. And tax forms in duplicate are all too real. So are the neighbors who leave their garbage cans in public view all week, and the dove that wakens you with its penetrating call at dawn, and the million other claims, noises and anxieties with which we are confronted every day. And is it any wonder, then, that we find it unconscionably hard—believers though we are—to take the claims of the New Testament with full seriousness, or to reach out as men once did to clutch them gratefully. It is such an effort, takes such sheer will, to be Christian now.

But Christ, we may be thankful, is determined to help us in our plight. That is what is meant by these seemingly weird words in the Testament: "Behold my hands and my feet that it is I myself," He says; "handle me and see, for a spirit hath not flesh and bones, as ye see me have." I know very well what intellectual problems a sentence like that puts before us: I find them standing brutishly before me too. And yet, at the same time, they are saying this: that Jesus Christ lives as a spectre does not, and takes extraordinary pains to tell us so. And therefore, "Behold I stand at the door and knock," He goes on, and is quite insistent that He will not be put off. Surely He is at least as real as a tax form and a dove.

II

And, if He is alive, something else follows. It certainly did follow for the disciples. I mean that He gave them a commission. He told them, as the "New English Bible" puts it, to "Begin from Jerusalem: it is you who are witnesses to all this." And they did exactly that, although we find it hard to believe, so poor was their record up to that moment. Peter, for example,

159

the unreliable enthusiast; and Thomas, forever obtruding his plodding, dull-witted doubts at the most crucial moments; and Nathanael, the cynic, wondering aloud whether anything respectable can come out of Nazareth; and the rest of that little company—mere names, most of them, with nothing memorable about their lives for any gospel-writer to fasten on and pass to us. What an odd assortment for Him to depend upon! And yet it was on them that He placed the most vital of all responsibilities, "that repentance and remission of sins should be preached in His name among all nations." He gave them a commission.

Does it shock you to be told that you are in their line? Their commission is yours. And I do not mean just that you and I are to be decent and kind and honorable, and all the other adjectives up to and including reverent. Everybody in the world is expected to be that! Tree-worshippers were kind, and Druids reverent to a fault. Your duty is far more arduous. "It is you who are the witnesses to all this." And what you have seen you are to tell. The Church lives for more than itself, must do so or its title to be Church is gone. We have no right, Professor Farmer finely says, to treat the Christian faith as a source of comfort without at the self-same moment acknowledging its claim.

And ghosts do not make claims like this. You remember how, in "Hamlet," the prince of Denmark follows the ghost of his father, the dead king, and when they are alone, and only then, the ghost speaks:

> I am thy father's spirit,
> Doomed for a time to walk the night,
> And for the day confined to fast in fires,
> Till the foul crimes done in my days of nature
> Are burnt and purged away . . .
> If thou didst ever thy dear father love
> Revenge his foul and most unnatural murder!

Revenge! And anyone who sees the play feels his blood freeze as he hears the terrible word: Revenge! But Jesus Christ says something very different. "Proclaim," He calls to us. "Be my witnesses. Show forth to all the world the love that entered it even through my death."

That is the commission of the Christian, at Easter time and always. He is a member, willy-nilly, of a missionary church.

III

So Jesus Christ is living; and so too He places before us an inescapable demand. But I ask you now to give consideration to another fact, a fact which is every bit as inescapable. It is the last word of the risen Lord that

160

Luke remembered, or heard of, and therefore is Christ's final benediction upon the eleven. "And behold, I send the promise of my Father upon you." In other words, He made them a pledge.

"I send the promise of my Father." Come what may, He means, the Holy Spirit will abide with you. As far as we can tell, He will stand to it; He always has. In 1568, for instance, a young man of eighteen, a Scottish reformer, was apprehended by the church authorities and sentenced to die. John Knox tells in his own words what happened next. The boy "at the first was faint, and gladly would have recanted. But . . . the Spirit of God, which is the Spirit of all comfort, began to work in him . . . and with a joyful voice, upon his knees he said, 'O Eternal God, how wondrous is that love that thou bearest unto mankind; for even now, when I would have denied thee and thy Son, our Lord Jesus Christ, thou, by thine own hand, hast pulled me from the very bottom of hell. Now do what ye please: I praise my God I am ready.' " And so he died.

Yes, yes, we answer—but who could do that now? Why, it is bad enough to go into an art gallery, and see there the pictures of the martyrs, with hideous wounds drawn to the life, and blood covering all. You tell yourself, when you stand open-mouthed before such works of art, that you —who are bothered terribly by hypodermic needles—could never stand it. To live in an age of faith is one thing; to live in an age of doubt is another. And besides, you offer with good reason, we who live in a gentler time are called upon to suffer no such martyrdom. Our martyrdoms have little glamor, and therefore are possibly even harder to bear: the endless succession of meaningless days; the depressing business, as it sometimes is, of growing old; the blur of loneliness; the flatness of a gadgeteering culture. So we wonder whether Christ's promise means anything at all, and set ourselves stoically to meet the harshnesses of life without it as bravely as we can. We feel no spiritual glow.

But that, our Lord returns, is to fail to take me at my word. It is to play games with my gospel, to treat it as a ghost story or as a barren ethic. I have offered you all I can. And if I live, my purpose is to live with you. And if I command, my longing, my dearest wish, is to give you my own power to help you in your daily obedience. "I will come in, and be with you, and sup with you." That's the Christian faith! "I send the promise of my Father." He doesn't haunt, you see; He pledges Himself. However can we be the same again when Easter tells us that?

Sermon Twenty-two

A KISS THAT SHOWED NO LOVE

Reverend W. Earl Strickland, D.D.

A Methodist Minister and President of Wesleyan College, Macon, Georgia

Dr. Strickland gives a simple, thoughtful, and effective account of the Crucifixion and the events leading up to it.

Born November 2, 1919, at Colquitt, Georgia, Dr. Strickland graduated from Emory University in Liberal Arts, then took his B.D. and M.A. there also. La Grange College conferred the honorary D.D. upon him in 1959.

He was ordained to the ministry of the Methodist Church in 1940 and had wide pastoral experience in the Methodist Church in Georgia, including pastorates at Brookhaven Church in Atlanta, 1941-1944; South Broad Street Church, Rome, 1944-1948; Sylvan Hills, Atlanta, 1948-1950; East Lake, Atlanta, 1950-1954; College Park, 1954-1959. He was appointed Superintendent of the Augusta District, 1959 to January, 1960, when he assumed the presidency of Wesleyan College.

He has served on many important boards and committees of the Methodist Church, was a delegate to the 1960 Southeastern Jurisdictional Conference of The Methodist Church, a member of the Education Committee of the Southeastern Jurisdiction, of the General Board of Missions, a member of the Executive Committee of the Georgia Methodist Commission on Higher Education. He was vice-president of Emory University Association, has been a visiting professor at Candler School of Theology, and a member of the faculty of the Southeastern Jurisdictional Pastors' School.

163

A KISS THAT SHOWED NO LOVE

As the needle of a magnetic compass turns always toward the north, the theme of Christian preaching through the centuries has turned with remarkable singularity to the crucifixion of Jesus Christ. Telling the story of Jesus has been largely a recital of the events relating to his suffering and death. The gospel writers themselves, judging by the amount of their narratives devoted to the close of Jesus' life, considered the whole of his story to find its meaning in its conclusion.

To ask what it was that killed Jesus has been a part of the task of Christian preaching in every age. And any attempt to provide more than a superficial answer must probe deeper than a mere recall of the incidents related in the four gospel narratives. The whips and the thorns, the cross and the spear were the immediate causes of his death, but they were themselves the symptoms of deeper issues. The accusing Jewish leaders, the deriding throngs, the callous Roman soldiers all combined to put him on the cross, but behind them all were the real culprits, the human attitudes, motives and concerns. Because these ultimate factors, which are recurrent in every generation, are mirrored so faithfully in the glaring cruelty of the cross, every age finds the cross to be its accuser.

Jesus was crucified by a kiss that showed no love. Judas betrayed Jesus with a kiss. "Now he that betrayed him gave them a sign, saying, 'Whomsoever I kiss, that same is he: hold him fast.' And forthwith he came to Jesus, and said, 'Hail, Master,' and kissed him." (Matthew 26:48-49) Why did he not point boldly an accusing finger at Jesus and say, "There's your man"? Did he think to hide the nature of the deed behind a symbol of love? Did he think somehow that only the soldiers would be to blame if his only overt act were a kiss? Had he by some strange process of rationalization persuaded himself that what he did he did in love?

That kiss that said love but meant betrayal has been repeated in a multitude of ways in the centuries since the crucifixion. Men have lavished their materials and skills on the erection of beautiful buildings that stand as monuments of adoration. Masters of language have composed rituals that recite the worshippers' profession of love in artistic cadences. And the craft of the musician has brought forth its glorias, its te deums, and its anthems to sing of love for the Lord.

But it is all too easy to think that one has served the Lord fully when he

164

has built a building. And the singing of songs and the recitation of prayers often substitute for the doing of the will of God. To memorize the right ritual, however, can never fully hide the betrayal of the principles of Jesus in the market place or in personal relationships.

Jesus was crucified by a question that desired no answer. In his interview with the prisoner Jesus, Pilate asked, "What is truth?" But Pilate did not wait for an answer. "Pilate saith unto him, 'What is truth?' And when he had said this, he went out again unto the Jews." (John 18:38) Why did Pilate not wait for an answer to his question? Was it that he preferred not to have his mind cluttered with answers contrary to his own opinions? Was he afraid that the truth might prevent his disposing of an unpleasant situation as expeditiously as possible?

How many times during the last nineteen centuries prayers must have been addressed to God by men who asked, "What is truth?" but who did not really desire to hear God's answer! Men go to services of divine worship presumably to discover the truth of God. They frequently persuade themselves that the projection of their own prejudices is the voice of eternal truth. Through the ages, Christ has been crucified repeatedly by the refusal of men to hear the answer to their most oft repeated question.

We are afraid of the truth, for intuitively we know that the truth would disturb our way of life. It would rob us of our cherished prejudices against other peoples. It would lay naked our unconscionable scheming for wealth and power and position at the expense of others. It would knock down the cheap idols which we have substituted for God. It would bring unrest in the midst of a people who have achieved a comfortable truce with materialism.

In nineteen centuries Christianity has failed to establish the kingdom of God on earth. It has not failed because God's answer to man's quest for truth was inadequate. It has failed because man has preferred his own answers.

I

Jesus was crucified by a vow that could lightly be broken. Peter promised that "Though I should die with thee, yet will I not deny thee." And yet by the dawning of another day Peter had denied his friend three times, even to the point of cursing and swearing that he did not know him.

Every time a person joins the church he vows this or some similar vow— that he will be loyal to the church and support it with his prayers, his presence, his gifts and his service. But how soon is carping criticism of the church substituted for prayer in behalf of the church! And how frequently are members of the church offended when someone dares to suggest to them that they give to the budget of the church and share their time in its program! A vow that can lightly be broken!

When infants are presented at the church for baptism the parents vow to teach the child as soon as he shall be able to learn the meaning and purpose of the sacrament. They promise to teach him the precepts of the Holy Scripture. They promise to lead him by precept and example into the practice of the principles of the Christian life. But for many parents the occasion is purely social in significance, and the family heirloom baptismal dress and the number of people on the guest list obscure the vows that are soon to be broken so lightly.

And what shall we say of that most significant of all human social institutions, marriage? At the marriage altar the Christian is asked: "Wilt thou have this woman (or man) to be thy wedded wife (or husband)? Wilt thou love her, comfort her, honor and keep her, in sickness and in health, and forsaking all other keep thee only unto her, so long as ye both shall live?" The vow is said. But its meaning for many people is gone almost as quickly as the flowers that beautified the sanctuary during the ceremony. The vows were said, but there were inward reservations. A vow that could be lightly broken.

II

Jesus was crucified by a watch that was not kept. In the garden of Gethsemane he said to his closest friends: "My soul is exceeding sorrowful unto death: tarry ye here, and watch." But "he cometh and findeth them sleeping." (Mark 14:34, 37) It is true that the disciples must have been quite weary. It is true that they hardly could have known how truly momentous this night was to prove to be, both for Jesus, and for mankind. Their intentions undoubtedly were quite honorable. And some men would even ask "What difference would it have made in the long run if they had kept the watch?"

And so ask we all. Our place of duty seems to us so insignificant that it hardly can matter if we are not faithful in its performance. A prestigious post would be different. But what earth-shaking difference will it make if I don't show up to teach that Sunday School class of boys. And who would ever know, or care at all, if occasionally my conduct is not morally correct. If I were premier or president, the situation would be altered.

And for nineteen hundred years Jesus' closest friends have failed to keep

166

the watch. Because a thousand friends of Jesus fail to do faithfully the little thing that is right, the big thing that is right seems impossible, and the big wrong prevails.

III

Jesus was crucified by a trial that did not try. He was condemned; but he was never really tried. Pilate said, "Why, what evil hath he done?" But the only answer was "Crucify him." (Mark 15:14) The purpose of the entire proceedings was not to try him but to condemn him. Every standard of justice was violated. He was arrested at night and killed in the early morning. He had no counsel, and his friends were intimidated. Even in a day when the miscarriage of justice was an everyday affair, Jesus' trial was so flagrantly a violation of the principles of right that Pilate felt constrained to try to wash his hands of the matter and absolve himself of blame.

But who are we to criticize Pilate? In what age of the Christian Church have we who professed to be Christ's followers been willing to give him a fair trial? We have paid lip service to Jesus' principles, but never in sufficiently large numbers have we been willing actually to try to live by them. After all, it is rather idealistic to talk about mankind being brothers, isn't it? And you know what would happen to anyone who did turn the other cheek, don't you? And, though it sounds good in church, it would be rather difficult to love our enemies, now wouldn't it? And so we continue, until Christ's way means nothing more than the way we wish to go. And another age witnesses the crucified Lord, who once again fails to receive a trial.

IV

The place of Jesus in history is secure. Even if some atheistic, materialistic philosophy of life should capture the governments of the world and should set out to re-write history to fit its theories, even then, surely, somewhere an honest historian would be found recording what Jesus has meant in the life of mankind. That he lived and that his influence was decisive for men and for people through many centuries cannot be denied by honest men. But what can be disputed, and is being disputed widely in some sections of the world today, is whether Jesus will be allowed to be a decisive factor in the framing of future history. One thing is certain, that the role of Jesus in the life of today and of tomorrow will be determined quite as much or more by his friends as by his enemies. He may be defeated as effectively through words of flattery that do not reflect genuine devotion as by unkind or critical words. He may remain enthroned on the altars of artistic churches and yet have no voice in the affairs of the world.

The Negro spiritual asks, "Were you there when they crucified my Lord?" Well, were you? More to the point, are you there among those who today are crucifying him?

Sermon Twenty-three

MAN'S QUEST FOR EQUALITY

REVEREND CLAYTON E. WILLIAMS, D.D., LL.D.

Minister, The American Church in Paris

For twenty-five years Dr. Williams has preached to and for Americans who live in Paris or who visit there. A native of Illinois, he attended Butler College and the University of Pittsburgh, then spent 1917 and 1918 in France as a YMCA secretary. In 1919 he joined the United States Air Force as an officer. He studied at the University of Paris and did social work at Chateau-Thierry in 1921. Later that year he returned to the United States and became assistant pastor of the First Presbyterian Church in Indianapolis. He entered Western Theological Seminary for four years, graduating in 1925, then went to be assistant pastor in Poughkeepsie, New York, 1925-1926.

He was invited to return to Paris as assistant minister of the famous American Church under Dr. Joseph Wilson Cochran. He directed young people's work and religious education there until Dr. Cochran resigned in 1933. Dr. Williams was then asked to become the minister. During World War II he returned to the United States. In these years, 1941-1945, he was pastor of the Seventh Presbyterian Church in Cincinnati. As soon as the war was over he returned to France and resumed his ministry at the American Church.

MAN'S QUEST FOR EQUALITY

"Do not take account of your own interests but of the interests of others as well. Have the same attitude that Jesus had, for though he shared the nature of God, he did not grasp after equality with God, but layed it aside to take on the nature of a servant."
Phillippians 2:4-6 (Goodspeed)

"We who are strong ought to bear the infirmities of the weak and not to please ourselves!"
Romans 15:1

Around the world today there is springing up a desire for some sort of democracy which will consummate the ideal of equality declared in the Declaration of Independence and referred to later by President Lincoln in his famous Gettysburgh Address. You remember the words: "We hold these truths to be self-evident, that all men are created equal."

As a matter of fact, though Thomas Jefferson considered it rooted in human consciousness, equality is an ideal which has arisen very largely in our western civilization and even then only recently. Slavery, class, casts, and aristocracy of blood have been accepted facts in most civilizations. True, some primitive communal societies have known a measure of equality among their members, but one cannot say that it is intrinsic to communal society since the one country which pretends to have the greatest communal life has the least equality and the greatest difference in both the privileges and economic advantages of its citizens.

But, as a matter of fact, the whole idea of equality is an elusive one and more of a dream than a reality.

We are all of us aware that we are not equal in natural endowment. One man has a strong heart and great physical resistance; and another has a frail body and no resistance. One can stand grueling labor in the hot sun and another breaks under it. One man has music in his very fingertips; another, like Gladstone, can only tell that the National Anthem is being played because everyone about him rises to his feet. One man has a quick mind and learns rapidly, another has to plod laboriously along the path of knowledge. One is born with deft fingers and an aptitude for mechanics, another's fingers are all thumbs and all mechanics a mystery to him.

Moreover, our inequalities tend to increase as life goes on because all

170

men do not make the most of their natural capacities. Life, in consequence, does not tend to make us equal but rather unequal.

Again, we speak of political equality and we cherish it as an ideal, but we know that that is a figment of the imagination, or perhaps a manner-of-speaking. We are the victims of machines and organizations and the oratory of demagogy. Only in a limited sense do we have equality before the law, as many will testify. The administration of justice is too complicated to do anything more than approximate equality.

Nor are we equal in advantage or opportunity. One is born in darkest Africa a slave child or in the isolation of the icy wastes of the Arctic, another has every privilege of cultural background and educational opportunity.

Neither are we equal recipients of God's providence. Even though His sunshine and rain come to both evil and good they do not come alike to all. We are individually the recipients of God's bounty and love, but not equally. We have equality only in our need. We are all equally in need of God's mercy and grace, and we are all equally the object of His concern and love. But the fact remains that we have not been created equal. It may be very good as a premise but it is not a fact.

I think I can safely say that we all recognize this and yet there are many of us who are not reconciled to it. There are many who feel deep down in their hearts that we should have been created equal. That equality ought to be, that men will never be happy until they have equality.

Now there is a sense in which this desire for equality has a legitimate basis. Men want to feel equal to others so as not to feel inferior to others. Nothing is so devastating to the human spirit as to be made the object of contempt and ignominy, to be stigmatized as inferior. All men have a craving for respect and anything that despoils a person's self-respect is vicious.

Jesus considered this so evil that He said, "He who calls another 'dumb' may be in danger of a suit for slander, but he who contemptuously despises a man and denies his essential value as a creation of God by calling him 'a damned-fool' (which is what the word Jesus used, literally means) will himself be liable to a hell of fire."

The judgment of that fire burns in our world today. It is a flame in the hearts of men in Algeria, and the Congo, and in Asia, and in Mississippi, and in South Africa. Men resent being considered second class citizens. Every man wants to feel that he, as a person, is entitled to the respect accorded to others; nothing so rankles in the human heart and creates a

171

burning sense of resentment and hatred as does the bitter insinuation that one is an inferior person.

That is what lies behind the passionate desire of the African nations to be admitted to and heard in the United Nations Assembly. And that is what lies behind the distorted arrogance with which they demand what they call their rights. This is where they are wrong. Equality is neither a fact nor a right.

But men could nevertheless accept the fact of their essential inequality if their essential dignity as individuals were respected and they were given equal consideration.

This ideal of equality, which we cling to so passionately, can result in making us feel inferior in another way, for one of the by-products of this idea that we should all be equal is the feeling that we should all be equally successful. That we should make good as our neighbor conceives of making good. And so we attach our efforts to being like some ideal person we have set up, oblivious to the fact that that person's life is quite different, his bent quite unlike ours, his capacities of quite another sort. And when we try to cudgel ourselves into becoming like this person, violating all our own natural capacities, and by a sheer tour-de-force, trying to push the square peg of our life into the round hole of his, it can only end (not in our becoming the other's counterpart, equal to him) but in our becoming frustrated and perhaps even neurotic.

That is the danger in believing that everyone should succeed as the other man succeeds, that everyone can be and should be equal to his neighbor in conforming to the commonly accepted idea of success. True success bears no relation to our being equal to the next person. That is merely "keeping up with the Joneses," which often means "going down with the Joneses." Success depends not on equality but on individuality— on difference. It is measured not in terms of common standards, but in terms of faithfulness to the best within us. And in the last analysis, respect must be won on that basis.

Again, there are some people who feel that equality is necessary because justice demands it. Now, like all half-truths, this conception lends itself to some very dangerous distortions, and this is one of them: that equality is synonymous with justice, that the only just basis for life lies in every man's having an equal share of things, whether of opportunities or possessions. There are some people who feel that if someone else gets something, they should have it too, and that if they can't have it, the other should not have it either. When my two sons were small and I gave something to one and not to the other, the latter would say, "It isn't fair! Ce n'est pas juste!" How often you have heard that?

172

Now that sense of justice is a valuable sentiment, but it is presumptuous and it is unrealistic. In the end justice just can't be worked out that way. Life is too complicated, too involved for us to simplify it that way.

Attempts have been made to apply justice in this manner and some of the greatest injustices have been perpetrated in consequence. Men cannot all be treated equally. Certain trade unions used to insist that all workers should have the same remuneration, irrespective of skill, industry or production; but they found that it often meant the end of superior workmanship. For it only served to breed indolence on the part of those who had no will to work and resentment on the part of the superior workman who wished to work better.

Equality is not a means to justice. And yet there are many who have a lurking feeling that the justice of God should issue in all men's having equal privileges, that God owes us equal advantages, and that we have a right to expect them from him. Many believe that if things go wrong, we have a right to believe that God will make it right for us, that it is coming to us.

Their idea of a sovereign creator is one who evens things up. Now Jesus believed in the legitimacy of rewards but He said that this was a false premise. We have what we have not as a right but by the Grace of God. We have no inherent right to anything. We all have more than we deserve. As Dr. Paul Scherer says: "God's textbook on economics starts out with the supposition that not only theoretically but very practically life belongs to Him. This world is not God's by human courtesy; it is His eminent domain." Taking into account all that we do, all our efforts, we are still only exploiting God's creation, and we are dependent on all the forces that make our effort possible. Life, air, warmth, the soil we walk on and the light by which we see. It is presumptuous to demand anything, above all to tell the Creator how he shall dispense his gifts.

A great deal of our trouble about equality stems from the fact that we want equality not because it is good but because it is good for us. We want equality for what it will bring us.

Very often it is our egotism that feeds our desire for equality.

You remember how the man who believed that God should mete out justice with a fine balance thought he saw an opportunity to get satisfaction through this new young Rabbi who spoke with such authority, and so he went to Jesus with his grievance saying:

"Rabbi, speak to my brother about our inheritance and make him even things up." To which Jesus, who saw deeper into the situation than this disgruntled brother, answered, in effect, "Who made me a divider over

173

you? I did not come to even things and make men equal in property or privilege. I came to help men make the most of the things which are theirs. You have missed the point. You are caught in the meshes of covetousness. Beware of covetousness. It will rob you of all peace of soul and all sense of true values, and in the end you will lose all that you have."

That is the heart of the trouble. If we center our life around ourselves and make the important question: "What shall I get out of life?" rather than "What shall I put into life?", life's inequalities will drive us to envy and misery. You see, if the former is the important question and we are out to get what we can for ourselves (no matter whether it be a good living or a fine education or what you will), we shall find ourselves concerned with getting our due and demanding our rights and becoming anxious about equality, getting as much as the next man gets.

But if the latter is the important question and we believe we are here to serve to the best of our ability, then equality will be of little consequence. We shall be more concerned with fulfilling our opportunities than with getting our share of things. Things will fall into their places.

Who ever heard of Thomas A. Edison wanting to get into the social register, or Wilfred Grenfell wanting to rank with King Edward the VII, or George Washington Carver wanting to be equal to James Farley, or Albert Schweitzer wanting the plaudits of President Auriol, or St. François of Assisi wanting to be equal to the Pope.

As a matter of fact they were all superior. St. Francis' pope is all but forgotten, but we put the little brother of the birds in the stained glass windows of our cathedrals, Protestant and Catholic alike. And both because of his skill and his rich spirit, George Washington Carver's help and counsel was sought by many of the best of his white contemporaries. Those men weren't concerned with equality.

Equality is a craven desire.

But inequality did not bother Jesus. He was a realist. He saw and accepted inequality of a kind as a fact of life—as a fact of the universe. He knew that there were five-talent men and two-talent men and one-talent men, and that the only equality involved in the situation lay in the fact that they were all recipients of gifts of the Master, stewards alike responsible for their faithful administration.

It is evident that God lays no great store upon equality and, rightly seen, equality is not a great boon. For in the Providence of God and by His Grace, it may very well be and often has been, that a man of one talent may live a fuller life and make a greater contribution to posterity than he who has five. God has often sought humble instruments for his riches. Are the scales by which he measures out His providences bound by man's superficial judgments of equity?

Men are not equal and we thank God for that. Else we should have no Beethoven and no Bach, no Milton and no Shakespeare or Dante, no Plato and no Augustine, no Galileo or Copernicus or Einstein, no Bunyan or Wesley, and the world would be infinitely poorer.

But the greatness of these men lies indisputably in their benefactions to mankind. Those who have superior talents are obligated to use them for the service of their fellows. Superiority means greater obligation as Jesus so well pointed out. Our inequalities involve not greater rights and privileges but great obligations and responsibilities for service.

Dives are responsible for Lazarus, Grenfell and Pasteur and Salk and Fleming are responsible for our health. Rembrandt and Botticelli and Cezanne and Manet are responsible for our having beauty. Soldiers and sailors and airmen are responsible for the world's security and order, and so it goes. "Those who are strong ought to bear the infirmities of the weak, and not to please themselves," as St. Paul says.

After all why all this concern about equality? Unless it be that we are concerned that others have it.

But really there is no solution to the problem that inequality presents, except the solution that Jesus suggests—that of superiority—superiority not of privilege and rights but of character, devotion and the spirit of love and service. This was taught by One, who, though He was rich, for our sakes became poor, who counted not equality with God something to be grasped after, but rather, who, knowing who He was and whence He came, took a towel and girded Himself and washed His disciples' feet, and went out to a cross, and forever proved the superiority of service and sacrifice.

Sermon Twenty-four

FACING NEW FRONTIERS

THE REVEREND LATON E. HOLMGREN, D.D.

An Executive Secretary of the American Bible Society and a Methodist Minister, New York City

This sermon was first preached at Christ Church Methodist in New York City on February 19, 1961. It was subsequently preached in the First Methodist Church of Buenos Aires, Argentina and in the Union Church of Lima, Peru. Dr. Holmgren travels abroad frequently for the American Bible Society, and his messages always contain a challenge to Christian people to become concerned with and involved in the proclamation of the gospel to the nations of the world. In this sermon he describes some of the serious obstacles confronting the spread of Christianity today and reminds us that we are probably falling behind in the struggle for the minds and souls of men.

A minister of the New York Conference of the Methodist Church, Laton Holmgren studied in Asbury College, took his theological degree at Drew University, and has done graduate work at the University of Minnesota and at Edinburgh University. Illinois Wesleyan University recently awarded him the honorary D.D.

For five years he was Associate Minister of Christ Church, Methodist, New York, then spent three years as minister of the Tokyo Union Church in Japan, the oldest English-language Protestant Church in the Far East. He played an important part in the rebuilding of this church after it was bombed during the war. He worked with the National Christian Council of Japan, edited the Japan Christian Year Book and was a consultant to the Japanese Foreign Office. He is now an Executive Secretary of the American Bible Society.

During the Korean war, he conducted a series of spiritual retreats for the United Nations Chaplains at Corps Headquarters near the front and visited POW camps where he distributed the Scriptures in Chinese to captured soldiers. He has made four trips around the world during the last ten years and most recently spent a month visiting churches and missions in eight South American Republics.

FACING NEW FRONTIERS

The World Day of Prayer has been observed in churches throughout the world. As the day advanced, beginning with dawn on the island of Tonga and continuing every hour from Tonga to Tokyo, from Bangkok to Beirut, from Leopoldville to Lima and from Washington to Waikiki, Christian men and women in one hundred forty-five countries prayed for the success of the Christian message and mission.

As my mind entered that orbit of intercession surrounding the earth, I could not escape the disturbing question as to whether, in fact, the Christian faith was prevailing in today's world, whether on the frontiers of the world—not the geographical frontiers merely, but the psychological, moral and spiritual frontiers of earth—we are actually winning in the desperate struggle for the minds and souls of men.

The apparent answer to that question is that we are not. Despite the astronomical sums spent by our government, despite the further large amounts sent by private organizations and philanthropies and despite the vast expanse—and expense—of the Christian world mission, we seem to be losing ground. James Michener, the celebrated author of plays and novels about life in the Pacific Basin, has recently said that we are losing approximately one hundred million souls a year to the enemy and that the point of no return, at this rate, will be reached within five to ten years. The plain truth is that even after two thousand years of Christian witness in the world, there are more non-Christians on earth today than there were on the Day of Pentecost.

What, then, are the reasons for the seeming decline of the Christian cause in today's world? What are the barriers we face which make our advance across world frontiers so difficult? There are several, but four in particular presented themselves to me as I joined in intercessory prayer for the Christian Church—four barriers, each a formidable obstacle, but each able to be transformed, with imagination and dedication, into a glorious opportunity for Christian evangelism.

The first of these is the exploding populations of the earth. The figures are frightening. We have reached a world population of two and a half billion souls after several thousand years, but we are told that by the end of this century, in less than forty years, the figure will have exploded to six and a half billion souls. The fastest rate of growth will be in Latin America, where there are already more people than in North America and where, by the year 2000 A.D. there will be twice as many people as in North America. The largest actual increase will be in Asia, where in forty years it is estimated that 60 per cent of the world's population will live.

All of this is too complex to understand. Let me put it this way: Every thirty seconds, or about as long as it will take me to complete this sentence, eighty-five persons are born in the world; forty-five persons die during that same period; leaving a net increase in the world's population—every thirty seconds—of forty persons! The sobering fact is that accessions to the Christian faith do not even approximate those fantastic figures. The net result is that every minute you are sitting in this church we are falling behind in our effort to win the world for Jesus Christ.

A second obstacle we confront is the advancing literacy and learning of the earth's peoples. Probably one of the most revolutionary events in our world today is the amazing spread of literacy and education. It is estimated that at least twenty million adults learn to read and write for the first time each year. In India alone there have been nearly one thousand colleges and universities formed since its independence in 1949. My own belief is that when future historians write the story of our age, long after the beneficent uses of atomic energy are as commonplace as the incandescent light, they will say far more about this being the era of literacy and learning than they will about its being the age of nuclear power.

One of the most exciting moments I have ever known was when I saw a grown man, a village chief, write his name for the first time in my presence. I had gone out to a small Indian village with a literacy team which had been visiting the place for several weeks. A kind of portable blackboard was set up in one of the village streets and the people sat in a large circle on the ground. After the lesson for the day, the teacher asked the villagers to come to the board, one by one, to show how well they had practiced the assignment of the week before—each one to write his own name. They arose in order and came, somewhat shyly, to write their names publicly for the first time. The last one to approach the board was the village elder. His movements were a mixture of fear and confidence. He was the chief but he must not make a mistake. He had the most to gain and the most to lose. I saw the old man's hand tremble slightly as he took the chalk and wrote slowly in his own language, "My . . . name . . . is . . . Samuel." Then, because he was the chief, he had done extra work and he added, now more firmly, "And my Savior's name . . . is Jesus Christ!"

As moving as that scene was, it depressed me to think that at that moment there were men of questionable intent and sinister purpose who

179

were moving rapidly to win the uncommitted peoples of the world, particularly those who are now learning to read and write for the first time. They are using vast expenditures, able craftsmen and determined methods to make their case and in many places of earth are successfully winning the day.

It is always a pleasure to find unexpected support for the Christian world mission from the tycoons of industry. Such an implied endorsement is contained in a remarkable little brochure by J. Peter Grace, President of the Grace Lines, entitled "It Is Not Too Late in Latin America." Mr. Grace doesn't mention missions by name, mind you, but he does speak strongly of the need for commitment and dedication to our task which will match the skillful determined methods of those who scoff at moral and spiritual values.

A third obstacle to the advance of the Christian faith is found in the rising revolutionary moods and movements of our day. We have all become so familiar with the cry of subjugated peoples that we hardly hear them anymore. Moreover, we are becoming discouraged with the results of our efforts to alleviate want. Despite all we have tried to do to lift depressed humanity in recent years, there are more men and women on the verge of starvation today than there were fifty years ago. Will you imagine that you heard a knock on your front door just now and that when you opened it you saw standing in his tattered rags one of the emaciated, diseased men of the earth. As you were about to offer the poor fellow a piece of bread, you noticed that standing just behind him was another just like him. And behind him still another, and another. That line of hungry distressed men and women at your front door this morning would reach around the world and return to your house, not once, but twenty-five times.

Bishop Rajah B. Manikam, one of India's great churchmen, puts it this way: "Millions of men and women in the East still live in inhuman or subhuman conditions. Two thirds of mankind is going hungry. In my country of India, millions go to bed at night with only a single meal a day. Ninety per cent of the Far East is undernourished. As for Africa, it is one of the biggest areas of hunger in the world. However, more food is being produced and eaten in the world today. But who is eating better? The ones who always have eaten well, while the eternally underfed of Africa, Asia and elsewhere continue to starve." Later in the same brochure, he writes: "While an American child at birth has an average life-expectancy of 67 years, the Asian child has an expectancy of only 30 years. Malaria strikes down a fifth of mankind. One million lepers are at large in India even in these days of miracles of modern medicine!" What a formidable obstacle to the free advance of the Christian gospel. I remember hearing Dr. Ralph Sockman say after his first visit to Asia that he now understands why it is that when the people of the world are offered four freedoms by one hand and four sandwiches by another, they will invariably reach for the sandwiches.

The fourth obstacle is the awakening ancient religions of the world. Everywhere we are seeing the revival of ancient faiths. Men are rebuilding their crumbled shrines, repairing their broken altars and even launching aggressive world missions. Islam last year sent four thousand missionaries to Africa. Buddhism and Hinduism are enjoying an unprecedented period of revival and renaissance. While we can only be grateful that men are everywhere trying to find the true God, we are dismayed to hear their preachers and prophets saying that the "East is spiritual; the West is secular." Christianity has been weighed in the balances and found wanting.

It has been the dominant world religion for nearly two thousand years and yet it has been unable to eradicate hatred and fear, to smother prejudice and bigotry, to banish cruelty and war. On the contrary, they are saying, the Christian nations have been the prime source of imperialism, the author of two world wars and now they threaten to unleash such destructive power that none may survive its holocaust.

As unfounded as some of these charges may be, they are being heard and believed by sober frightened men in many places on earth and represent a further difficulty in presenting the central truths of Christian faith to the world.

If these are, in fact, the conditions which confront us on the world's frontiers, the question must be answered as to where we may find the dynamic and the determination required to cross these frontiers—better yet, to capture them for Christ and His cross.

To answer that question I call your attention to a story in the Book of Acts about two of our Lord's first disciples who had sufficient dynamic and dedication to "turn the world upside down." The story, from the New English version, goes like this:

"One day at three in the afternoon, the hour of prayer, Peter and John were on their way up to the temple. Now a man who had been a cripple from birth used to be carried there and laid every day by the gate of the temple called 'Beautiful Gate,' to beg from people as they went in. When he saw Peter and John on their way into the temple he asked for charity. But Peter fixed his eyes on him as John did also, and said, 'Look at us.' Expecting a gift from them, the man was all attention. And Peter said, 'I have no silver

181

or gold; but what I have I give you: in the name of Jesus Christ of Nazareth, walk.' Then he grasped him by the right hand and pulled him up; and at once his feet and ankles grew strong; he sprang up, stood on his feet, and started to walk. He entered the temple with them leaping and praising God as he went. Everyone saw him walking and praising God, and when they recognized him as the man who used to sit begging at Beautiful Gate, they were filled with wonder and amazement at what had happened to him." [1]

In that story there are some striking lessons for us who confront a world full of despairing men very much like the poor fellow at the Beautiful Gate. Let me speak of three.

Consider, first, that the faith of these early disciples was wonderfully creative. These men had not yet substituted convention for conviction. They always seemed ready to do the unexpected if it held any promise of relief, recovery or redemption. The conventional thing in passing the poor wretch at the temple gate was, of course, to drop a coin in his lap. But not Peter and John, for they saw how inadequate a remedy that was for man's real need. On the contrary, Peter surprised him by saying, "I have no silver and gold." How unconventional. How disappointing. How completely unproductive.

Of course, the reason for their unusual approach to human need was that they had been with Jesus, the most unconventional of men. He was always seeing uncommon possibilities in common men. They well remembered the very first day they ever saw Him. They were rough, coarse fellows working at their nets. We would have passed them by as unworthy of membership in our church. But He saw that they had unusual possibilities for God's kingdom and He invited them to follow Him. Or that other day when he was preaching on the Galilean hillside and the little children, irresistably drawn to Him, had left their mothers and were playing about his feet. The disciples afraid that He was being annoyed by their chatter and play tried to chase them away. But He stopped them. "Don't do that," He said in effect, can't you see that in these little ones God has wonderful plans for His kingdom?" Or again, that other day when the man who had been born blind was brought to Him for healing. The disciples began immediately to speculate as to who may have sinned so badly as to cause the man's blindness. "That isn't the question," said Jesus. "The question is, what can this man become if God's power is allowed to reach him." Then he touched the man and he saw. He was always doing that kind of surprising thing.

182

So it has ever been with men of faith. They have always had a way of doing the unexpected. Abraham bravely left the known for the unknown. Moses staunchly forsook the security of Egypt for the hazards of the wilderness. Joshua launched his surprise attack on Jericho and captured the city without "firing a shot." St. Francis, the frail friar, forsook the comforts of his wealthy family to walk in poverty among the family of nations. Kagawa, a modern version of the medieval monk, startled his friends and neighbors by leaving his aristocratic home for life in the slums of Kobe. Not one of these men depended on silver and gold to achieve his ends or fulfill his ministry. We would probably be making very much more progress in meeting the world's needs today if we had more of the kind of wonderfully creative faith that dares to say, "We have no silver and gold, but . . ."

Notice, second, that their faith was tenderly compassionate. These first disciples had not yet substituted apathy for sympathy. Even though they had no money to give the poor beggar at the Beautiful Gate, they were not indifferent to his desperate plight. "I have no silver and gold, but what I have I give you." They simply could not be complacent in the presence of human suffering.

Once again, the secret of their compassion was their close companionship with Jesus. They had been near Him on those many occasions when He "looked with compassion on the multitude." There was the unforgettable day when He was surrounded by scores of suffering people, pushing and shoving, trying to get His attention so they might be healed. Among them was one feeble woman, unable to walk any longer, who crawled through the crowd until at last she could barely touch the hem of His garment. "Who touched me?" he said. In that pushing crowd, everyone was touching Him. But no, here was someone in special need who must not be overlooked. "Who touched me!"

Or that other day when still another crowd of sick and lame surrounded Him in the street, each man shouting to get His attention. But one poor fellow, alone and blind, was unable to find his way through the crowd and so sat wearily at the edge of the road pitifully crying, "Lord, Lord." And He said, "Who called me?" In that shouting throng everyone was calling Him. But no, here was someone who needed special attention. "Who called me!" It's that kind of quivering sensitivity to human need that always characterized Him and that made those who had been close to Him so tenderly compassionate whenever they saw suffering humanity.

Surely one of the greatest words in the New Testament is the word "compassion." Not mercy, with its accent on judgment. Not pity, with its accent on condescension. But compassion, with its accent on love. How much real compassion do we feel for suffering humanity in our world?

A very striking summary of the dimensions of human need in our day appears in Dr. Stringfellow Barr's little pamphlet entitled "Let's Join the Human Race," in which Dr. Barr suggests that in order to understand conditions over a large part of the world, we pretend that we are to be born today, along with two hundred thousand other persons being born each day. Where, we do not know, but, he says, "There will be only one chance in twenty that you will be born in the United States and about the same chance of being born in Soviet Russia. You will probably be colored—black, brown, or yellow. If you are born colored, you will probably be born in a country which has recently revolted and thrown out the white folks, or is still trying to do it. If you are born in Africa, you are likely to learn the maxim, 'Never trust a white man.' You have only about one chance in four of being born a Christian. It is far more likely that you will be born a Confucian, a Buddhist or a Mohammedan.

"If you are born in India, you have only a little better than a one-to-four chance of living more than a year and if you survive babyhood you have only a fifty-fifty chance of growing to maturity. If you are born colored, the chances are overwhelming that you will be sick all your life—from malaria or intestinal parasites, tuberculosis or even leprosy. You will probably be weak from hunger and at times you may experience such a famine as to be willing to eat the bark off a tree. Again, if you are born colored you have only a one-to-four chance of learning to read. You will most certainly work on the land and most of what you raise will go to the landlord, but also to the local moneylender and interest rates may be from thirty to one hundred percent." [2]

That kind of world desperately needs the kind of tenderly compassionate faith that Peter and John had when they said, "Such as I have, I give . . . I give . . . I give unto you."

Finally, notice that their faith was thoroughly committed to Jesus Christ. "I have no silver or gold; but what I have I give you: in the name of Jesus Christ of Nazareth, walk." He was the real secret of their power. He was the measure of their conviction; He was the object of their devotion. In His name, they found they too could heal the sick, lift the lame, help the weak and feed the hungry. Consequently nothing else really mattered to them except that they discover and do His will. With them, this was a matter of life and death and must become so with us if we are to share their power in today's world.

Someone once asked a disciple of Buddha what had been the secret of

---

[2] Copyright, 1950, by the University of Chicago.

the great man's life. The disciple seized the surprised seeker by the neck, plunged his head under water and held it there until the startled man came up sputtering and gasping for breath. Then the disciple said, "When you want righteousness as badly as you just now wanted air, you will understand the secret of the master's life."

A friend of mine told me recently that he had just signed a letter which he had earlier dictated to his foreign-born secretary who often had difficulty with our strange language. What he had said in the dictation was that "We must put our insights into action"; but what the letter said when written by the secretary was "We must put our 'insides' into action"; That, I should say, was a definite improvement over the original. Until we are ready to put all we have, inside and out, into the struggle for the minds and souls of men we shall never be able to capture the new frontiers of the world for Christ and His cross.

Not long ago I stood in Bishop Dibelius's pulpit in East Berlin. I could still hear the echoes of his courageous pastoral letter which had been read to the congregation—and to all the congregations in East Germany—a few days earlier. In it he had recited the fundamentals of the Christian faith; he had reviewed the noble history of the Christian Church; and he had called his dwindling flock to a courageous stand against the steady pressures of a government determined to smother their witness and suffocate their spiritual lives. He closed that service with Luther's great hymn now more relevant than ever:

> Let goods and kindred go,
> This mortal life also;
> The body they may kill
> God's truth abideth still,
> His kingdom is forever.

Here, then, is the answer to our question as to where we shall find the dedication and the dynamic to face and cross new frontiers that we face across the world. They are to be found in men so thoroughly committed to Jesus Christ that His purpose is always before them and His presence is always within them. To such men, whose faith is wonderfully creative, tenderly compassionate and thoroughly committed we say

> Rise up, O men of God,
> The Church for you doth wait.
> Her strength unequal to her task,
> Rise up and make her great.[3]

---

[3] Copyright, The Presbyterian Outlook.

Sermon Twenty-five

GOD HAS NEED OF YOU

Reverend John G. Ferry

Minister, St. John's United Church,
Church of Canada, Vancouver, British Columbia

John Ferry comes from a church-oriented family. His grandfather was a saddlebag preacher for the Presbyterian Church on the Canadian frontier and one of the early champions of the Church Union Movement in Canada. Two of his uncles, Ebbie and Asa Ferry, were ministers of The Presbyterian Church U.S.A., and a cousin, Frankie Frodsham and her husband and family have returned to Canada from troubled Angola, where they were doing missionary work for The United Church of Canada.

A graduate of The University of Saskatchewan, Mr. Ferry studied Theology at St. Andrew's College. Like many of his fellow theological students, he spent each Sunday during his college and university terms preaching somewhere in rural Saskatchewan, sometimes returning to college by freight train in order to make Monday morning classes.

Shortly after graduation Mr. Ferry was privileged to attend the second assembly of The World Council of Churches as press representative for The Saskatoon Star Phoenix. This marked the beginning of an interest in religious journalism which has continued through the years. He has contributed articles to most of the leading publications in Canada, including *Liberty, Maclean's, Toronto Star Weekly,* and *The United Church Observer,* and contributes several sermons a year to "The Quiet Hour" feature of *The Family Herald.* He has also contributed to *The Pulpit, Christian Century, Modern Bride, Life Today,* and many others, and is a professional member of The National Writers Club.

For the past five years, Mr. Ferry has been minister of St. John's United Church, in the heart of downtown Vancouver. Also he is public relations convener of The Vancouver-Burrard Presbytery, convener of publications for British Columbia Conference, and chairman of the management committee of The Pacific Regional Literature Depot of The United Church of Canada.

GOD HAS NEED OF YOU

> "Rise and enter the city, and you will be told
> what you are to do."
>
> Acts 9:6

As God needed Abraham and Moses, Peter and Paul, so He needs you. In the same realistic sense in which He visited these men in time past and gave them a specific task to perform in the interests of the Kingdom, so likewise has He a specific task for you.

From the very beginning of the religious story of mankind God worked through specific individuals to accomplish His good purposes. He spoke to Abram, challenging him to go out to a land that He would show him, that He might establish a nation from his seed. He spoke to Moses, challenging him to lead a disorganized mob of slaves out of bondage into the freedom of the Promised Land. He spoke to Peter, challenging him to leave his fishing nets to become a fisher of men. He challenged Saul of Tarsus to leave off his persecutions and instead to carry Christ's message of salvation to the nations of the world.

These men were chosen of God to do His bidding, whatever the personal cost might be. But have you ever stopped to consider that God, in a similar sense, may be calling you? He has work for you to do and He challenges you to do it. It is surely a tragedy that as in the Scriptures, so in daily life we are often unaware of our election to a place of responsibility in the service of the Lord our God.

Saul of Tarsus failed to recognize Christ's plea. When we first meet him in the book of Acts we find him in open rebellion against Christ and His Church. Finally the risen Lord confronts him before the gates of Damascus, and in an experience, vivid beyond all description, he hears Christ say, "Saul, Saul, why do you persecute me?" Suddenly aware of the blindness of spirit which had been his, Saul fell to the road and said, "Lord, what wilt Thou have me to do?" Saul the persecutor died at that moment, and from the dust of the road there arose Paul, the Christ-appointed apostle to the Gentiles.

The light which he tells us lit up the sky, was really the light which set his soul aflame, for he was the only one dazzled by it.

Religious experience is the same now as then. Christ today speaks to your heart, He strives to enkindle your spirit. As He found Saul of

Tarsus in the midst of a company bound for Damascus and singled him out for active service, so from the midst of your friends and associates he calls saying, "Come and follow me. I have need of you." What remains is for you to become receptive to that call; to cry out, "Lord, what wilt Thou have me to do?" Then immediately, as you respond to God's challenge, you will find sweeping over you an overwhelming feeling of inadequacy, and you'll say to yourself, "How can I, a very ordinary man, be of service to the Lord?" But you will not be the first to feel this way.

Once a young man of Judah stood before the altar in Jerusalem, overwhelmed by the impending disaster which he felt sure must come upon his nation with the death of the good king Uzziah. But as he stood there mourning for his king, he caught a vision of the King of kings, and his train filled the Temple, and a voice spoke to this young man's spirit, challenging him to become God's spokesman. But Isaiah's immediate response was: "I can't, I'm unworthy. I'm a man of unclean lips, and I dwell amongst a people of unclean lips. Lord, how could you think of me?"

But the Lord took a live coal from off the altar and put it on the young man's lips, a symbol of purification, and He said, "Be thou clean." The challenge was issued a second time, "Who will go for me?" And Isaiah replied, "Here am I Lord, send me."

The late Lloyd C. Douglas, in one of his earlier novels, *Forgive us our Trespasses,* has as the hero of his story a cynical, rebellious youth by the name of Dinny Brumm, who has allowed the injustice of circumstances both real and fancied to poison his soul. His hatred for those who have wounded him, and his mother who died at his birth, is boundless. As a journalist he becomes a brilliant satirist, scoffing at all that people have held in reverence for five thousand years. Until one day he discovers a letter in a secret compartment of his desk, written for him by his mother before she died. The letter explained that the hatred which once had ruled her life was overcome as she entered into the bargain which God offers in the Lord's prayer, "Forgive us our trespasses as we forgive those who trespass against us."

Dinny Brumm, the cynic, decided to give his mother's faith a trial. He is rewarded by being reconciled with those he once despised, finding that he is now able to respect them in a way he previously found impossible. But most of all he is rewarded with a new thrill in life, a sense of power and accomplishment, and an inner sense of peace and wellbeing born of his fellowship with God that was unknown to him before.

Dinny Brumm had ceased to kick against the pricks, and was aware of the call of God, saying to him, "Come my friend, I have need of you."

Though to the casual observer it may seem that few are chosen by God from amongst the many, the reverse is actually true. Each of us at one time or another have sensed God's call, imperative upon us. But like Isaiah, or Paul, or Dinny Brumm, we have been slow to respond. Yet once we have accepted His challenge it brings new life to us, and we experience a sense of spiritual enrichment that was not ours before.

Our natural inclination is to then go out and share this good thing that has come to us with all we meet. And that is precisely what our Lord would have us do. This is our response to His call for service. He wants us to spread the glad tidings of His kingdom.

For this great purpose he has appointed each one of us to an individual task. What he wants us to do is not vague. It is specific. There is a distinct task which God has in mind for you, a task that no one else on the face of this earth can perform. For He has made you uniquely what you are. He has given you the power to envision what, with God's help, you might become. If then you fail to respond to His challenge, His kingdom is that much poorer, for there are no substitutes. Who can do for God the task He has appointed you to do?

But, you say, how can we know what that task is? St. Paul asked the exalted Christ what He would have him do. Christ replied, "Rise and enter the city, and you will be told what you are to do." That initial response is the most important step. God will lead us if we will but follow.

But in order that we should know assuredly what God would have us do it is necessary, in prayerful meditation and with as much honest objectivity as possible, to review the talents which He has given us. Perhaps you are a ten talent person, perhaps only five or three. Perhaps your talents can be measured in material ways. Perhaps in special training or natural aptitudes. But whatever they may be, realize that God didn't give them to you accidentally, nor indiscriminately. The Lord of Hosts, Whose purpose extends even to the life of a sparrow, has a vital interest in the native abilities with which He has endowed you, and the accomplishments and skills which you have achieved as a result. He grieves when you misuse those talents and treasures, or bury them in the earth. He would have you invest them to the glory of the Kingdom and the joy of your own soul.

Did God fill your heart and soul with music? How can you use that talent to praise Him and to enrich the age you have been called to serve? Did God give you an intellect which makes study and research a pleasure? How can you use it to return thanks, and to lift the shroud of darkness and ignorance from the world of men? Did He make your fingers sensitive so that they are skilled in some art or craft? How can you thank Him, and

190

invest that talent in His interest, so that the blessings of His Kingdom may be extended to others? In other words, what is your particular talent and how have you held it in relation to the God who gave it to you? Assess your talents carefully, prayerfully, for it is through them that God issues His challenge unto you saying, "Come, I have a task to be done for which you are peculiarly fitted. I need the abilities and the unique qualities of personality that you alone possess."

George Eliot expressed this truth in the poem "Stradivarius," in which she has the great violin maker say:

> Tis God gives skill,
> But not without men's hands:
> He could not make Antonio Stradivari's violins
> Without Antonio.

God has chosen you for a special task. Rise and follow Him, and it will be revealed what you are to do.

Sermon Twenty-six

A CHRISTIAN FAITH

REVEREND RALPH E. KNUDSEN, TH.M., TH.D.

*A Minister of the Baptist Church and Dean, and
Professor of New Testament Literature and Interpretation, Berkeley Baptist Divinity School, Berkeley, California*

Dr. Ralph Knudsen was born in Harlan, Iowa, in 1897. He graduated from Des Moines University in 1923 and from the Southern Baptist Seminary in 1928. He received his Th.D. degree from Berkeley Baptist Divinity School in 1938.

Ordained to the ministry in the Baptist church in 1925, he held pastorates at Glasgow, Polson, and Bozeman, Montana. He was minister of Central Church, San Francisco, from 1935 to 1939, and of Universal Church, Seattle, from 1939 to 1943.

Since 1943, Dr. Knudsen has taught at the Berkeley Divinity School. In 1946 he became Dean. He is president of the Berkeley-Albany Council of Churches, trustee of the Spanish-American Theological Seminary, and San Francisco Bay Cities Baptist Union.

A CHRISTIAN FAITH

The statement, "Jesus Christ is the same yesterday, and today, and forever," from Hebrews 13:8, is one of the great affirmations of our Christian faith. It is lucid, positive, direct, understandable, and inclusive in its latitude and meaning. The compass of the words is staggering in scope and depth of design for the Church and for the world. As a matter of fact, the words contain the bases for faith and Christian life for any moment in history.

I

The name, Jesus Christ, which introduces the statement is the minimum as well as the maximum for Christian faith and life. This is the point at which God meets man in the most dynamic moments of history and human experience. The two names tell essentially all that can be known of God, and all that is needed for faith, "for in Him dwells all the fulness" of God in revelation. The terms, Jesus Christ, state definitely what makes Christianity a distinct and inimitable religion. At a student conference an Indian student asked Dr. Stanley Jones what Christianity had which other religions did not have. Stanley Jones answered, "You haven't Christ." This is precisely the reason Christianity is different; we do have Jesus Christ, who is central in the whole structure of Christian faith.

The name, Jesus, reminds us of the One who walked among men, taught them, loved them, and did good to all who sought Him. He is the One who in humility of spirit but with depth of understanding gave meaning to our comprehension of the Heavenly Father. It is in the presence of this One we affirm in elation, "We have found Him," or in deep confession utter in subdued words, "My Lord and my God." Faith finds sufficient dimensions in such declarations concerning Jesus as the inescapable and irrestible expressions of experience. Christ is the name which gives meaning to our salvation in fellowship with God. In the two names "Jesus Christ" we are thrust into the very depth of all we can mean by Christian faith and life, for here is the center or existential focal point of all history for all mankind.

194

The text is easily anlyzed and is a delight for the preacher for it suggests its own logical development. It mentions clearly three dimensions of faith: first, a faith which is rooted in the actuality of history—"yesterday"; second, a faith which is competent to help man in the tensions of contemporary life—"today"; third, a faith which provides the basis of a courageous hope—"tomorrow." These dimensions stretch across all man knows of time in its continuing unfolding in life and history. "Yesterday" reflects the actuality of human experience in time which has passed and beyond recall. "Today" suggests the present, where we live and struggle, in the most relevant period of life. "Tomorrow" declares time in terms of eschatological hope which is essential for confident faith today.

History does have a sober word for those who have courage to search and patience to listen. The process whereby history is debunked does not in the least change the facts of history nor the importance of that past upon today. History is not merely the record of events, nor an inventory of great personalities, but the impact of all of life as lived then being consciously or unconsciously operating through the continuity of life into every present time. We cannot escape the past and in many ways we are unconsciously fashioned by it. It is not necessary to review history to establish this fact, for yesterday is vitally meaningful and directive for us today.

American history and life are immeasurably more meaningful today because of those stalwart Pilgrims who came to our shores in 1620. Plymouth Rock symbolizes a point of history in our yesterday which bequeaths character and godly purpose to this country which has developed out of diminutive beginnings. True, it is only a rock on which are some figures but these silently remind us of men of courage, daring, faith and a firm resolve to establish a new home where freedom for worship shall be a reality, and where home shall be man's sacred shrine. We who live in and enjoy America today should never cease to be grateful for these ideals in our historic heritage.

The little land of Palestine, destitute of resources and opportunities for freedom or wealth, has contributed more to the world historically and morally than the many larger and richer nations of that period. It was in this land that the prophets emerged to startle their own age and every succeeding age with their clearness of purpose, their demand for moral integrity, and their understanding of God's will for Israel and all mankind. No nation in history has produced such intellectual and spiritual giants whose words are still pondered and whose truths are still believed. They were part of yesterday which lives in actuality in the world of our today.

One need only mention the name "Jesus" as an historic figure in yesterday to make clear the importance of what yesterday means today. He was and still is the most controversial person who ever lived and the most radical religionist of history. His teachings are minutely studied and His life is the ideal of man in his highest moments of unselfish living. His unselfish and sacrificial giving of self for others is the greatest challenge ever presented to man. The disturbing statement to love God with the total being and one's neighbor as one's self strikes the height of Christlike accomplishment and the sublimity of concerned human relations. The whole world has been immeasurably blest and benefited because He lived. To disregard yesterday is indefensible, incomprehensible, and irrational, for we are the children of history and cannot escape from that which has taken place in time.

The tendency today is to speak in extravagant terms of our changing world. It is a changing world on the superficial level where man can bring about changes, for such changes can only take place in the areas where man has been able to invent things. There are great depths of life where man cannot by his own ingenuity occasion changes of importance. When I visit my boyhood home in Iowa I always spend a time in the country cemetery on the hillside, not because I enjoy cemeteries but because during the lapse of time between my visits friends of other days are laid to rest on this quiet hillside. I am always reminded that changes do come for some have departed from this order of life. H. F. Lyte, the hymn writer, expressed this truth, "Change and decay in all around I see." There are also the great unchangeables in the world and life which give permanency to cosmic existence. One never tires of a beautiful sunset where the Eternal Artist blends the colors of the spectrum into delicate and indescribable hues which no human artist can approximate. The mountains stand "tall, wonderful and grand" with strength and majesty reaching into the blue heavens with the enduring qualities of the eternal hills. The waves of the sea continue to wash against the beach in quiet ripples or in thunderous billows echoing the music of the deep. Love is the greatest constructive force in the universe and the prime essential for life on its unfathomable creative level. These unchangeables are not subject to the modifications of life which man directs but are inherent in the very fabric of the cosmos.

It is in a world built on such dimensions that Christian faith today finds the facts of history so meaningful. The Christian faith is rooted in a person who lived and worked in yesterday. A knowledge of what that history says

196

is essential to know what it can mean for us today. The history of yesterday tells us of Jesus who lived among men and taught them timeless truth about the Heavenly Father. His very life was an acted revelation of the God of love and mercy. Only two facts of this revolutionary past can be mentioned: One, He did something for people. A casual reading of the story reflects the true meaning of the statement about Him, "He went about doing good." (Acts 10:38) The people who really encountered Him were changed in spirit and in life. An analysis of the disciples reflects this fact for one learns that Peter was changed from a cursing fisherman to one who dared to face magistrates for His sake, that John a son of "thunder" became the exponent of love for all people, that Matthew the collector of taxes and the keeper of tax records became the writer of a great gospel. The list might continue to include the sinful woman at a well in Samaria, who after talking with Jesus returned to the city to tell her friends, "Come, see a man who told me all that I ever did. Can this be the Christ?" (John 4:29) Any encounter with Jesus in the long ago brought transformation to those who dared to believe and follow Him. Someone has well said that whenever one encounters Jesus in His actuality he becomes either a "cynic or a saint." New life came to those who met Jesus yesterday.

The second fact is found in His always relevant teaching. He taught many things in that first century but only two can be considered here. He set love as the basis for all faith and life and inclusive of all activity in relationship. This love must first of all be toward God, "you shall love the Lord your God with all your heart, and with all your soul, and with all your mind" (Matthew 22:37), and then toward one's neighbor, "you shall love your neighbor as yourself." As a matter of fact such love is so fundamental that "on these two commandments depend all the law and the prophets." (Matthew 22:40) Such conception of love had never been taught and such teaching of love had never been lived in actual human situations before. A second truth in his teaching was forgiveness. He taught man to forgive and related Divine forgiveness to the genuineness of human forgiveness; "for if you forgive men their trespasses, your heavenly Father will also forgive you; but if you do not forgive men their trespasses, neither will your Father forgive your trespasses." (Matthew 6:14-15) These were sober words penetrating conscience then as well as today. In His ministry He often said to depressed and defeated man, "thy sins are forgiven." It is love and forgiveness which make reconciliation an objective reality between God and man and between man and man. Reconciliation is the great need of every age and this was a vital reality in His teaching.

197

It is useful to review the past if one does not remain there and attempt to live in that past. The past with all its wonders and romanticized reconstructions can never be recaptured in the present. We should learn the lessons and mistakes of the past but always remember that it is gone and gone forever. We must take from the past that which helps us live today in the most meaningful and useful way. It does seem at times as though the history of yesterday should help men today to escape the errors and utilize the good. The trend in much of contemporary life gives little encouragement to believe that we are serious students of the past. Some mistakes could not be repeated so consistently historically if men were serious students of history.

The world has, of course, changed much since the time of Jesus. His was a simple and a slow moving world. There were no cars, no planes, no motor boats, no telephones to hurry them about in a mad race with time to get places and return exhausted and confused. They did much because they had time to think and to act in harmony with such contemplation. We move with rapidity and then try to ascertain exactly what it all means. We are much like the man in a city who ran nearly a block to catch a bus and when he had sufficient breath to ask a question, he said to the conductor, "where is this bus going?" It seemed to be more important to be going somewhere than to know where that might be. There are some who would like to change the life and teachings of Jesus to make them conform more to our contemporary understanding and desires. Jesus has been interpreted all the way from a high salaried executive to a great social radical to conform Him to our ideas, activities or ideals. Some of His teaching has been demythologized so as to bring it into harmony with our scientific understanding of man and his world. Our contemporary process often leaves Jesus much less Jesus than He was in the history of the first century. If the process of demythologizing must be applied then some areas in our contemporary ways of expressing common things need to be demythologized before they become matters of history. The time spent on secondary aspects of the life and teaching of Jesus might better be utilized in the discovery of meanings which are easily comprehended but unwillingly obeyed, for such would mean a radical transformation of much contemporary living.

The New Testament presents Jesus as the One who is doing today precisely what He was doing yesterday. That which was His basic interest, concern, and purpose then is the same now. The way to real life has not changed, for such life demands faith and obedience, two qualities which contemporary man finds difficult to accept. We live under the false illusion that we have something to contribute to God's plan for His world in terms of its inner structure and meaning. In that intellectual fallacy we are the inventors of new religions, new psychologies, and new philosophies which we presume should contain truth for man's inner revival. The rapidity with which we project new ideologies and cults is staggering and to say the least frightening. We assume we can do God's supreme task through right thinking, right actions, directed intercommunication or dialogue, incessant activity or withdrawal from the world. In the last few years we have tried everything from tranquilizing pills to Zen-Buddhism, without evidential consequences.

It has been the hope of the hopeless that our own ingenuity would provide an improved way to happiness and purposeful living. Many new machines are even utilized to assist. Those who cannot find a partner for marriage can now have their names placed in uni-vac and out will come the selected partner through the process of machine action. Such a method saves much time and money, but how absurd and unprofitable, for actual human love making in this most thrilling adventure. The machine as perfected today is a marvel and can do what at times seems human, but it is still a machine. An incident is reported in which a well known magazine was involved in a national program to secure subscribers. The names and addresses were being processed for mailing through an I.B.M. machine. The machine stuck at a certain name and a sheepherder in a Western State received six thousand invitations to subscribe to the magazine. The people in the little town into which the sheepherder's mail poured were all excited about the amount of mail he received. After opening a few hundred of the letters the sheepherder responded by saying, "I give up, I subscribe." A machine cannot do the work of man unless man is at hand to keep the machine functioning properly. We have literally tried everything but God.

III

In such a tension torn and confused age Jesus stands as the One who brings the transforming changes to life in redemptive reality, and teaches us how to truly live. Man's numerous attempts to change life have failed again and again. It is only God the creator of life who can renew life in Jesus Christ. The true story of the Christian Church is the story of men and women who have found in Christ newness of life, yes, life itself. It would seem as though our many failures ought to convince us that only in the love of God and the self-giving of Jesus on the Cross can life be re-created and specified abundant. Jesus Christ is God's way to life which can be lived above the changing pattern which comes from the mind and hand of man.

The contemporary world has many wise and helpful teachers and we do know much which previous generations did not know. Perhaps the test of knowledge is not how much is known nor how many things have been invented to enhance and ease the life of man, but rather what is actually taking place in the spirit of man, to his own inner self and to his integrity of character. What is actually happening to man's human knowledge of the will and purpose of God? The teachings of Jesus still remain as the highest teaching for man, for his redemption and service. It is in this Jesus and His teaching that we find the way to God's heart of love and the only basis by which man can live with man in sanity and usefulness. It is in love and through forgiveness that reconciliation becomes a potent reality. There is no greater need for man as an individual or for man in corporate union then reconciliation which is the very heart of the message of Jesus. Unless reconciliation can become increasingly an actuality the world may find itself facing an unwanted extinction. The crucial experiences of the world and the faith experience of the Church affirm the truth that Jesus Christ does match this day with that life and truth which can bring to contemporary man that which His inner spirit demands and without which he remains restless and an alien from God. Christian faith is as contemporary as each new morn in the gospel of Jesus Christ, a Gospel which gives meaning to life and a creative purpose for living in the disturbing present.

IV

It is a common fault of man to worry about many things, the least of which is not the future. There are two areas which seem to be of major concern. First, the desire for security demands and receives much thought and time in our present consideration and design. It is often difficult to adequately delineate what is meant by security. It is somehow related to one's tomorrow if something should happen today to delimit earning capacity or old age overtake us. The scramble for sufficient protection through insurance, or well provided pension plans, or secured savings all seem to be an integral part of contemporary security. No one would criticize careful planning for the future but when it becomes a mania it has assumed unnecessary proportions. Perhaps a reason for such agitation is induced by man's insecurity as well as the Church's trivial faith in God who does provide enough for all His children, but who does not make provision for all the greeds of man. This is not to suggest carelessness or lack of fore-

200

sight but it does suggest more dependence upon God who knows our needs. The major problem is not in God but in selfish man who seeks to secure and control more than he or his can ever need or use. Security is real today but should not be the primary driving force in life. Second, the growing and destructive force of fear in life paralyzes growth and work. There are so many things we fear in ourselves, in our communities, and in our world. We fear so many things which never do, nor can happen. Fear leads to worry and devitalizes personal strength for that which is the good and the right. We are afraid to live and we are afraid to die. It is only in love, the love of God, that fear can be overcome, for "perfect love casts out fear." (I John 4:18) Fellowship with God in Jesus Christ helps one live with a minimum of fear because it has been displaced by a greater force, the force of love.

Tomorrow is the time about which we are concerned and about which we would like information. What H. G. Wells called "The shape of things to come" is hidden from us in the mystery of life and time. Many changes will come in that tomorrow, changes which will be revolutionary in science and in mechanics. No one can tell where we will be able to go, nor the speed with which we will go, nor the time saving devices which will be ours to use. It is certain that the things which count will not change: God, Jesus Christ, man, and the deepest reality of his spirit for fellowship with his creator. It is reasonably certain that man will never find a force so powerful nor so creative as love which is at the heart of God and indispensible in His world. Assurance can be found in a faith which believes and knows that when tomorrow comes, which may bring good or evil, Jesus Christ will be there to meet us and to give us His Presence and help. The Christian should not fear when this assurance is rooted and determined in the One who is the same tomorrow as He has been today and as He was yesterday. No more assurance is needed than this, that as tomorrow comes He is there to meet us, for when we have Him we have enough for any situation in life.

We need not elaborate schemes which plot the course of all events in that tomorrow whether it be near or far removed. God gives us no scheme but He does give us Himself and that in the fulfillment of hope. Much energy has been dissipated in trying to blueprint the future and, "determine times and seasons" but without avail. History should teach us of the futility of such planning and such interpretations. It is enough to know that when our tomorrow comes He will be there even though it be through the valley of the shadow of death. A Christian faith should provide such

Sermon Twenty-seven

RELIGION WITHOUT RESERVATIONS

REVEREND EDWARD HUGHES PRUDEN, TH.M., PH.D., D.D.

Minister, First Baptist Church, Washington, D. C.

Dr. Pruden was born in Virginia in 1903. He graduated from the University of Richmond in 1925 and from the Southern Baptist Seminary, Louisville, in 1928. In 1929 and 1930 he did graduate work at Yale and in 1931 received his Ph.D. from the University of Edinburgh. The University of Richmond gave him an honorary D.D. in 1932.

Ordained to the ministry of the Baptist Church in 1935, Dr. Pruden had a church in Petersburg, Virginia, from 1930 to 1935. In 1936, he was called to his present pastorate.

In 1935 and 1936 he was guest teacher at the University of Shanghai. He is head of the board of founders of that university, a trustee of the University of Richmond, a member (and past president) of the American Baptist Convention, American Baptist Foreign Mission Society. He is director and past president of the Washington Federation of Churches.

Dr. Pruden is author of *Interpreters Needed,* has contributed sermons to several books, served as Washington correspondent for *The Christian Century,* and contributed articles to religious journals.

RELIGION WITHOUT RESERVATIONS

The stirring story from the book of Daniel to which we shall turn our attention today might well be called "the story of a religion without reservations." The scene is laid in Babylon during the days of Israel's captivity. Even though the Hebrews were a captive people, they soon demonstrated to their captors that they were men of unusual ability and integrity, and a number of them were selected to occupy places of leadership in the life of the nation. One of the most conspicuous was Daniel who was chosen to assume large responsibilities, and who was looked upon with unusual respect. It was Daniel who suggested the names of three other young Hebrews, and the king appointed them to places of leadership over the people. These three were Shadrach, Meshach, and Abednego.

It was not long after these appointments that Nebuchadnezzar authorized the construction and erection of a gigantic golden image over one hundred feet in height, and everyone, at the sound of the musical instruments, was commanded to fall down and worship this image. It is quite evident from the story that the image possessed no significance in itself but it became significant when it became known that it had been erected in response to the king's decree. Worship of the golden image became, then, a test of patriotism and loyalty. That is one of the dangerous things about a state religion. Any independence of thought or action is considered to be disloyalty to the state. The Roman Empire looked with great suspicion upon the early Christians because they would not worship Caesar. The mob threatened Pilate when he refused to condemn Jesus instantly, and called into question his patriotism by saying to him, "If you do not grant our request, you are not a friend of Caesar's." They undertook to convince Pilate that Jesus was a rival king who was dangerous, not only to the religious traditions of the people, but to national stability and safety. The British king, as well as the Church of England in the seventeenth and eighteenth centuries, regarded with suspicion all Dissenters and Separatists. And even in colonial America, Roger Williams of independent mind and convictions, was not only looked upon as an enemy of the church but also as an enemy of the state. In Japan, prior to 1945, Shintoism was a state religion with the Emperor as its head, and winning of converts to Christianity was exceedingly difficult because loyalty to any other faith seemed to be disloyalty to the state. So it was in the land of Babylon, and this situation made the position of the three Hebrews all the more difficult and all the more dangerous.

As can well be imagined there was much jealousy among the natives of the land regarding the sudden prominence which had come to these captive Israelites. They murmured among themselves, wondering why they were not considered sufficiently wise to occupy these places which had been given to strangers. Inevitably they began to search for ways by which they might bring these Hebrews into disrepute. In the course of time it was noted that the Hebrews did not bow down and worship the king's image. This seemed to provide grounds on which they might be accused, so those who were determined to remove them from their places of leadership, went to the king with their complaints, and he was furious. We are not surprised since such disobedience struck at his pride. His orders had been disobeyed; his image had been disregarded; his commandments had been ignored. He threatened these Hebrews with dire punishment. He described the furnace of fire and threatened them with its torture and death. Alexander Maclaren, the great British expositor, commenting upon this incident, says that Nebuchadnezzar literally opened the doors of the furnace and let them feel the heat as he described to them what would happen if they did not obey his command. And then he uttered a word of blasphemy against the one true and living God. He said, "Who is that God that shall deliver you out of my hands?" That is always the boast of pagan national leaders. Disregarding any god other than themselves, they refuse to acknowledge any moral restraint or any spiritual influences.

We are told that during the years of the Second World War when the heads of nations were discussing how they might pool their forces against the enemy, someone reported that the Pope of Rome had offered certain suggestions, and instantly Stalin asked, "How many divisions does he have?" Which is another way of saying to any group of Christians, "If you can't produce mighty armies and material weapons, you have no strength whatever." So Nebuchadnezzar ridiculed the Hebrews concerning their God. Then there follows the courageous reply which is one of the high points in Old Testament history: "Our God is able to deliver us, O King," said the three young Hebrews, "but even if he does not, we will not serve your gods nor bow down before your golden image."

This reply is especially refreshing when we compare it with what our reply might have been under similar circumstances. I am quite sure many of us would have rationalized the situation and come up with some very resourceful compromise by which we could have obeyed the command of the king and still preserved every appearance of religious fidelity. Such a compromise would not have been acceptable in the sight of God, but we would have made ourselves believe that we were maintaining our religious integrity. For the three Hebrews, however, there was no compromise and there was no retreat. As a result, Nebuchadnezzar became so angry that the expression of his face changed; which is another way of saying that he became livid with rage; and at his instructions the three Hebrews were thrown into the furnace ablaze with fire. We are told that their faith was amply rewarded, and that they were miraculously spared. The truths contained in this inspiring story of courageous faith are numerous, but I should like to give special attention to three of them.

Observe in the first place, that Christians today, like the Hebrews in Babylon, are constantly under pressure to conform to existing patterns of life and thought. Even here in America where we pride ourselves upon our hard-won liberty, it is not easy to be true to one's convictions. We speak of our country as the land of the free and the home of the brave, but one has to be exceedingly brave if he would act freely under all circumstances. How hasty we are to label all who dare to be different as "odd-balls" or "squares." But strangely enough it is the "odd-balls" and the "squares" who have made history. To save my life I cannot recall the name of the judge who sentenced John Bunyon to twelve years in prison in Bedford jail—I doubt if there is a person in the congregation who recalls his name—but all of us know John Bunyon and rejoice in his witness to his faith. He is included in the stained glass windows in our church not because he gave in, but because he held out. I suppose the average person in Bedford at the time said, "Why on earth doesn't that fellow Bunyon do what other clergymen are doing and go to the proper authorities and get a license to preach. Why be difficult about it?" And all the while John Bunyon was not trying to be difficult; he was standing for a principle—a principle which was very vital then and which we honor very highly today.

I cannot possibly recall the name of the colonial authorities who banished Roger Williams from the Massachusetts Bay colony, but I have a vivid recollection of what Roger Williams stood for and what he accomplished in his refusal to submit to the oppressive requirements of his contemporaries. Christians in the first century were called people of the way—a way which was different from the ordinary way of living. They constituted a minority. They entertained different attitudes of mind and spirit from the average person. They were set apart because of the spirit which dominated them. Certainly we are not to be deliberately obstinate or unnecessarily difficult, but we are to take to heart the command of Scripture to "Come out from among them and be ye separate, saith the Lord." The

206

Christian today needs great courage to withstand the pressures of a pagan world, and such pressures are always around us, but if we insist upon the right to obey our consciences, that courage is never without its exceeding great reward.

You will notice in the second place, that the people of God have no guarantee of escape from pain and suffering even when they do what is right. The three Hebrews did not suffer for some crime they had committed but simply for their loyalty to the God of their fathers. Some of the psalms are most comforting when rightly understood, but most misleading when misunderstood. For instance we read, "A thousand shall fall at thy side and ten thousand at thy right hand, but it shall not come nigh thee." Then some of us jump to the conclusion that that means that we, as the people of God, occupy a little circle of God's favor and that we will be spared the normal pain, suffering, and sacrifice which other people are called upon to endure. This is not true. However, there is a great deal of truth in what the psalm implies, namely, that if the people of God avoid certain practices and habits which are dangerous and destructive, they will be spared the consequences of such folly. The sober individual, for instance, will never know the disgrace of the drunkard. Certainly the Bible does not teach that the people of God are immune from suffering. The prophets of Israel, those seemingly nearest to God, were among those who suffered most. John the Baptist, the last of the great prophets, suffered as all of us know, at the hands of a wicked king. Stephen, one of the most Christlike of the early disciples, was stoned to death; and later, many who were seeking to maintain their faith in spite of all opposition, were burned at the stake. Jesus Christ, the fairest among ten thousand and the One altogether lovely, was crucified upon a cross. Christianity is no refuge for weak persons. It is an opportunity for those who are prepared to make courageous decisions and render sacrificial service. It does not save us from suffering; it gives us strength and courage with which to face up to suffering, wherever and whenever it may come to us. Jesus went to great pains to be sure that those who would follow Him knew exactly what discipleship involved, and finally, He said, "Behold, I send you forth as sheep in the midst of wolves." Doing what is right, and maintaining one's relationship to God, does not protect us from the unpleasant and painful experiences of a normal life.

Then you will notice finally, that the Christian philosophy of life is not conditioned on ideal circumstances. The Hebrew children seemed to be saying in substance, "We would like to bear testimony to our faith under ideal circumstances, if that is possible, but if these circumstances are not possible, then we will bear our testimony anyway." This is indeed a religion without reservations. Several years ago I preached a series of sermons on Sunday nights regarding the Christian home and marriage, and I undertook to set forth the ideal circumstances under which a marriage might be supremely happy and a home might remain intact. I was somewhat startled one night when one member of the congregation came up after the service and said, "What about those who are already married, and whose circumstances are far from ideal; who married perhaps without taking into account the things about which you have been speaking; or who were not sufficiently alert mentally to consider such things for themselves?" It was then that another sermon came into being regarding the message of the Christian faith for those who must live under unideal circumstances, and who in spite of such situations can still find happiness, peace, and great satisfaction.

Life itself does not always provide ideal conditions. Sometime ago I saw that remarkable play entitled, *Sunrise at Campobello*, and whatever we may think regarding the political philosophy of Franklin D. Roosevelt, we cannot help but admire his remarkable courage in the midst of a great physical handicap. The play opens just as he returns from a swim in the cold waters off the coast of Nova Scotia, where his summer home was located. During the hours of that night he was stricken ill and was paralyzed to such an extent that he was practically helpless. His mother wanted him to return to Hyde Park and be an invalid for the rest of his life; to be waited on by servants; to retire from the ordinary demands of life completely; but one of his trusted friends pled with him not to do it, but rather to make every possible effort to get back on his feet and resume his place in society, making full use of his talents and fulfilling his ambitions. Occasionally, when everyone else had left the room, sitting there in his wheelchair, he would try to get out of the chair and get to his feet unaided, only to fall flat on his face, then crawl back into the chair and try it again. Then at other times he would get down on the floor and crawl from one chair to the next, trying to exercise his muscles and regain some of his strength. Finally, he did get back on his feet, and fulfilled the mission which he felt he had been born to assume. Life does not always provide ideal circumstances, but some of the greatest achievements in history have been accomplsihed by those who have made courageous adjustments to life's unavoidable circumstances. And perhaps the handicaps, and the pain, and the suffering, constitute a challenge which called forth their best, and which made of them persons which they never could have been under more favorable circumstances.

Nor is our Christian experience always an ideal experience. We falter and fail; we go back on our promises; and we prove disloyal to God, to loved ones, to friends, and to our professions; and the natural impulse is to give up in despair and be filled with remorse, as though there is no hope; but the Gospel has a glorious message for such persons. They are reminded that this need not be the end of the story. Those who recognize their transgressions, repent of their sins, turn from their evil ways, seek God's forgiveness, and open their hearts to His spirit, become new creatures, and by the grace of God can be better Christians than they have ever been before. Someone wrote a poem years ago with a line which said that the bird with the broken pinion never flies as high again. That just is not so. Physicians tell us that sometimes when a broken bone is repaired that the repaired part is the strongest part of all; and that people who have had heart lesions, when the lesion is healed, discover that that is the strongest part of the heart. Do you wonder then, that the Gospel is called good news, coming to men in their hopelessness and despair? It tells us that if we are willing to receive Christ and appropriate His power we can be stronger and more useful, and have more of God's grace then ever before.

Surely this is the message to which we have dedicated ourselves, and the message we would share with all mankind in a day of fear and confusion. We would probably prefer that life would surround us with only favorable circumstances; that we would be spared all pain, suffering, and sacrifice. God could do this for us if He considered that to be the best environment in which to produce a Christian life, but evidently He does not, and so we will make spiritual adjustments to life as we find it, and render our supreme service, not in spite of the handicaps involved but because of them.

Our God is able to save us from life's fiery furnaces, but if not, we shall refuse to bow down and worship the idols of compromise, expediency, and despair. For He who has called us out of darkness into the light, has called us to something better than that.

Sermon Twenty-eight

OUR ULTIMATE RULERS

REVEREND RALPH W. SOCKMAN, PH.D., D.D., LITT.D., LL.D.

Minister Emeritus, Christ Church, Methodist, New York, New York, and Preacher on the National Radio Pulpit

This sermon on leadership in our nation was delivered by Dr. Sockman on Lincoln's Birthday, February 12, 1961, before the Chicago Sunday Evening Club in Orchestra Hall, Chicago. In it he discusses the function of world leaders, of government and the place of Christians.

Ralph Sockman was born in Ohio, is a graduate of Ohio Wesleyan University, did his theological work at Union Theological Seminary, New York, and took his Ph.D. at Columbia University. His doctoral dissertation was in the field of history, which he often calls upon to give perspective to his preaching. He preaches all over America every year, counsels and corresponds with thousands of people. His National Radio Pulpit congregation is numbered in millions and is probably the largest in the world.

In 1916, while still studying at Union and Columbia, Dr. Sockman became associate minister of Madison Avenue Methodist Episcopal Church; in 1917 he was invited to become the full-time minister, where he has remained for forty-four years. He is the Director of the Hall of Fame for Great Americans.

He is the author of many books, including *The Higher Happiness, The Un-employed Carpenter, The Paradoxes of Jesus, Date with Destiny, The Highway of God*, and *How to Believe*. He has received the honorary doctorate from numerous universities and colleges, including Ohio Wesleyan, Wesleyan University, Rollins, Florida Southern, Washington and Jefferson, Northwestern University, Miami University, Columbia University, and Duke University. In 1941 he gave the Lyman Beecher lectures at Yale, and during 1947-48, he was Visiting Professor of Homiletics at Yale Divinity School. He is President of the Church Peace Union and, since 1928, has been chairman of the World Peace Commission of the Methodist church. He is a member of the Harvard University Board of Preachers and is chaplain of New York University.

OUR ULTIMATE RULERS

On this anniversary of Abraham Lincoln's birth I should like to speak with you about the matter of leadership. As life becomes swifter and more dangerous the choice of leaders becomes more imperative, and as our government grows more complex they come nearer to each of us. When Lincoln was a young man the residents of Illinois were a long way from the seat of our national government in Washington. When it took such long hours and even days for news to reach the Mississippi and the St. Lawrence, local committees could carry on quite a while almost without contact with our national government. But now that the acts of Congress passed at five o'clock in the afternoon are known in the new state of Hawaii at noon of the same day, now that the national government concerns itself with every aspect of life from elementary education to the care of the aged, and now that the government has in its employ more people than it had in its population at the beginning, we, the people, are becoming more and more aware that we must give attention to our rulers.

The person who is not concerned about the leadership in our nation and in the United Nations is not a good citizen. And certainly he is not a good Christian. Jesus enunciated the Christian principle of rulership on His way to Jerusalem for the triumphal entry. Jesus had refused a crown offered by His countrymen to lead them in a rebellion against the Roman Empire. But He kept talking about the Kingdom of God. And His disciples had the hope that He was going to set up some kind of rule and assert His authority. The mother of Zebedee's sons, James and John, came to Jesus and asked, "Command that these two sons of mine may sit, one at your right hand and one at your left, in your kingdom." She wanted them in Christ's cabinet. Jesus replied, "You do not know what you are asking. Are you able to drink the cup that I am to drink?" The sons, who had accompanied their mother, answered, "We are able." Then Jesus said to them, "You will drink my cup, but to sit at my right hand and at my left is not mine to give, but it is for those for whom it has been prepared by my Father."

When the other ten disciples heard of this request they were indignant at the two brothers. Then Jesus called them to him and laid down a basic principle. He said, "You know that the rulers of the Gentiles lord it over them, and their great men exercise authority over them. It shall not be so among you; but whoever would be great among you must be your servant

212

. . . even as the Son of Man came not to be served but to serve." (Matthew 20:25-28)

Note first that the Christian motive for ruling is to serve. This principle of seeking rule in order to serve was so revolutionary that the contemporaries of Jesus did not comprehend it. His countrymen would have rallied around Him in a revolution to wrest the power from the Roman overlords and restore the privileges and properties to the Jews, but when He talked about a cross instead of a crown they could not follow Him. If Jesus had been a rebel leader seeking power and plunder, Pilate would have understood Him. But when Pilate asked Him, "Are you a King?" Jesus replied that if His Kingdom were of this world then would His followers fight. Pilate was bewildered and probably thought Jesus was a bit addled. What would a king want but power and riches?

And think how Judas misunderstood Jesus. Judas was the treasurer of the little company of disciples. Perhaps he expected to control the exchequer in the new kingdom Christ was to set up. When Jesus refused to lead a political revolt, Judas was either disillusioned by Jesus' seeming lack of power or else he thought he could force Jesus to display His power by having Him arrested. Jesus was betrayed and crucified because He was not the kind of king His people expected. His contemporaries could not understand his kind of rule.

And after nineteen centuries Christ's principle of ruling to serve is not very well comprehended or accepted. To be sure, we in free countries like England and France, like Canada and the United States, roundly condemn the dictators like Khrushchev and Trujillo who seek power for plunder, and the fanatical rulers like Hitler and Castro who get drunk with power. We have advanced to the point where candidates for public office must profess that their desire is to serve the public good. We call our officials public servants. And it would seem that an increasing number of high-minded persons in both political parties accept office with a sincere desire to serve. But the cynical view still persists that politicians seek power for themselves and to the victor belong the spoils.

Also, when nations seek to extend their rule over other countries, men take it for granted that their motive is to gain rather than to serve. When the Soviet Union asserts that its desire is to serve and improve its satellites, the free world points sarcastically to plundered Poland and bloodied Hungary. And when the United States extends its economic relief and technical help programs, the communist countries insist that our motive is selfish.

Well do I recall a conversation in 1946 with a member of our Embassy staff in Moscow. We were standing by the window of the American Embassy looking out at the Kremlin. Our representative said, "I do not believe the word 'charity' still exists in the Kremlin vocabulary." The communist revolution came out of a czaristic governmental regime and an autocratic state church, both of which ruled for power rather than service until the peasants no longer believed in genuine charity. They impugn the motives of anyone who pretends to give. In every hand which offers help they see an axe to grind. Seeing self-interest as the only motive of others' conduct, the communist rulers reach out no trusting hands to other nations and eventually resort to purging trials among themselves.

We must not permit the Christian motive of service to be impugned and destroyed in America. We must honor those officials who do sincerely desire to serve. The cynical concept of politics as a game of greed and patronage must be corrected by a more determined effort to weed out the grafters. The fault lies as much with those who seek favors from the government as with those who grant them. Our government has become such big business that it cannot rest on rotten foundations. Our whole citizenry must have a new consecration to honest service.

We need warning signals on this highway of life, and we certainly need them now. May I read some lines from "Variety," a magazine not frequently quoted in the pulpit. They were written recently by Roland Gammon, an advertising man, with editorial experience on such magazines as *Life* and *Pageant*. Here are the lines: "Silently, contagiously, sometimes inside and sometimes outside the law, the national cheating habit deepens; contract kickbacks, shady deals, political grafting, media payoffs, business embezzlement, income concealment, labor feather-bedding, capital price-fixing, farm over-payments, shoddy workmanship, venal journalism, academic cribbing, and perhaps worst of all . . . an American stampede away from responsibility." Maybe that's overcolored, but there is truth here. We believe in free enterprise in America. Then under God let's keep our enterprise free from corruption and graft, that we may have the spirit of service, the spirit which was in Lincoln, the spirit of those who gave their lives for our liberty.

When we think of the bounties with which God has endowed this good land, when we think of the privations of the pioneers in developing it, when we think of the blood which has been poured out to preserve our laws and liberties, how swinish seems the spirit of those who would feed at the public trough, fattening on the taxes paid by honest citizens and prostituting a public trust into a selfish profit. To be decent, and certainly to be a Christian, "whoever would be great among you must be your servant, even as the Son of Man came not to be served but to serve."

Let us go a second step and see that the Christian ruler must not only de- sire to serve but help others to serve. Some thirty years ago a minister over- heard his two little children talking across the room from their beds before they fell asleep. The little boy, who had an inquisitive mind, asked his sis- ter some three years younger, "Why do you think we are here?" The little girl replied, "Dad says we are here to help others." The lad then added, "But why are they here?" Yes, when we talk about the rulers serving the people, let's remember what the people are here for. This, as Lincoln said, is a government of the people, by the people, for the people. If, as Christ said, those who would rule must serve, how about those they serve?

A good government is one that helps its citizens to help themselves. It should help to make them self-reliant, self-supporting, industrious. But if it is a Christian government, it must do more. It must help its people to help others by keeping alive the spirit of service and charity. Paul in his let- ter to the Galatians puts into the same chapter these two injunctions: "Each man will have to bear his own load." And then this also: "Bear one another's burdens and so fulfill the law of Christ." The spirit of going out in compassion to others must not perish if America is not to lose her own soul. There is no government subsidy that can take the place of human kindness.

Every person should be sufficiently self-respecting to support himself in- sofar as it is possible. But there are some things even the most self-respect- ing and self-reliant of us cannot handle by ourselves. If every person in Chicago had a good well in his own yard, you would not have a water sup- ply adequate for Chicago without city cooperation. Disasters come to the best of us which sometimes call for help beyond our own strength. If we had to do everything for ourselves I would not be here tonight. I would not have gotten out from under the snowdrifts of New York to come to this sun-kissed city of Chicago! We just have to do some things together. That is what must be kept alive in this country by our leaders. These things call for governmental organization and aid.

A Christian leader not only serves but also spreads the spirit of service. Last May in *The New York Times*, Professor James MacGregor Burns of Williams College wrote an article entitled, "Test of a President." He dis- cussed such factors as availability, campaigning skill and others. But he said that the office of president is above all a "place of moral leadership." And Dr. Burns declared that moral leadership requires at least five things.

First, it requires conviction. Does the man stand for something? Is he a leader of thought or is he an opportunist veering with the wind of popular opinion? Under the burden of public office a leader must be sustained by some ungirding convictions.

Yes, we need convictions also in the pressure of private living. Sweden, one of the most socialized governments of the world, with no poverty and no hunger or unemployment, has one of the highest suicide rates in the world. A Christian, whether ruler or one of the ruled, needs faith to live by as well as food to live on.

Secondly, for moral leadership is required the capacity to inspire. Not only must a person have convictions but they must glow from within. I have a friend who is such a ready talker that he talks too much. His wife has a pungent wit, and she said this year he should make a New Year's resolution to count twenty before he speaks, because in this jet age to count ten is not enough. And he does need to count more before he speaks. Nevertheless he does have a kindling power to his speech. He always invigorates me. We need people who can inspire others. Yes, we should weigh our words before we speak; but Jesus said, "The words that I have spoken to you are spirit and life." Clement Atlee once said of Winston Churchill's oratory, "Words at great moments of history are deeds."

Third: To be a good president or a good private citizen we must have a grasp of human events. We must see what we do in the light of their time and place. Take a very homely illustration. Suppose I went to a basketball court at your high school tomorrow night and I saw a young fellow and I said to him, "My dear fellow, you look sick. You ought to be in bed." It might be an act of kindness, might save him from serious illness. But suppose I went to a friend of mine here in Chicago tonight who was recovering from a long illness, after weeks in bed sitting up for the first time, and I said to him, "My dear fellow, you look sick. You ought to be in bed." Precisely the same words, but in one place they would be kindness, in the other place they would be cruelty.

In 1922 I was on a tour of Europe with a student crowd and we came one night to the Austrian city of Innsbruck. It was at the time that the Austrian currency had depreciated to almost nothing. You could buy a whole sheaf of it for a few American cents. That night in a public restaurant one of our American students, in the spirit of what he thought was harmless fun, took a high denomination of Austrian currency, rolled it into a taper, and from the candle on the table lighted his pipe. Quite a harmless thing if done in Chicago or New York, but it almost started a riot that night in Innsbruck. It was a reflection on the national pride of the Austrians. Yes, I repeat, to be a good president, a good private citizen, we must have a grasp of human events, read the signs of our times, as Jesus said.

Also, there must be a fourth factor in moral greatness, namely commitment. "This is something more than intellectual conviction; it is a pledging of one's heart as well as mind." A leader must be consecrated to the public good.

But, said Dr. Burns, this quality of heart depends on one final requirement for presidential greatness, which is capacity for growth. Never more than now did we need to heed the words of James Russell Lowell:

> New occasions teach new duties.
> Time makes ancient good uncouth.
> They must upward still and onward
> Who would keep abreast of truth.

Professor Burns summed up his article on the "Test of a President" by citing Abraham Lincoln. New Yorkers who listened to Lincoln at Cooper Union that snowy night in February, 1860, must have felt that he did not look like presidential timber. He was homely and awkward and he spoke with a prairie accent in a high-pitched voice, and his shoes hurt him. He had been defeated for office. But as he spoke and warmed to his argument, the critical New Yorkers began to see that he was a man of burning convictions, a personality with a capacity to inspire, a thinker with a grasp of events, a public servant with a deep sense of commitment, and above all a man humble enough to learn and manifest his capacity for growth.

In these days when we are restudying our national purposes and goals, let us take a longer and deeper look at the qualities of the persons selected to lead us. Never more than when they were uttered almost a century ago do we need to pray the words of J. G. Holland:

> God give us men! A time like this demands
> Strong minds, great hearts, true faith and ready hands;
> Men whom the lust of office does not kill;
> Men whom the spoils of office cannot buy;
> Men who possess opinions and a will;
> Men who have honor; men who will not lie;
> Men who can stand before a demagogue
> And damn his treacherous flatteries without winking;
> Tall men, sun crowned, who live above the fog
> In public duty, and in private thinking.

But remember, in this "government of the people, by the people, for the people," God does not give us such men sent down from above. He summons us to help raise them from among us. "Whoever would be great among you must be your servant . . . even as the Son of Man came not to be served but to serve."

Having seen that Christ's principle of ruling is to serve and that Chris-

217

tian rulers should serve in ways that help others to serve, let us see whether these principles really work.

When I used to read these words of Christ, "Whoever would be great among you must be your servant," I was wont for a long time to think this statement was just a counsel of perfection, that Christians in the church should honor the ones who serve, and that in the Kingdom of Heaven the servants will be accounted greatest. But I have changed my mind. I think this principle of Jesus works in the here and now. When we have the spirit of service, we are on the way to the rich abundant life Christ came to give.

And if we look around clearly, we can begin to see the truth in Jesus' words: "Blessed are the meek, for they shall inherit the earth." The meek are not the weak, timid little souls who go around with downcast eyes and inferiority complex. The meek are those who look up to God and feel humble in His presence. The meek are those who are modest enough to know that they do not know it all and hence are forever learning. The meek are those who are godly enough to seek for their duties before they shout for their rights. The meek have the true humility defined by Dr. Frank Crane, a popular press columnist a generation ago: "It is the wish to be great and the dread of being called great. It is the wish to help and the dread of thanks. It is the love of service and the distate for rule. It is trying to be good and blushing when caught at it."

There are two contrasted ways of gaining rule. One is to go out by force or domination and make others subject to you. But the trouble with that kind of domination is this: it makes the subject restless and he wants to throw off the yoke, and that kind of rulership doesn't usually last very long. Italy went into Ethiopia. Her rule did not last long. Japan went into China. Her rule did not last long. And my inner conviction is that some day the communist domination of China will pass too. The other way of attaining mastery is to set out to serve others until they crave your cooperation. The latter is Christ's way, and it is the rule that lasts.

The contemporaries of Christ did not comprehend His principle of ruling by service, and the world today, even Christ's own church, still seems to measure greatness by social prestige and power over others. During his lifetime a person may be rated by the number who serve him. But after his death he is remembered by the number he served.

Napoleon made himself master of France and most of Europe by the power of his marching legions, but Louis Pasteur made himself the servant of France and the world in fighting the germs of disease. And the serving Pasteur out-lives Napoleon. The strutting Mussolini dominated Italy for a decade, and some of us in those 1930s thought we needed a Mussolini here. Signor Marconi put his electrical wizardry at the service of his nation and the world. Mussolini was hung by the heels, but Marconi is still hanging in the world's Halls of Fame. Albert Schweitzer goes into Africa to heal the natives. Khrushchev goes into the Congo to dominate and divide, but Schweitzer will be revered for his service long after Khrushchev is forgotten.

If our Bible can be believed, if the testimony of history can be trusted, Jesus was right when He said, "Whoever would be great among you must be your servant . . . even as the Son of Man came not to be served but to serve." The dictators are gone, the Caesars are gone, but

> Jesus shall reign where'er the sun
> Doth its successive journeys run,
> His Kingdom rule from shore to shore,
> Till moons shall wax and wane no more.

Those who serve are those who ultimately rule. And the Son of Man outlives the demagogues and dictators. He, the Christ, is the ultimate Ruler of life.

Sermon Twenty-nine

DON'T RESIGN FROM LIFE

Reverend Norman D. Fletcher, D.D.

*Minister, Unity Church, Unitarian, Montclair,
New Jersey*

Dr. Fletcher has worked for the underprivileged in New Jersey, Kentucky, Florida, and Maine. In collaboration with Clara Olson he wrote *Learn to Live*, about experiments in gearing education to the needs of the low-income groups of these states. In 1937 he worked with Professor James Alexander of Princeton University and Rockwell Kent, the artist, in publicizing the publication of "The Denial of Labor and Civil Rights in Hudson County, New Jersey."

Norman Fletcher attended St. Lawrence University and Canton Theological School. St. Lawrence conferred the honorary D.D. upon him in 1936. He has worked with the N.A.A.C.P. and is a member of the Consumers League of New Jersey.

DON'T RESIGN FROM LIFE

Modern man, it is said, will not face death. Everything possible is done to lessen its rigors and, when it comes, to make it seem unreal. The efforts of the contemporary mortician seem not only to lessen what has happened, but to make it appear that nothing has really happened at all!

Back in 1931, Mary Austin wrote a book she called *Experiences Facing Death*. She wrote this book on the premise, as she put it, that "Deep within life is the need to orient itself toward death." I do not recall that there was any more than one edition of this book. Modern man does not want to "orient (himself) toward death." Cyrus Sulzberger, formerly head of *The New York Times*' foreign service, has just published his book, *My Brother Death*. It has been likened to Burton's famous *Anatomy of Melancholy*, published in 1621. My melancholy guess is that Mr. Sulzberger's book will reach that bargain counter known as "Liggett's Delight." For modern man will not face death.

It is equally true that modern man will not face life. Just as there are some people who resign from the human race by refusing to concern themselves with human problems, so there are some people who resign from life by refusing to live it, resign that is to say in favor of existence.

William Lyon Phelps wrote a little book called *Happiness* something over thirty years ago. He was very clever in giving it that title. Everybody wants to be happy. The book went through at least twenty-six printings in five years. Nevertheless it had in it some sound medicine for living which must have surprised many of its readers who were merely bent on being happy. Wrote Phelps, "There are people who carry their happiness as a foolish woman carries a purse of money in her hand while walking on a crowded thoroughfare. The first man who is quick with his fingers, nimble with his feet, and untrammelled by conscience, can and will take the purse away and disappear with it. He will have separated the woman and her money. Now if one's happiness is like that, dependent on an enemy's volition, on a chance disaster, on an ill wind, and any one of a thousand accidents to which we are all exposed—then happiness can be lost."

If Dr. Phelps were alive today, I am sure he would agree that he was talking about life as well as about happiness. We can lose our life as we can lose our happiness by misconceiving it, by making it "dependent on an enemy's volition, on a chance disaster, on an ill wind, on any one of a thousand accidents to which we are all exposed." We can lose our life or, to keep to the figure of this discourse, we can resign from life by reducing it to politics, economics, the physical sciences, technology, climate, and environment.

Here, then, we have the first indication of how it is people resign from life. They do so (and aren't we all tempted) by *reducing* it, by trying to live it as if it were something much less than it is. Some do this with deliberation; it is a matter of their basic philosophy. Others do it unconsciously, because they have no worthy philosophy, only a low and menial one which is implicit in their attempts to live.

"Man does not live by bread alone." We still call bread "the staff of life." We cannot do without bread; it is necessary to physical continuance. But it is not enough. When we think it is enough or act as if it were enough, we are not living but existing. We have resigned from life as surely as a man who has committed suicide. This does not mean that we should have no concern for those who have no bread or not enough (and how great a proportion of the world's inhabitants haven't enough bread!). But we should not fool ourselves, as many of us are doing, that when we all have bread and bread enough, we shall all be living.

This idea that life is to be equated with existence, reduced to bread, lived as if it were a matter of things, automobiles, houses, clothes, and all that, and the more the better, this description of the good life as "living it up," is not only not living it up, but really not living it at all. It is resigning from life in favor of existence. I am not saying we should all try to exist on a crust of bread, though having to do so for a few days might help some of us. I am no ascetic. I am not saying we should regret our necessities or even some of our luxuries. But I am saying that he who does not resist the constant pressure to make more and more luxuries into necessities, who does not find a line to draw somewhere, will soon be the victim of things which will be in the saddle riding him, and he will soon discover, or worse never discover at all, that he has resigned from life!

The reduction of life to existence is carried on not only by a practical, every day materialism, but by a philosophic materialism that arises largely from a preoccupation with or overemphasis upon science, especially the physical sciences. All is reduced to the test tube and the equation. The beauty of the rose is solely a matter of fertilizer. A great person like Jesus of yesterday or Schweitzer of today, or indeed some loved one in our own family, is to be accounted for, and hence reduced to, his physiological makeup and the political, economic, and climatic conditions of his environment.

This is to say nothing against science per se. Einstein of yesterday and Loren Eiseley of today never reduced life to the categories of physical science. They, and others like the mathematician Bronowski, contend that reality in general and life in particular cannot be reduced to the conventional and accepted terms of orthodox science, but is of such tremendous depth that "symbol and metaphor" as Bronowski says, "are as necessary to science as to poetry." But many people are back in the crude science of the nineteenth century; they want to reduce life to grossly limiting terms. They think they are "thinking," that they are being "exact," when after the notion of some of the semanticists they define their terms, and by defining they mean not merely to set off what is defined from something else, which is a highly rational procedure, but to reduce it to its smallest proportions.

Nathan Scott, Jr., reminds us that the philosopher Hobbes "wanted a plain, straight-forward language purged of all the rich ambiguity of Elizabethan and Jacobean diction—the kind of language that Thomas Sprat in his *History of the Royal Society* (1667) called "a close, naked, natural way of speaking . . . bringing all things as near the mathematical plainness as they can." Well, Shakespeare was an Elizabethan, and who came nearer to an adequate description of that aspect of life we call love, Shakespeare in "Romeo and Juliet" or Mr. Sprat's mathematician? I say Mr. Sprat's mathematician rather than mathematicians because I do not wish to be unfair. Mathematics, properly conceived, is not a matter of reduction, certainly not higher mathematics!

Matthew Arnold long ago protested against this habit of reduction, particularly the notion that life is to be described in limited and lowly terms. "More and more mankind will discover," he wrote, "that we have to turn to poetry (all art I would say) to console us, to sustain us. Without poetry our science will appear incomplete and most of what now passes with us for religion and philosophy will be replaced by poetry." Poetry, drama, and all the arts, as well as science, are needed if we would describe life with even the beginnings of adequacy. I shouldn't wonder if this was why Robert Frost was invited to read one of his poems at the recent presidential inaugural. Imagine a poet invited to a strictly political affair, and not just to be present but to read one of his poems! Perhaps the inaugural wasn't thought of as a strictly political affair, but rather as a moment in our national life embracing more than the merely political. I take Mr. Frost's presence at that occasion to be a good omen!

But, alas, the reductionists are still among us and hard at work. It is not strange, in a world where life is confused with mere existence, equated with

224

physical continuance—a matter of bread and bread alone, things and the more the better—that much contemporary literature and drama celebrate the absurdity of life, the emptiness and meanness of life, the fragmentized, disintegrated, frustrated, morbid agonized existential character of life. It is natural and logical that this should happen. We should have long since expected it. It is the fate of those who resign from life.

People resign from life also by unconsciously or deliberately adopting the notion that life is for youth and consequently slowly peters out as one grows older. Actually this is a phase or aspect of the habit of reduction. It is not surprising that many people, millions upon millions I imagine, have accepted this notion of life, and, worse, put it into definite, day to day practice in their own lives. It is not surprising not only because, as the old hymn puts it, the "woes of life o'ertake us," problems increase, troubles multiply, miseries proliferate, but because this notion is a prominent piece of furniture in our national pattern.

I was talking the other day with a Chinese student at Columbia University, the most cosmopolitan of all places save the United Nations itself, who had been in our country for a year. When I asked the familiar question about his impressions, he said that over and above all he saw was our universal emphasis on youth. "Everything in your country," he said, "is for youth. Nothing is for old age. Your ads are all in terms of youth. Clothes, soap, automobiles, even medicine—all for youth." I reminded him that occasionally the telephone company pictured grandpas and grandmas getting a call across the nation from their married son or daughter, but he thought this very much of an exception. "In our country," he went on, "we honor age." Being at the moment in a highly argumentative mood, I replied that perhaps in his country, and the East generally, old people were deferred to altogether too much whereas in this country young people were deferred to, or emphasized, too much and that possibly what the world needed was some position in between. Unfortunately I had to terminate our interesting conversation abruptly and dive down into the bowels of the earth for the subway which to my oriental friend must have seemed typically occidental. But I thought about our conversation all the way home. And the more I thought about it, the more I thought that the accent on youth has not only put clothes, soap, and automobiles, medicine, and much else over on us in increased quantities but also, without meaning to, put over on us the idea that youth's the time and the only time for life, or that life is for youth and consequently slowly peters out as one grows older. No wonder, then, that people, little by little, resign from life (It is resignation by default.) so that when they come at last to die they are not resigning from life, which they have done long since, they are merely resigning from existence!

There is only one greater mistake that can be made and that is to misconceive life from the first. But it is a mistake that is great enough! When we think life is for youth only, we have sentimentalized our youth. When I think of how little I knew as a young man, how worried I sometimes got about making myself into anything worthwhile, how frustrated I became on occasion, how many cavernous pitfalls stretched out ahead of me and how stupidly I fell into some of them, I stop sentimentalizing about my youth, and throw into the wastebasket the notion that life closes in upon one and it is less rich today than it was in the yesterdays. I know that some of the things that interested me "then" do not interest me at all "now," and that some of the things that interested me "then" interest me vastly more "now," for I have come to see these things in new and infinitely greater proportions. Why ever should we expect in middle age and old age to delight always in the same things we delighted in as children, or young people? "When I was a child, I spoke as a child, I felt as a child, I thought as a child; now that I have become a man I have put away childish things." And God be praised, or life be praised, that this is so.

People who feel that life is something that peters out as we grow older are confounding loss of interest or delight in some particular experience with loss of interest or delight in all experience. Let the past go. Let that part of it fall away that will fall away. There are many more interests to be taken on, many more delights to be experienced. Moreover we are in far better condition to appreciate these interests, to enter into these delights, than we were in former years. We have more experience, we are more sensitive, we have more depth of being—unless, of course, we have made the mistake of resigning from life. The life of the adult is so much richer than the life of the younger person that there is no comparison possible! Life stretches out on every hand, infinitely outward, infinitely downward in the sense of depth, infinitely upward, and the longer we live the more aware we are of this infinity.

Some of us have probably not read Cicero's "De Senectude" since we stumbled through it in the Latin class in college. But it would be well if we did, even if we had to use a "trot" or a translation. Listen to the noble and perfectly true words: "As I like a young man in whom there is something of the old, so I like an old man in whom there is something of the young, and he who follows this maxim will possibly be an old man in body, but he will never be an old man in mind." No, nor in spirit! Assuredly he will not resign from life!

Perhaps it may be said that I have made one mistake in this discourse! I have been talking all this long time about not resigning from life, why it is that some do just that, why perhaps we all of us do at times and to an extent, but I have not defined life, or if not defined, set forth its essential character. But of course I don't think I have really made this mistake for, as you must be aware, I have implied something at least of what I mean by life, set it forth indeed in part at least rather explicitly all along, and on the other hand I have deliberately left the concept of life to the last because I want to have this concept uppermost in our minds.

Life, reality, is infinite. Go down any path and it stretches on into infinity. Suppose you search for truth. Is there any end to it? Can you say at any time I have the truth, the whole truth, and nothing but the truth? Not if you live to a thousand years! Suppose you set out to appreciate all the beauty there is in the life of the universe. Can you do so? Can you come to the time, no matter how active you are and sensitive you become, when you can say: I now fully appreciate all beauty; I have exhausted it? Suppose you search for goodness. Suppose you set out to appreciate all the goodness of history, all the good people in our time. Can you exhaust that? Suppose you try to embrace goodness and live it day by day. Can you ever say: Now I am a good person, I can never be any better. There is no more goodness for me to realize? Most certainly you cannot and you would be insufferable if you ever took such an attitude.

I am not saying that all is truth, all is beauty, all is goodness. Far from that. There is evil and plenty of it. But we shall be better prepared to handle evil if we see the infinite character of life—that truth, beauty, goodness are inexhaustible. Life is a mystery. Our science and our philosophy have probed it, made helpful discoveries, and accumulated a vast amount of knowledge about it. But the more discoveries they have made, the more knowledge they have accumulated, the wider and deeper and higher the mystery is. That is why Bronowski says that "symbol and metaphor are as necessary to science as to poetry and goes on to say that science and art should not be opposed but in league with each other. All science, all art, all music, all literature, all psychology, all sociology, all philosophy work, or should work, together, that we may know more and more of life, of the totality we call reality. And the more they work together the more they see the need of it, for there is no end to what they are working on.

Actually, therefore, instead of our very bad habit of reduction we should cultivate the habit of expansion! Instead of mistaking existence for life we should see even existence, finite existence, over against the infinite character of life. We protest against our preoccupation with things. But things are a part of life and partake of its infinite character. There is nothing wrong with a thing per se. It is only when we see the thing in a very limited way, as just this or merely that, and not in terms of the infinite mystery. A flower is a thing. But what a thing! You have studied botany, but do you know all about that flower? You can give botanical names to all its parts. You can tell your neighbors what kind of fertilizer you used in the growing of it and precisely how you tended it. But have you told the whole story of how it came to be? It is, after all, a long story, and a very wonderful one. And we do not know the whole of it. It extends back, as all things do, into mystery.

Tennyson, you remember, plucked a flower and held it in his hand and thought about it. This thought so carried him out into the infinite character of life, of which that flower partook, that he said that if ever he *knew* that little flower "all, and all in all" he would know "what God and man is." If he felt that way about a flower, about plant life, whatever must he have felt about human life, about a human being!

Don't resign from life! Don't mistake life for existence! Don't think that what you have in a test tube, what you can see and measure, what you can reduce to an equation, extremely valuable though all this is, is life, all of it, or the essence of it! Let us be like Thoreau who said, "God himself culminates in the present moment, and will never be more divine in the lapse of all ages." Thoreau did not need to go to Paris, or London, or Berlin, or Tokyo, or even Boston. Looking toward Walden, Thoreau said, "I think that the richest vein is somewhere hereabouts; so by the divining rod and their rising vapors I judge; and here I will begin to mine."

It is not that we should not travel but rather that there will be small use of it if we cannot go out into our own backyard and say: The mystery and wonder and grandeur, and inexhaustible character of life is here, "here I will begin to mine." Let us say the same thing of the first person we meet, and the whole gamut of human association. This is life, wider than I can ever know, deeper and higher than I can ever perceive, more infinitely varied than I can ever comprise. "Here I will begin to mine." I will know, experience, and appreciate all of it that I possibly can. I will not resign from it by default or otherwise. I will not make the mistake of those pathetic creatures who, as Emerson said, "live on the brink of mysteries into which they never enter, and with their hand on the door-latch they die outside." No, I will renew my allegiance to life. I will lift the latch, and go in, and on!

Sermon Thirty

FOUNDING OUR FAMILIES IN CHRISTIAN MARRIAGE

REVEREND WILLIAM FREDERICK DUNKLE, JR., D.D.

Minister, Grace Church, Methodist, Wilmington, Delaware

Dr. William Frederick Dunkle, Jr., is the Senior Minister of Grace Church, Wilmington, Delaware, one of the well known Methodist churches of the East. He served in Florida and Virginia before coming to Wilmington in 1948.

He received his education at the University of Florida, Emory University, and Union Theological Seminary. American University in Washington in 1951 awarded the D.D. to Dr. Dunkle. In 1950 he was Exchange Minister for four months in London, in 1951 he represented American Methodism at the World Methodist Conference at Oxford University. He has also traveled widely in Europe and in the Middle East. In 1953, following the Korean truce, Dr. Dunkle was invited by the Defense Department to conduct preaching missions for two months in the Far East for the U. S. Air Force.

He served as Chaplain of the Virginia Senate in 1946, is a Trustee of Wesley College and a member of the Commission on Worship of the National Council of Churches.

He was Contributing Editor of *The Florida Christian Advocate*, one of the compilers of "The Book of Worship" of The Methodist Church, and one of the authors of "Strength for Service," a widely distributed devotional guide during World War II.

FOUNDING OUR FAMILIES IN CHRISTIAN MARRIAGE

"What . . . God hath joined together, let no
man put asunder."

Luke X:9

One of the cleverest sermon titles I ever heard is this, "Marriage Is What Two Make It." But, far more than *two* make or break modern marriages. There is a social sundering of what God has joined every day in American life. This, then, is not a sermon to husbands and wives alone. This is a sermon to the whole Church, for the Church's service of marriage rightly begins on a corporate, congregational note: "Dearly Beloved, *we* are gathered together here in the sight of God—to join together this man and this woman in Holy Matrimony." Not the minister alone, not even the attendants or witnesses, marry a couple. Rather, here is the Church, gathered in God's sight, mindful of His presence, usually assembled in His House, prayerfully engaged in the establishment of a Christian union between two people. Our great Protestant doctrine of the priesthood of every believer is never more clearly implied than in the marriage service: All of us make a marriage. And when we do, we found a family.

On this day which increasingly is being observed by American Protestantism as the Festival of the Christian Home rather than Mother's Day only, let us see how that ancient classic of devotion, "The Order for the Solemnization of Matrimony," outlines our faith about Christian families.

I wish I had time to suggest some of the ways we, as a Church, could improve the marriage services in which we mutually participate. I might point out, for example, how much more symbolic of spiritual sensitivity it would be if we always stood reverently in God's sight during a marriage service rather than craning curiously for a sight of a bride or a bride's dress. Or again, briefly, I could wish that instead of having soloists sing the Lord's Prayer, especially the somewhat sentimental setting currently in vogue, the whole congregation always could voice its prayerful participation in the Service.

But the more important point I make is that what we as God's Church do in beginning a Christian family through the Marriage Service, we must continue to safeguard thereafter. All of us, as a Church, share in making a marriage; all of us, as society, can share in breaking a marriage. If we are God's agents in uniting a man and a woman, we must be equally His

230

servants in protecting that divine union. The Christian Church has a responsibility to prevent any man from putting asunder what God has joined.

Just where are our responsibilities in this? Again we may look to the ancient ritual.

After the opening statements clearly define the corporate nature of worship in the marriage service, the betrothal vows come next. Originally, this part of the Service may have taken place years ahead of the wedding itself. That is why the marriage vows in the next paragraph seem largely repetition.

It is still true that later marriage promises can only reflect the standards young people develop, or fail to develop, all through their dating days. Marriage vows repeat courtship's values. When we pray our prayers in church at a marriage, we may be praying too late unless we have been mindful of the environment out there in society in which our young people meet their mates.

What kind of environment is it? What does it teach boys about girls, and girls about boys? Sex without sanctity! Romance without realism! Promiscuity without purpose! To croon moon, spoon, and June endlessly in shallow triteness and think them love's only vocal vocabulary! Who puts asunder many a modern marriage? For one, the man who paints the cover girls on most magazines; still more, the man who prints the lewd nudes on the calendars everywhere current. Or the man who writes Hollywood's blatantly suggestive advertising copy. Or the author of the sex-sodden novel. Or the cheap songster who makes a hit parade of banality. Or could it be the Christian citizen who silently accepts such social sores and acquiesces with an indifferent shrug to low levels all about him? How can we grow *holy* matrimony in unhallowed mud?

Not that I am offering to lead any movement back to unrealistic Victorian taboos, let me insist. But the most liberal Christianity must nevertheless always oppose the salacious and the licentious in the society of its day. And, more positively, Christianity in our time needs to found its faith on more than Freud if it is to salvage sex, needs to lift up Christ's clean code of continency, needs to offer a purity which is not mere prudery!

What shall we do? First, let me urge that we invoke our ancient power of prophetic protest. Our Roman Catholic friends have demonstrated the Church's influence through their Legion of Decency, and the very word "legion" bespeaks the fighting faith necessary to combat such evils as assail society today. Whenever God's Church dons the armor of Christ, the hordes of hell hear the challenge of our word and are warned. Let us

231

speak up and speak out! On this Mother's Day, let us pledge ourselves to resent and resist every cheapening of womanhood in current fads and fashions. Let us demand of publishers that books and papers and magazines stop flooding filth in the name of literary realism. Let us stay away in droves from plays and pictures which portray crass or criminal plots. Let us refuse to have our homes invaded by radio and television programs which destroy the very values of household holiness. Yes, let us cry havoc, make a tumult, raise a clamor for cleanliness! The time has come for the Church to cease its silence.

To be specific, there is a bill pending now in Congress (sponsored in the House by Representative John Dowdy of Texas and Representative Edward H. Rees of Kansas, and in the Senate by Senator Olin Johnson, chairman of the Senate Post Office Committee) which would strengthen the powers of the Postmaster General to bar indecent and obscene matter from the mails. It has been introduced by the Senate's Juvenile Delinquency Investigating Committee. It deserves a letter of support from you to our members of Congress.

Or to call you to the attack from another quarter, let me tell you about some correspondence published recently in a Northamptonshire newspaper which has reached me from England through the columns of *The Methodist Recorder*. The Rev. Ronald J. Bradwell in protesting against crude and nude shows as current in Britain as in America had written to insist that people seeking amusement will laugh just as readily at clean humor as at smutty jokes. The newspaper editor in commenting on Mr. Bradford's communication agreed, but defended the producers of burlesque shows by saying, "The fact is, sex sells, and clean shows usually lose money." If we stay away from what is rank or rotten, we ought to support commercially what is wholesome and refreshing. Good shows must sell tickets. Christians ought to buy them. An enthusiastic support of what is good is the surest defeat of what is bad.

Of course, it is far less dramatic, and even less emotionally satisfying as an expression of the Church's determined indignation, but the tireless tutelage of truth to youth is our surest insurance that wholesome betrothals will lead to holy marriages. But, we teach best when we prove our precepts with exalted example, when we translate Christian creed into clean code. We ourselves are the society into which our children are born and in which our teenagers experience emerging maturity. Let us demonstrate by our own actions and attitudes how we hallow the procreative potential that is called sex. Merely negative commands to youth will never restrain and control, but we can be positive about our teaching that sex is meant for

232

purposeful partnership with a parental God, that it is a high and holy endowment by which men and women are united to each other and to God. We must answer youth's questions without evasion, understand with sympathy the emerging urge of youth, and refuse to call dirty or shameful what the marriage service describes as "representing unto us the mystical union that is between Christ and His Church." Christians who are not teaching the serious sanctity of sex are not witnessing to the whole gospel or the holy gospel. Our Christ was *conceived* . . . was *born!* Our God is a *Father!*

But let me pass on. Marriage is more than sex, more than parenthood even. Indeed, its holy estate is not established for young people only. This formula of faith we are reviewing today recites how matrimony was "instituted of God in the time of man's innocency," yet the marriage vows themselves contemplate the hard, even harsh eventualities which imperfect people inevitably experience in an imperfect world. There is a growing-up process expected in every successful marriage, a passage, not always wholly pleasant, from honeymoon couple to homebody and housewife. Failure to make this translation or transfer gracefully, intelligently, maturely, and above all religiously is the failure factor in far too many modern American marriages.

Our marriage service warns us solemnly and specifically about this. It admonishes us that matrimony should not be "—enterprised, or taken in hand unadvisedly, but reverently, discreetly, advisedly, and in the fear of God." And then it points out in considerable detail how what we hope may be better may turn out to be worse, that instead of richer we may be poorer, and that sickness instead of health may be our fate.

This isn't the language of Hollywood, is it? But it is the language of life, and Christians can make it the language of love.

And the Church can help make it so by its whole message. The ceremony of a wedding ring is a perfect illustration. You know how it is done (and I could wish it were never done twice in any marriage service, for repetition weakens the dramatic climax); first a man puts a simple circle of purest gold into a woman's open hand, and she in turn passes the ring to the officiating clergyman who offers the Church's prayer of blessing and then hands the ring back to the man. Finally, the circle is completed when the groom places it upon his bride's finger forever in the Name of the Holy Trinity. The circle of gold has circulated from hand to hand, encircling irrevocably this man, this woman, and God's Holy Church. This is the wedding, the *welding* if you please, of earth and heaven, of physical and spiritual, of man, woman, and God which holds fast as long as life lasts.

233

Isn't that the Church's total message?—that we are always in the circle of God's grace, that His are the encircling arms of an imperishable Providence, that better or worse, richer or poorer, sickness or health as they all come can never separate us from the love of God which is in Christ Jesus!

Yes, but the circle is so often sundered. We let ourselves be severed from our assurance of God's loving care. It is man's doing and his undoing. There is the man—the movie magnate who peddles romance that isn't real. There is another—the advertiser who tempts us to think that we can buy enough things to make us happy and who fools and befuddles us with the fancy that "gracious living" is the same as the life of grace. He is kin to the stylist who stultifies woman's simple, honest beauty with artificialities of dress—or undress—militating against all modesty. Then there is the politician who promises a prosperity all out of proportion to sound values and cuts the security from beneath our homes. Oh, the men who put asunder what God would join are many! But chief of them all is the churchman whose own faith has faded. His failure to make his Christianity a strong, working way of life robs his own marriage of stability under stress. What may be worse, he robs the world waiting around him of a workaday witness by which the marriages of other men might be strengthened. Marriages in America cannot thrive on sophistication, on artificiality. Once again Christians must evangelize with forceful faith a pagan age. The morals and manners of America must be brought under Christian judgment. We must defy with our faith the cult of happiness which has no regard for holiness. We must start meaning the prayers we pray in the marriage service, and start translating those devotions into disciplines that witness, that transform and redeem society.

For devotion, doctrine, and discipline are the elements of Christianity. The marriage service expresses them all. Perhaps the sentence in this lovely sacramental which says most clearly what I have tried to say in this sermon is found in the closing marriage prayer. A man and woman have plighted their troth, and then assumed inviolate vows. Their very first act as husband and wife is to kneel in prayer. Then it is that the minister speaks to God for the whole Church after this wise: ". . . send Thy blessing upon this man and this woman, whom we bless in Thy Name . . ."

Yes, we bless them. Only in God's Name can we bless them, to be sure, but we, all of us who are God's Holy Church, do bless them. We bless them when we hold fast the sound doctrines of personal purity and teach them to our children. We bless them when we permeate our age with deep devotion to beauty, to truth, to goodness. We bless them when we march under discipline as soldiers of Christ against all that is wrong and false in

if those starving foreigners were in our midst, we would not let them fall
and die of hunger.

If we really had seen for ourselves the distended stomachs of starving
children, surely we would not have been so callous as the rich man in Jesus'
story.

There are I think two things to say in reply to this. First, the man in the
story did not really see the beggar either. For he is revealed as being far
from an insensitive brute a little later in the story. His trouble was not
hard-heartedness essentially; it was blindness. My task this morning is to
make us see the pleading faces of the hungry.

Secondly, the world is smaller now and the starving peoples of Africa
and Asia are in fact at our very gate. Trouble in Europe produced a war that
we could not ignore. We saw that the Japanese lived very near us when
bombs fell on Pearl Harbor.

It is a small world and the starving indigent beyond the narrowing
oceans lies at our gate.

This story that Jesus told is sharply parallel to our case and moment. If
so, let us follow on in the story. "And it came to pass that the beggar died."
That hardly needs be emphasized. A starving man will die and relatively
soon.

But Jesus went on to say: "The rich man died also and was buried." We
sometimes forget that. With all his fine clothes, with all his good food, his
end is the same as the other.

And in his story Jesus imaginatively pictured the ultimate destination of
the two men. The poor man was carried by the angels to "Abraham's
bosom." What an economy of words he used—no attempt to satisfy vain
curiosity as to the kind of place it was—Abraham's bosom, a personal paradise of comfort and joy.

And when the rich man died he found himself in Hades or Hell. "And
being in torments, seeth Abraham afar off and Lazarus in his bosom."

At last he sees the beggar. He recognized him as that man he had passed
by many times beside his gate, but had never really seen before. "And
he cried and said, 'Father Abraham, have mercy on me and send Lazarus
that he may dip the tip of his finger in water and cool my tongue for I am
tormented in this flame.'"

All his life he had had servants to do his bidding so now very characteris-
tically: "Send that fellow Lazarus to help me."

Abraham said, "Son (notice the combination of affectionate address
with ultimate severity) remember that thou in thy lifetime receivest thy
good things and likewise Lazarus evil things: but now he is comforted and

thou art tormented, And besides all this, between us and you there is a great gulf fixed."

Let us not lose ourselves just now in theological speculation about heaven and hell, their geography, their justice, or in any details of the imaginative story. Essentially the point of Jesus' story was that there had been fixed a gulf or chasm between the beatitude of Lazarus and the torment of the thoughtless rich man.

No one could cross the chasm if he would. This is no sentimental tale. It is full of horror, even worse than the details of Dante in the *Inferno*. By his actions in this life an impassable gulf had been fixed. Terrible finality. This from the lips of the gentle Jesus.

And, artist that Jesus was, he lets us see that this rich man was no cruel beast or villain. For notice what he says next: "I have five brothers. Send Lazarus to warn them lest they also come to this place of torment." He forgot himself perhaps for the first time when he thought, "Help my brothers."

But Abraham replied: "They have Moses and the Prophets, let them hear them." Once more the rich man pleads for his family still on earth: "Nay father Abraham, if one went to them from the dead, they will repent."

Surely if an apparition came to us today, the ghost of an Indian boy who fell yesterday on Calcutta's streets, pleading for his fellows—surely we too would change. If the wraith of a Moorish woman who fell last night on the streets came now to us and we heard her plea, surely we would repent.

But would we? Listen once more to the word of Abraham, his last word, with great finality: "If they hear not Moses and the Prophets, neither will they be persuaded, though one rose from the dead."

And we have that one beyond Moses and the prophets. We have the word of Jesus too to speak to our hearts and minds. If we won't hear him, there is no hope that any means could persuade us to notice that man at our gate.

But you and I profess the name of Christ. Is our need that we should be more stirred to sympathy for the starving world. Do we not recognize that how we respond to the world's need is of final significance in our spiritual destiny?

Perhaps we need no more persuasion. I trust that that is so. Our trouble is not hard-heartedness. I hope it is not blindness either. I see him there "that man at my gate."

But what must I do specifically? Can't we hear ourselves in the rich man's thoughts: "If I feed him, I'll have all the beggars in the city at my door." "If I give him the wastage from my table, what will I feed my pigs? You don't want me to slaughter my pigs, do you?"

And losing ourselves in the economic complexities of poverty and hunger, of oversupply and waste, of too much here and too little there, we shake our heads and say to ourselves, "It is morbid to go on thinking like this—I will turn my mind to more pleasant thoughts."

But we who profess Christian faith dare not turn away from the man at the gate. And yet as I return from a recent visit to one of the free and uncommitted nations—a nation which for some years now we have been supplying with food and technical assistance—I have the feeling that our Christian Churches, and individual Christian men and women in this rich and comfortable nation, are not making a sufficient witness to our nation that we ought—we have an obligation to share generously of our abundance with a starving world. To the rest of the world, we look fat and fearful; not Christian and generous. And I wonder in terms of the parable whether by our indifferent self concern we are not *fixing* a great (impassable) gulf between us and that eternal comfort which is the gospel's promise to the faithful.

Recently the President asked from all the American people sacrifice and support in the face of the political and military threat to our country and to the western alliance. Congress and the people have responded with a unanimity born of well founded fear. But at the same time, there has been before the Congress a new Foreign Aid Bill which languishes in Committee.

It is true that we cannot expect the nation made up of all kinds of believers and non-believers to act like a Christian Church. But may we not expect the Churches in our country to act like Christian Churches?

Where is the flood of letters to the Congress, pressing for this Bill? Where even is the informed and steady support of our own Christian programs to meet this desperate human need—such as Church World Service of the National Council of Churches and the Division of Interchurch Aid of the World Council of Churches. Where are the Christian public witnesses in plush golf and yacht clubs standing up for Christian generosity as an obligation?

As I am brought swiftly back from the great poverty of Morocco to the lush luxury of our life, I cannot put out of my mind this awful story of Jesus about the rich man and the beggar Lazarus at his gate. Some of us who find ourselves in positions of church responsibility in this nation have been severely criticized for talking too much politics and economics and (as they say) "forgetting the gospel."

241

Good God, what is the gospel? Surely the God who so loved the world to give his Son to die for it lays upon us an obligation to respond to that love beyond what we are doing?

Is not this the very heart of the obligation of Christian profession—to serve in Christ's name the desperate needs of all God's sons?

There is, I remind you, as I close another picture parable that Jesus told: It is the end of the world. The King speaks: "Come ye blessed of my Father, inherit the Kingdom prepared for you from the foundation of the world: for I was an hungered and yet gave me meat. . . ."

Then shall the righteous answer Him saying: "Lord, when saw we thee an hungered and fed thee . . ." And the King shall answer and say unto them: "Verily I say unto you, inasmuch as ye have done it unto one of the least of these my brethren, ye have done it unto me."

Sermon Thirty-two

AFRICA'S NEEDS
AND AMERICA'S HOPES

REVEREND DONALD SZANTHO HARRINGTON, S.T.D.

Minister, The Community Church (Unitarian), New York, New York

Since 1944 Donald Harrington has been minister of the Community Church in New York. For the first five years there he was junior minister with Dr. John Haynes Holmes; since 1949, following Dr. Holmes' retirement, he has been in charge of the church. Dr. Harrington was born in Newton, Massachusetts, and attended Old First Parish Church (Unitarian) in Waltham. He attended Antioch College and the University of Chicago. He received his theological training at Meadville Theological School in Chicago and became minister of First Unitarian Church in Hobart, Indiana. In 1938 he was awarded the Cruft Traveling Fellowship and went to Europe to study at the University of Leyden for a year. While there he also visited the Universities of Marburg, Kolosvar, Oxford, and Cambridge. He has traveled through most of the countries of Europe. In 1939 he and the Reverend Vilma Szantho, the first woman to be ordained to the ministry in Central Europe, were married by the Bishop of the Hungarian Unitarian Church in Budapest. He and Mrs. Harrington returned to the United States in the fall of 1939, and he became Minister of the People's Liberal Church in Chicago.

During the winter of 1960-1961 Dr. and Mrs. Harrington made an intensive study tour of Eastern Europe and Israel as well as East, Central, South and West Africa. At present he is Chairman of the American Committee on Africa. He is also a member of the American Association for the United Nations' Commission to Study the Organization of the Peace. In 1959 he received the honorary degree of Doctor of Sacred Theology from Starr King School for the Ministry in Berkeley, California.

"Africa's Needs and America's Hopes" was given March 12, 1961, in the Community Church, New York.

AFRICA'S NEEDS AND AMERICA'S HOPES

Africa is today like a giant dark question mark, a sizzling time bomb under the rest of the world. Our attention is focused upon Africa for we realize that what happens there will affect us all the rest of our lives. But, until very recently, we didn't regard Africa as being very much our concern. It was the concern of Britain, France, Belgium, Spain, and Portugal—but not of America. Despite the fact that ten per cent of our American citizens come from African ancestors, we have not felt especially concerned, nor have they. It was a Negro poet who wrote, not very many years ago: "I am an American. What is Africa to me?" But now the American Negro, and every American, knows that Africa is something to the American Negro, and so are the Africans. The American Negro can stand a little straighter now that he sees Africans marching upon the world stage at the United Nations, and being treated with the respect that is their due. All of us Americans now have to reckon with a new importance in Africa and show a new interest ourselves. The day of neglect is rapidly passing. We are building embassies and consulates throughout the African continent. We are beginning to pay attention, because we know that it is important for us to do so.

If Americans in general have neglected Africa, we liberal religionists have even more. While the Presbyterians and Baptists, the Methodists and Congregationalists, and even the little storefront sects were sending missionaries, teachers, doctors, and nurses out to Africa, we were taking a superior attitude. We were looking down our long, New England noses. That may be a hard metaphor for some of you to take, and saying we didn't believe in conversion, which isn't true; but it was an excuse for not doing anything. The result was that on that great continent there are today only two Unitarian Centers, one European oriented and the other African. Both of them are weak and desperately in need of sympathy and help that they are not yet getting from us. Our liberal religious unconcern has been worse than that of Americans in general. It was our realization of how deeply we are involved in the fate of Africa that took Mrs. Harrington and me on a long journey starting in Egypt, going down through East Africa, over into Central Africa, through the Congo and French Africa into West Africa, and finally . . . home. I want this morning to try to summarize briefly what appeared to us to be Africa's greatest needs and then

244

to examine how far these needs may correspond with America's ideals and hopes.

Africa's needs are so dramatically obvious that it would take one who is either stupid or terribly blinded by self-interest to fail to see them. They stand out on every hand, and shout, so that one cannot miss their significance. In essence, they fall into five basic categories.

First of all, the African feels he needs FREEDOM—he needs independence from colonial rule, an opportunity to share in the determination of his destiny, and to feel that his destiny is in his hands, as an African. One finds the evidence of this need in a tremendous passion for freedom throughout the length and breadth of Africa. From Egypt on down and in every part—it is dramatically in evidence. If you ask the African whether he would rather have political independence or economic well-being, the answer is instantaneous, political independence!—for it holds the key to economic well-being and every other kind of well-being. When you drive along the roads through East Africa, through Kenya and Tanganyika, even though you have a white, European face, the Africans walking along the road from one place to another, whether they be children or old people, raise their hands in the sign "V" and shout, "Uhuru.—Freedom!" When you drive through Nyasaland, the cry is "Kwatcha—Rise up"—with the sign of the thumb upraised. When you go into the Central African Federation you find the greeting that flows from one person to another, as you and I say "Hello" or "Hi," is: "Freedom! ! !"—with the response: "Now! ! !" And I think that there is nothing more thrilling than to hear a vast crowd in one of the West Africa countries, using that interestingly different African pronunciation, "Free—Dom—Free—Dom—Free—Dom! ! !" as though the reiteration of the word would satisfy some terrible pain and anguish within their souls. There can be no question whatsoever but that Africa needs, and wants, and must have freedom.

We have got to understand that the prerequisite for any effective work in Africa during the next quarter century must be sympathy for the independence movements and for their leaders. Of course, our great problem is that our NATO allies have been giving ground grudgingly before the African Nationalists. They still wield enormous influence in all the areas of Africa and they still have absolute control in many of them. These NATO allies of ours bitterly resent, not only what they call American interference, but even American interest in the problems of Africa. They certainly resent and protest expressions of sympathy for African national-ism, even though their own policies have moved far and fast in support of ultimate independence in recent years. Until now this has tended to lead the United States to keep "hands off" and often to fail to respond to the cries for help that have come from the African lands. We did not respond when Guinea cried for help. We did not even acknowledge the plea of Sekou Touré; and the result was that Guinea turned to the Soviets from whom help was forthcoming immediately. Now, we are worried and alarmed, and we cry that Touré is a Communist; but it is not so. If he leans in that direction, it may be because he learned from us that we were not ready to respond to a plea for help. This is the problem that we face in the world at the moment; the resentment on the part of our allies if we show interest, and try to help, and, on the other hand the great need of the Afri-cans for the help that we could give.

Perhaps the most dramatic evidence of our dilemma was our stance during the first part of the Fifteenth General Assembly of the United Na-tions when, on important question after important question concerning the Africans, we either abstained or took the opposite position from the one they hoped we would take. This was generally not from the dictates of our own minds and hearts, but because we were afraid of disturbing our re-lations with our NATO allies. When the watered-down resolution calling for the ultimate independence of all areas of Africa came up, we ab-stained. When there was a resolution calling for a reporting to the United Nations of what was going on in areas administered by foreign powers, aimed primarily at the Portuguese, we abstained! When there was a ques-tion of the election of a non-permanent member of the Security Council, we supported Portugal, the nomination by our Western allies and the worst, unrepentant colonialist in Africa. We supported Portugal against our best friend in Africa—Liberia. It so bothered one of the Liberian delegates that he said to a friend of mine, "I feel like shaking every American I see." I could go on, for on question after question we either voted against the Africans or we placed ourselves in the equivocal position of abstaining on what they felt were the most important questions before the world today. It has seriously compromised us in their eyes.

Perhaps the most important question of all was that of the recognition of Kasavubu's regime in the Congo. We took the lead in pushing through the United Nations the recognition of Mr. Kasavubu's regime, though vir-tually all of the African and Asian States asked us to wait until the United Nations Conciliation Commission could report on the real situation there. We, nonetheless, pushed ahead; we had our way; we won the friendship of Mr. Kasavubu and some others, but at the price of the understanding and support of almost every other African and Asian leader. It was a very great price to pay. I can report that in our traveling through Africa we found very few African leaders who had very much good to say for Mr. Kasavubu, Gen. Mobutu, Mr. Tsombe, and Mr. Kalongi. These men, who are now desperately trying to get together on the island of Madagascar, represent to most Africans the things they are most afraid of in this emerging situation—secession or fragmentation along tribal lines and division between one another, submission and subjection to continued colonial rule, and rule by assassination. They have become symbols of these negative forces rather than symbols of national and tribal unity, which most Africans feel alone can save them in the new Africa that is emerging.

Thus, in our actions in the United Nations, we seem to have done almost all of the wrong things. One can only hope that now there may be a shift in policy and we may draw closer to those who should be our natural allies.

Mr. G. Mennen Williams uncovered, quite by chance, the real problem in Africa and showed how important it is that we should find a way to support the aspirations for independence and ultimate union of the African Nationalists. He said in a statement which must have seemed reasonably mild to most Americans that America stood for a policy of "Africa-for-the Africans." By "Africans" he meant the people who live in Africa, whether they are white or black or somewhat in between . . . the people who make Africa their home. It seemed like a truism, but there ensued a great hue and cry both in Africa and in Europe. As one leader said, "If Mr. Williams doesn't understand the difference between a European and an African, he doesn't know anything about Africa at all." In a sense, this is true. Far too many of the Europeans who live in Africa do not think of themselves as Africans; they do not want to be called Africans, nor do they acknowledge that Africa should exist for Africans. For them Africa and the Africans exist for the Europeans. We cannot afford to be associated in any way with this point of view. I am glad that Mennen Williams spoke out, for I think that we all learned something in the response to what he said. So, I say the first great African need is for freedom, for independence for her territories. Later there will come a union of those who have become independent—a broadening African union which will join them together. If America wants to work in Africa, she must sympathize with this need.

The second great need of the African is for education. It is hard for us to imagine, here where education is omnipresent, but in Africa the opportunities for education are very slim. One finds primary schools, mostly run by the churches, enough primary schools to accommodate in the first eight grades, half of the children. What happens to the other half I have no idea. There are almost no high schools at all—for the Africans. There is one government high school, and there are two small religious high schools in the whole of Northern Rhodesia. In Tanganyika 300,000 children come into school at the first grade, 30,000 go into school at the fifth grade, about 300 into high school and about 150 graduate, matriculating for college . . . not because they are stupid, but just because the schools are not there! The moment it became known that the Harringtons were interested in education for Africans, and somehow the news spread like a prairie fire, we were waited on day and night by young people wanting to come and study in the United States.

I've been studying some of the statistics with respect to education for Africans. We have in the United States today, according to the Institute for International Education, 1,192 African students from south Sahara Africa. When I was in Kenya, Tom Mboya, the outstanding African leader in Kenya, estimated that in Kenya at that moment there were something like one thousand students who had graduated either that year or the two years before with certificates from high school that could matriculate into college, but there was no place for them in their own land. There are a few scholarships available in Great Britain, but most of them would like to study in the United States. The principal bottleneck, however, is at the secondary or high school level. I don't know how many African students we shall make it possible to come to the United States this coming fall, but I have to say that I see no provision yet for more than at most 150. I must report also that, while we were in Africa, Mr. Kwame Nkrumah of Ghana announced that 3,000 Ghanians would go to study science in the Soviet Union. Mr. Nasser has announced from Egypt that room would be made at his university in Cairo for 2,000 African students, with full scholarships. Mr. Oginga-Odinga, who is the Vice Chairman of the major political party in Kenya and who is politically oriented toward the Soviet Union, came back from a trip to Russia and China and announced that he had 2,000 scholarships available for Kenyan students, and about £30,000—$75,000—to pay for their travel to the Soviet Union!

These students would rather come to the United States, if for no other reason than that they can speak English here and not have to learn a new language. The great question is whether we will find a way to make it possible. We must find a way! We must find a way to bring them, by supporting the air lift program of the African American Students Foundation that has in the last two years brought almost half of the students that have come to this country from Africa. We must secure more scholarships in our colleges and universities. We must find a way to open up that bottleneck at the high school level, bringing into our families and public schools some of those students who are ready for secondary school and who want so desperately to go on with their educations. Their countries so desperately need them.

III

In the third place, there is need for progress in the interrelated areas of agriculture, industry, and community development. I say these are interrelated, because as a matter of fact you cannot concern yourself with the transition from subsistence agriculture to cash cropping in any part of Africa without concerning yourself also with the re-development of village life. And today you cannot think of the re-development of a society which remains economically at a very primitive level without integrating into the process the development of small industry and ultimately big industry. We have the great opportunity in Africa of standing at the very beginning of a great and complicated process, which needs planning and thinking through in African terms, and which can be prevented from running away in any single direction. Because the process is just beginning, it can be guided more intelligently than it can any other place on earth. Again the great question is whether we will find a way to work with the Africans to make this opportunity something of which the world can be proud. In this particular task we must help in so far as it is possible, through the United Nations, using the agencies of the United Nations and not depending too much upon programs which are in the control of our allies who have been colonialists for so long. For, unfortunately, they are not deeply trusted by the Africans, and the work will not go as it ought. They cannot see the task through African eyes. We need an international agency with strong support from America.

249

In the fourth place, the African needs respect and understanding. Perhaps the greatest failure of the European in Africa, is that he is somehow unable to look the African in the eye with mutual respect. This creates all kinds of problems of which we became painfully aware the moment we entered the African continent itself. Really, so much depends upon the look-in-the-eye, and it is this that somehow is not right, as far as the British and colonialists in general are concerned. When we got to Nairobi we made it a point, as we walked along the streets or paths, to greet the African, to say "hello." We were astonished that very often there was no response to our greeting, just a look of astonishment on the African's face, as though this were the last thing he expected from someone with a white face —a greeting! We had a rather puzzling experience. We had learned to speak a few words of Swahili, the language spoken among the different tribes in East Africa. "Hello" in Swahili is "Jambo!" And so, as we walked along, we would say to Africans coming the other way "Jambo!" But there was no response. I asked a friend of mine, an African, why there was no warm reaction to the greeting "Jambo!" He explained that it had been the British custom not to speak to the African in English, nor to encourage his reply in English. This was too uppity. The rule was to speak to him in Swahili, and make him reply in kind. So that for me to try to speak to him in Swahili was an insult, which brought this strange, cold reaction.

One of the things we noticed was that just looking at Africans as human beings would elicit from them a response of astonishment, a kind of reaction like this. ". . . this man is different! . . . this man sees *me!* . . . He doesn't look upon me as a piece of the furniture." This would be followed by a growing warmth and willingness to talk, to communicate, and to share interests, ideals, suffering, and pain. The great failure between the European and the African in Africa today is the failure of understanding. It is not impossible to get through, but it is very hard, and very often the European simply does not make the effort.

Sometimes we were greatly angered by the arrogance we saw. I remember, for example, one day sitting on the outdoor terrace in front of the New Stanley Hotel in Nairobi having a cup of coffee in the morning, we saw an English settler berate—before everybody—one of the African men who wait on the table, saying, "come here . . . you stupid! Can't you get anything straight? . . . Don't act more stupid than you are! . . ." and then remarked loudly to his friend, "You know, the South Africans know how to treat these people!" It was at the table right next to us and was a little more than Mrs. Harrington could bear. At that point, having had all she could take, she said in a loud, clear voice: "I love the British—at home!" Of course, it is wrong to lump all people into any category, but in settler Africa one often becomes angry at the inability and unwillingness of the white man to reach across the race line.

The African wants respect. He wants to be treated as an equal. He needs understanding. In a very real sense, the African, as compared with the European, is at a stage of cultural development that is roughly equivalent to the adolescent. This does not mean that all Africans are adolescent—far from it—but the culture is at that stage. By and large the African today, in his culture, is like all adolescents—capable of daring, and dreaming great dreams, and expending enormous energy for the realization of his dreams. But, if he is frustrated beyond endurance, he is also capable, like all adolescents, of very destructive behavior. He needs, from the West, not condescension, but counsel—not goading, but guidance—not to be told what to do, but to be helped to find his own way and to stand on his own feet. Like all adolescents, he needs above all to be respected, to be loved, to be encouraged, and to be treated with patience and understanding. And he needs to be spared constant, carping criticism for minor faults and failings which he himself sees only too well.

This is his fourth great need—respect, understanding, and to be treated as an equal.

V

And fifth, and finally, the African needs to be helped to preserve and reassert that unique something that he still possesses that he calls the "African personality." It is a quality of spirit, or soul, if you will, that tends to wash out under the impact of the West. Yet, it is something that is so deep and sure and significant that everyone talks about "the African personality" from one end of the continent to the other, and it is easy to recognize it in almost every African. One of the great reasons for my going to Africa was to try to understand the "African personality" and to try to think of ways in which we might help the Africans to preserve it.

Let me try to tell you what I think the "African personality" is. It is a quality of innerness, that is made possible by the fact that the African, by and large, still lives in a very simple and uncomplicated village society in which what he has and what he is correspond, in which his inner self is not fragmented into a million pieces nor distracted in a million different directions. You remember that Laurens Van der Post once quoted an

251

African chief as saying that the difference between the European and the African is that the European *has* and the African *is*. It is this quality of is-ness and inner-ness, of self-possession and self-understanding that is tre-mendously strong within the African and that I think constitutes what we call the "African personality." It gives the African an enormous dignity and a sense of oneness between the inner man and the outer expression, a oneness that exists in a living and direct relationship between the man and what he possesses, the person and what he does. Let me give some illustrations. The recreational life of the African is not an audience kind of recreation—he doesn't watch other people dance and play and act out dramas. His recreation is participatory. Whatever it is, it's done together. There is nothing more delightful than to see Africans at a festival on a Sunday afternoon, with traditional African dancing in which everybody takes part. There are drummers, with drums of all sizes, shapes, and sounds, and players of bells and gongs and gourds, and then there are the women who dance, women with babies on their backs, and little girls dancing along-side of their mothers making exactly the same motions, which they've learned by the age of three. Off to one side the men are dancing, dancing alone, dancing with fierce contortions that require an enormous expendi-ture of physical energy, with steps and gestures that are intricate and beau-tiful. When Africa dances, everybody dances; nobody stands to watch, every-body dances!

In clothing, every woman makes her own dress, and makes it in her own fashion. She turns her scarf in a special way that expresses her personality. The men in West Africa are dressed in their handsome Keuti cloth togas, each cloth woven to each man's personal specifications. I think of the day we spent up-country in Ghana and how we met a village goldsmith. Our experience with the goldsmith taught me a great deal about Africa and Africans. I asked him what a goldsmith could do in a small village, and he told me that a goldsmith was a very important man even in a small vil-age. Among other things, he must make for each of the young girls as she grows a pair of earrings. It is the father's job to find the gold and bring it to the goldsmith; it is the goldsmith's job to suit those earrings to that par-ticular girl with all the artistry of which he is capable. But he confesses that he cannot do this by himself; he has to have an inspiration; he has to have some help. So, the father must hire a praise-singer. The praise-singer comes on the day that the earrings are to be made, and he sings the praises of the goldsmith and of the beauty of the girl and somehow, out of the com-bination of the two, if he is a good praise-singer, beautiful gold earrings emerge. Before I knew anything at all about the goldsmith, I was admiring the girls' and women's earrings, for they all are different, all unique, and all beautiful. When I knew how they had been made, I knew why they were so individually becoming and exquisitely beautiful. It would be sad to substitute some mass-produced earrings for these that are so integral to the purpose for which they are made.

One of the things which everyone who goes to Africa remarks on is the way the women of Africa, and sometimes the men too, carry heavy loads upon their heads. Often I've heard the Europeans say, "See how primitive they are! They haven't even discovered the wheel!" There are plenty of wheels to be seen on every side. I think the reason that the Africans still carry their burdens upon their heads is a psychological as well as an economic one. There is somehow a correspondence between the person and the load. If you don't believe this just sometime watch an African woman with a load upon her head walking like a queen, talking, and gesturing, and then try to imagine the same woman with a wheel-barrow. I suppose the day of wheels will one day take over in Africa, but I hope that first an effort will be made to find a way to preserve the good in the old, the marvellous congruity between the inner man and the outer environment which still remains there now. These things may disappear if an adequate effort is not made to preserve them in the days ahead. Perhaps there is no better way, over the long run, to help the Africans than to help them to preserve their African souls. There is no greater gift they can give to us than the essence of their "African personality," which has values which we seem to have lost.

These, then, are the five great areas of need: Independence, Freedom, Education, development of Agriculture, Industry and Village, Respect and Understanding. And finally they need help in the preservation of the "African personality." The African spirit and soul, not only for the African, but for all the world. Do not these correspond with America's hopes and dreams? Are we not the land of freedom and independence? Do we not believe in educational opportunities for all? Do we not hope to build a civilization in which community development and industry and agriculture go hand in hand, and have we not here much to learn that will ultimately be of help to all? Do we not believe in respecting all equally, regardless of race? And do we not preach the uniqueness of every man, and reassert the dignity of every human spirit? This is why I say that Africa's needs and America's hope correspond, and that there is every reason for us to help the Africans in the days ahead. Africa's needs are a challenge, a challenge to the finest of America's hopes! To meet that challenge will require thought and vision, sacrifice and solid effort, in governmental policy, in private organizational work, and in individual concern. If we are worthy of our great heritage we will rise to meet that challenge!

Let us pray: Give us the courage, Oh God, to face our own failings. Give us the heart and hope to make them right with new great deeds of good. Help us, hand-in-hand with our brothers across the seas, to build one great new world of Brotherhood. Amen.

Sermon Thirty-three

NEGATION AND AFFIRMATION IN LIFE

Reverend William Baillie Green, Ph.D.

A Presbyterian Minister, Chaplain and Assistant Professor of Religion of Vassar College, Poughkeepsie, New York

A graduate of Baylor University, Dr. Green received the Bachelor of Divinity degree from the Louisville Theological Seminary in 1951, and the Master of Theology degree from Union Theological Seminary in New York in 1953. While at Union he served as assistant minister of the First Presbyterian Church in Mt. Vernon, New York. In 1953, he was ordained to the ministry by the Presbytery of Westchester, Synod of New York.

After receiving the Ph.D. degree from the University of Edinburgh in 1955, he served as Assistant Minister of the First Presbyterian Church in Youngstown, Ohio. He was a member of the Religion faculty at Lafayette College in Easton, Pennsylvania, during the academic year 1956-1957. Dr. Green joined the faculty of Vassar College in 1957 as Assistant Chaplain and Instructor in Religion.

NEGATION AND AFFIRMATION IN LIFE

"For the Son of God, Jesus Christ, whom we
preached among you . . . was not Yes and No;
but in him it is always Yes."
II Corinthians 1:19

In the first chapter of the epistle we know as II Corinthians, St. Paul defends himself against the charge, occasioned by a change in his travel plans, of being fickle and unstable. After stating a good reason for the change, he writes: "Do I make my plans like a worldly man, ready to say Yes and No at once? As surely as God is faithful, our word to you has not been Yes and No. For the Son of God, Jesus Christ, whom we preached among you . . . was not Yes and No; but in him it is always Yes."

In this passage St. Paul makes a profound statement regarding the human situation, on the one hand, and the Gospel of Christ, on the other. As far as man is concerned, everything is Yes and No. But in Christ, it is always Yes.

Nothing is more characteristic of human life than the tension between Yes and No. One is reminded of the words which a poet has ascribed to God at creation:

"I will leave man to make the fateful guess
Will leave him torn between the No and Yes."

Sometimes it is one; sometimes the other. Often it is both at the same time. It so happens that in recent days the No has been more frequent and more compelling than the Yes.

This is an age of Negation; or, as someone has called it, the "beat generation." And that seems very apt for the disenchanted, nihilistic viewpoint which prevails among so many young people. They voice a rebellious No to parental authority; a resentful No to teachers and counselors; an indifferent No to social and political responsibility; a sullen No to the ultimate problems of life and the world; a defiant No to religious traditions and institutions, even to God Himself; a belligerent No to past, present, and future.

But such negation is not limited to a single age or class. This summer I saw an advertisement in a Chicago paper for the Cloister Inn on North Rush Street. Now the Cloister Inn is the meeting place, according to the

256

ad, for the most interesting representatives of Chicago's "hip set." And for those who haven't heard, the hipsters are the frozen faced, the unexcitable, the sharp-tongued, and corrosive-penned, to whom nothing is sacred. It all began, according to Herbert Gold, with the effort of the self-conscious urban Negro to overcome his characterization as a happy, emotional, Bible-shouting, jazz-loving person, and to parody instead the negative, uninvolved diffidence of sophisticated city life. This sort of nihilism was then reimitated by urban whites until the whole phenomenon rebounded among all types of city dwellers. Mort Sahl, Jonathan Winters, and Dave Gardner are now among the better known and more representative hipsters.

All of us, regardless of age, are being called upon to say No. And it is an urgent, convincing call. It comes from contemporary philosophy in the works of men like Jean-Paul Sartre who picture existence as utter darkness and loss. It resounds in modern art which so frequently depicts man a a mechanical creature, put together with bolts and nuts, or, at best, as a bag of splintered flesh. It echoes in today's literature and drama, as for example, in the writings of Kafka, the early Eliot, O'Neill, Tennessee Williams, and Arthur Miller. It breaks forth in music in the restlessness and dissonances of Stravinski. It sounds even in the pronouncements of science, particularly in the findings of depth-psychology from Freud on. It would seem that the whole of modern culture reaches its convergence and climax in the call to world and self negation.

Now, there is something very honest and daring and realistic about the so-called "beat generation" and their older counterparts. It takes courage to say No when heretofore men have said only Yes. As compared with the naive optimism of the previous generation—a generation which believed in automatic, inevitable progress—the present emphasis is surely to be praised. Men in every discipline have peered into the depths of life. They have seen its deserts and jungles. And they have had the courage, in the face of an unrestrained Yes, to pronounce a despairing No.

This No and the call to negation must be taken with the utmost seriousness, especially by those of us who stand within the Judeo-Christian tradition. For our religion at its best has recognized the necessity of dealing honestly with life; of seeing its demonic as well as its divine aspects. Prophets of both synagogue and church have experienced the paradoxical character of human existence. They have registered the tension between negation and affirmation. But their message has often been rejected. The true prophet has been attacked as a pessimist and defeatist and driven out of the religious community.

For instance, the deafness of modern Christianity to the inevitable No

257

has forced many creative artists with their profound realism into religious exile. It is sobering to consider that the majority of great figures in literature, art, music, philosophy, and science have found it necessary to withdraw from or remain outside the church in order to preserve their creative integrity. Surely this is in some deep sense a serious and tragic judgment on the institutional church.

While giving due weight to the No, let us remember that it is not the only word. We cannot live by negation alone. And those who try, end up by saying Yes to nothingness, or by affirming the meaning of meaninglessness. Soon or late, we must say Yes to something, even if it is only the utter futility and vanity of life.

The recognition of the need for a positive stance is one of the most significant developments in recent literature. Take the writings of Albert Camus, for example. In his earlier novels, Camus delcares that absurdity is the fundamental condition of human existence. That all life must be lived in the agony of despair. However, in a more recent novel, *The Fall*, Camus' hero Jean-Baptiste Clamance seems to be taking tentative steps in the direction of affirmation. To be trying—though obliquely, anxiously, and with much hesitation—for a Yes that moves beyond a previous devastating No.

This movement is more obvious in some of the novels by our young American writers. I have in mind J. D. Salinger's deeply sensitive *The Catcher in the Rye*. The protagonist is sixteen-year-old Holden Caulfield who, knowing that he is about to flunk out of prep-school, suddenly decides to leave and before going home to spend a carefree two days in New York. The novel centers around what he saw and experienced during those two days, and his melancholy struggle to find himself.

Holden's initial response to all that he has known of life is hatred and despair. What most distresses him is the "phoniness" in everybody and everything. Here is an instance: At prep school he lived in a new wing of the dormitory given by an alumnus who had made a fortune in the undertaking business. This man, whose name was Ossenburger, returned to speak in the school chapel. And like so many chapel speakers he was corny and long-winded. He started by telling jokes and ended by urging the boys to do as he did, that is, think of Jesus as their "buddy" and not be ashamed to pray to God whenever they needed help. "That killed me," said Holden. "I can just see the big phony . . . shifting into first gear and asking Jesus to send him a few more stiffs." And here's the rub, as Holden sees it: they are all like that—classmates, teachers, preachers, parents, girl-friends, even prostitutes—all phonies! At bottom he senses an insincerity, dishonesty, evasiveness in human relationships which drives him to the black pit of despair.

Finally when his ten-year-old sister Phoebe—the only person whom he feels really understands him and from whom he hides nothing—asks him what he really wants to be, Holden recalls having followed a little boy down a street. And the child was singing to himself "If a body catch a body coming through the rye." Holden tells Phoebe that he would like to be a "catcher in the rye." These are his words:

> . . . I keep picturing all these little kids playing some game in this big field of rye and all. Thousands of little kids, and nobody's around—nobody big, I mean—except me. And I'm standing on the edge of some crazy cliff. What I have to do, I have to catch everything if they start to go over the cliff—I mean if they're running and they don't look where they're going I have to come out from somewhere and catch them. That's all I'd do all day. I'd just be the catcher in the rye.

So Holden has moved from his initial and profound No toward an equally serious and redemptive Yes.

What about us? Shouldn't we be moving in the same direction? It won't be easy and it need not be a means of escape. It can be an expression of freedom, of understanding, and of maturity.

How are we to accomplish this? How do we move from negation to affirmation without sacrificing personal integrity? How balance the No and Yes without surrendering the truth which each represents? The answer seems to me to be suggested in the latter part of our text: "For the Son of God, Jesus Christ, . . . was not Yes and No; but in him it is always Yes." As much as to say: In Jesus as the Christ the weary struggle between Yes and No, between negation and affirmation, is resolved and overcome through the power of God himself. Thus, Christ is God's ultimate Yes to man. And when we find that God has said Yes to us, we are able to affirm ourselves and our world in spite of everything which drives us toward negation.

Elsewhere, St. Paul has spelled it out in these familiar lines: "If God is for us, who is against us? He who did not spare his own Son but gave him up for us all, will he not also give us all things with Him? . . . Who shall separate us from the love of God? Shall tribulation, or distress, or persecution, or famine, or nakedness, or peril, or sword?" (Here St. Paul has catalogued some of the more immediate threats which might have led in his day to nihilism and despair. Bring it up to date with your own list of the external dangers which confront us.) "No," continues St. Paul, "in all these things we are more than conquerors through him who loved us." (Through him who has said Yes to us.) "For I am sure that neither death, nor life, nor angels, nor principalites, nor things present, nor things to come, nor powers, nor height, nor depth . . ." (Here again we would not be violating the sense of the text to include some of those things which most seriously threaten us. Such things as doubt or certainty, despair or faith, truth or falsehood, goodness or evil, religion or irreligion, our past, or present or future. Then follow it with that all inclusive "Or anything else in all creation.") ". . . will be able to separate us," declares St. Paul, "from the love of God in Christ Jesus our Lord."

This is the wonder and mystery of the Christian gospel: The pre-eminence of God's Yes which enables us in our age to assert the final meaningfulness of all life. Exactly how it should apply in your case, I cannot say. I only know that no genuine affirmation is possible that is not somehow related to the Divine Yes.

Sermon Thirty-four

CHRIST AND POLITICS

REVEREND LAMBERT F. BROSE

*A Minister of the Lutheran Church,
Missouri Synod, and an executive of
the Armed Services Commission of
the Missouri Synod, Washington,
D. C.*

Lambert Brose is an accredited White House correspondent for *The Lutheran Layman* newspaper. He attends the Presidental news conferences regularly, and has been recognized frequently for questions by both former President Eisenhower and President Kennedy.

Mr. Brose is Director of Publications of the Armed Services Commission, The Lutheran Church-Missouri Synod. He edits the Commission's publications, *Loyalty—Christ and Country, Double-Time,* and is managing editor of *The Lutheran Chaplain.* The Washington, D. C., clergyman writes "Washington Observer" in *The Lutheran Standard,* official magazine of The American Lutheran Church, and "Capitol Views" in *The Lutheran Layman*—monthly columns looking at the Washington scene from the religious viewpoint. His series of three articles entitled "Combating Communism Effectively" were published in *The Lutheran Witness* and the *Congressional Record.* Mr. Brose has held pastorates in Los Angeles and Laguna Beach, California; Milwaukee, Wisconsin; and Duluth, Minnesota. He is a native of St. Paul, Minnesota.

"Christ and Politics" was delivered on the Lutheran Hour over NBC and the Mutual networks on July 10, 1960. Senator Warren G. Magnuson had it printed in the Congressional Record of August 30, 1960.

CHRIST AND POLITICS

"What do you think about the Connally amendment?" I asked six of my friends recently.

Five of them looked at me dubiously. Then they asked, "What's the Connally amendment?" or quickly changed the subject. Only one stopped to discuss the matter; he was a political columnist.

During the weeks immediately preceding the next nation-wide or state-wide election, voters will display considerable interest in the campaign: How sincere does a candidate's voice sound? Does he "look like a candidate should"? And there will be great interest on the part of certain groups in issues that will affect them particularly—health insurance for the aging, for example. But, judging by the past, most people will not know much more about the issues in general than did my friends about the Connally amendment, one of the vital problems facing our nation and the world. And, in those years when we do not have a general election, the political ignorance of the vast majority of citizens is appalling.

Is this too pessimistic an appraisal? Let me point out that these friends I asked about the Connally amendment were all very active members of Christian churches. The successful functioning of our form of government depends so much on an informed citizenry that it is tragic when any considerable number of citizens is ignorant of political issues. But when church people, whose religion teaches them to be good citizens and all that that implies, are that way, it is alarming indeed.

A Washington clergyman once made a statement in this connection that sounds a little shocking at first. He said: "Anyone who isn't interested in politics isn't much of a Christian." But when you think about it, there is a lot of truth in it.

Politics affects almost every area of a Christian's life. In his role, first, simply as a citizen. Consider the food he eats, for example. You would not think there would be much politics involved in that, but millions of votes in the next election may hinge on how much—or how little, if any—the candidates say our government ought to guarantee farmers for the food they grow. And what about the air we breathe. Think of the politics involved in trying to pass anti-smog and other anti-air-pollution laws.

Politics even affects the very church life of some of us. The question of whether church-supported schools should be tax-exempt has been on the ballot in a number of states. I doubt that you can think of a single day-to-day activity of a Christian that isn't vitally affected by politics. However, it's the religious motivation for a Christian's participation in politics that we would like to stress in this message, "Christ and Politics."

Christ's great mission is not, obviously, a political one. That is clear to us today. But when He walked upon this earth as the God-man, He had to tell the people forcefully that His Kingdom was not of this world. They were looking for a political messiah who would lead them in a political revolution against the Roman government.

Christ came into the world to live, suffer, and die that men might have forgiveness of sins—that, believing in Him, they might live eternally. He came to seek souls. His interest in politics was purely a subordinate one, but it was there! And it is important!

Jesus was interested in politics because it is political government which can make this world a more orderly place in which to live—so that the all-important work of preparing men for lasting life might be hindered as little as possible. Christ, our God, ordained that order in the world should be maintained by government, although he did not decree what form that government should take. Seeing to it that whatever system of government we choose is as efficient and good as we can make it is what Christ expects of His followers. And that we do through our participation in politics.

Let's see how this ought to work out in our lives today. The Savior has told us that our great mission is to "preach the Gospel to every creature." There is no mention here of politics, but the implication that Christ's followers are to take part in politics is there, nevertheless. In order to preach the Gospel as efficiently as possible, we must try to clear away all obstacles that are barriers to preaching it.

War is certainly a hindrance to world-wide mission work. A Christian obviously wants to do everything he can to do away with war—individually and through his church—for humanitarian reasons. But think how much more effective that effort is when the entire machinery of government is set in motion for peace. Assuredly the individual Christian also has the responsibility to do everything he can politically to influence his government toward working for peace—not a cowardly peace, which would allow godless communism to take over the world bit by bit, destroying men's souls as well as their bodies, but a *just* peace.

Or, take the problem of world hunger. It is often pointed out that three out of every five people go to bed hungry every night of their lives—that sixty per cent of the world's population is trying to stay alive on the protein equivalent of *one thin slice of ham a day.*

Again a Christian wants to do all he can to try to help these people out of sheer humanitarian impulses. "For God so loved the *world*," says the Bible. That includes the whole man, also his body.

But a Christian has a higher purpose than that. The Christian says, "It's hard for a man to listen to the Gospel of Jesus Christ when his empty stomach cries out so loud he doesn't hear the preaching." Hunger stands in the way of a man giving attention to the needs of his soul.

A Christian wants to do all he can to allay the world's hunger—through secular agencies and through his church. But think how many more people can be reached when our government throws open its granaries of surplus grains to feed the world's hungry. There are perplexing problems involved, of course—such as the danger of upsetting the world grain markets. However, this is exactly where a Christian's political responsibility comes in. He is to do the hard work of studying this subject. Does not human need, for example, take precedence over political expediency? A Christian should study the matter as much as he can and then seek to influence his government—through his representatives in Washington and through his vote—to do what he thinks best to break down this great barrier to hearing the Gospel.

When a Christian realizes how extremely important political action can be in making the world a better place in which to live—not only for a safer, more pleasant life on earth, but especially in speeding the march of the Gospel—then he assuredly will want to tackle the hard work of taking part in politics. Then he'll want to inform himself on political issues. That is hard work. It takes a great deal of will power, for example, to break the habit of skipping the editorial page in order to get to "Li'l Abner," or "Ask Abby," or the sports pages.

Then he'll want to study *both sides* of the issues. Most people like to think of themselves as being "open-minded." Yet I wonder how many of us make it a practice to read a daily paper expressing a political viewpoint that's different from that of the paper we usually read.

Moreover, a Christian then will want to *vote*. Not only in national, but in state and local elections. After all, it is you and I—the citizens of this nation—who, in the long run, govern this country; through our votes. A system of government such as ours works successfully only when its citizens work successfully, by voting responsibly.

Yes, a Christian, feeling perhaps that God has given him certain special gifts and abilities, may decide that he ought to run for public office.

A recent survey showed that seventy-three per cent of American parents interviewed do not want their sons or daughters to "enter politics" mostly

264

because they think that politics is "dirty." When one realizes how much our system of government depends upon having good men and women in public office, that is a frightening situation. Of course there's dirt and graft and corruption in politics. Just as there is in the business world, in the unions, in the professions—in any human endeavor.

A Christian's job is to clean up the dirt—wherever he finds it—also in political life. "All that is necessary for evil to triumph is that good men do nothing," said Edmund Burke.

A Christian can be a tremendous influence in politics by informing himself on the issues and voting responsibly and by taking part in local politics. And the higher he goes, the more influence he can exert.

I've heard the old cliché that the last word in every politician's speech is "God." Undoubtedly religion is used as a cloak of hypocrisy by many a politician just as it is by many a businessman, union leader, farmer, and professional man. But when a Christian politician really lives his Christianity, he can be a powerful leaven in the affairs of men.

There is one other matter—and it is the most important—that I would like to call to your attention in connection with "Christ and Politics." The activities mentioned so far can be engaged in by any qualified citizen, Christian or non-Christian. But there is one thing only the follower of Jesus Christ can do. Only he can pray to Christ, the almighty God, who has the power to change human hearts.

When the Holy Spirit enters a man's heart through the Scriptures, and gives him faith that Jesus Christ, by His sacrifice on Calvary's cross, has forgiven his sins—when a man really believes this—his whole life is changed. Out of love for his Savior he tries to lead a better life in every area of his activity, including his political life. And the more the Gospel is preached, the more human lives it changes, the stronger the family, the community, the entire nation become.

What an incentive for us in this day of widespread juvenile delinquency, of admittedly low moral standards on every level of society, in this Age of the Payola! No matter how gloomy things seem to be, a Chrisitan is an optimist. He has hope. He is assured that the Gospel of Jesus Christ "is the power of God unto salvation to every one that believeth."

Sermon Thirty-five

MISTAKES I HAVE MADE IN RACE RELATIONS

REVEREND WILLIAM O. BYRD

*Minister, First Methodist Church,
New Orleans, Louisiana*

William O. Byrd is a native of Meridian, Mississippi, and a graduate of Louisiana Polytechnic Institute and of Southern Methodist University.

He has been pastor of Methodist churches in Bonita and Farmersville, and of the University Methodist Church in Lake Charles, Louisiana. He served three years as an Army chaplain, eighteen months overseas, part of the time with the 82nd Airborne Division as Parachute Infantry Chaplain. On his return, he was pastor of First Methodist Church, Arkadelphia, Arkansas, then for four years he was at First Methodist Church, Pine Bluff, Arkansas. He was called to New Orleans in June, 1960. This sermon was delivered in New Orleans to an interracial group during the crisis there and was published in *The Pulpit*, February, 1961.

MISTAKES I HAVE MADE IN RACE RELATIONS

I have a confession to make.

And they say that confession is good for the soul—yet I wonder if that is why I confess. In fact, I hardly know why I review these things, except that they must be said by someone—for good or for ill. So, while confessing, I seek no absolution so much as I seek answers. They may not be easy answers—but answers at any cost—for I am hurt and bewildered. I must confess mistakes I have made in race relations. Mistakes of omission and commission. Will you hear my confession, please?

My first mistake was to be born in this time. Perhaps in the dear, dim days beyond recall I would never have faced this problem—but I picked the wrong century in which to be born. I shouldered my wrinkled way into this world in 1916. I was weaned during the war—that shining crusade to make the world safe for democracy.

Now, after forty-four years, with another world war and a Korean "police action" (strange—the casualties are just as dead whether we call it police action or war), we are threatened with nuclear holocaust. This one, if it comes, may be the war to end all worlds—at least as we know them. Now the question is how to make our much proclaimed but much less practiced democracy safe for the world.

And in such a world, shrunken into neighborhood by jets and communication media, we must have brotherhood; we must act "Thy Kingdom come" or we shall be blown to kingdom come. There is no place to hide. This is a world in which "Little Rock" can be hissed by Indians in Peru and Africans in the Congo. I have heard that hiss, and I know that "no man is an island, no man lives alone."

And this is my sin, my mistake, for to be born in a time such as this is to know that I am a part of a world in which "Little Rock" and all the other symbols of man's inhumanity to man is possible. And I cannot ignore it, nor live with it any longer:

> The times are out of joint . . . O cursed spite
> that I was born . . . to set things aright . . .

Who? Me? Reared on beautiful words—"World safe for Democracy," "Four Freedoms," "United Nations"—on these was I nourished.

And I believed them, for the time demands belief, and that was my first mistake in race relations. Hear my confession, please!

It was a mistake to be born of my particular parents. I should have chosen more wisely. They were of Scotch-Irish stock, with the sturdy Protestant faith. They were rather ordinary, yet amazingly good and independent people, driven by an unrelenting Puritan conscience. My "Mom" (bless her) really believed, and loved, everybody. She could master the stately language of the King James version of the Bible, but she never did learn how to pronounce the simple word, "Negro." To her dying day she called them "Nigras," with a Mississippi accent, and loved them—"in their place"—with all of her Scotch-Irish heart.

"Pop" was more lenient in law, if not in love. In fact, he could "bend" the law when it got in the way of his Scotch (and I don't mean blood). But others knew, and understood, and joined him in saying, "Don't sell it to the Nigras—they can't handle it like us Southern gentlemen."

But both of them, Mom and Pop, taught me to know the virtues of honesty, fair play, etc. They saw that I attended Sunday School, and that I learned to sing:

> Jesus loves the little children,
> All the children of the world,
> Red and yellow, black and white,
> They are precious in His sight,
> Jesus loves the little children of the world.

And I sang, and I believed them, and that was my mistake. Hear my confession, please.

It was a mistake to be born in this particular country. No man who wants to remain "exclusive" should ever select America as the land of his birth. Even deep in Mississippi, that "Magnolia Jungle," and later in Louisiana, the growing mind of a child could not help but be aware of the breath of freedom. For in those days, before the citizens came to their senses and gave their schools to the tender "protection" of the governor, a growing boy could hear such exciting words:

> We hold these truths to be self-evident . . .
> that all men are created equal; that they are
> endowed by their Creator with certain
> inalienable rights . . .

And they told me that in America it was true, and I believed them, and that was my mistake.

Of course, I should have known better, for "Bubba," my almost constant playmate away from home and along the river bank, wasn't in my room at

269

school. His skin was darker than mine, even when mine was dirty with Mississippi mud. But I ignored that, and I believed the teachers because, you see, I really wanted to believe those beautiful words. And that was my mistake. Hear my confession, please!

It was a mistake to be reared in a small southern town. And perhaps here was where I really went wrong. No one, not even Mom, thought it strange to have me play with Bubba and his friends; or, to have "Aunt Cindy," Bubba's mother, to walk with us across the hot pavements to buy candies for all—share and share alike—not separate, but equal!

For years I did not know that I was "better" and that, while we could sit side by side on the curb and eat our candies, Bubba must never, never sit down in the house. And yet they said, "Son, always play fair, always be honest, do unto others as you would have them do unto you. . . ." And I believed them, and that was my mistake.

Of course, I *am* grateful for one saving grace. I could not join the Boy Scouts (my folks couldn't afford the uniform, they said), and so I never had to unlearn all the "impractical" words of the Scout Law. But my friends did, and they said they believed them, and that was *their* mistake.

And so my sins pile up. Time would fail to tell them all. The tragic mistake I made, as a product of such a background, when I chose my life work—the ministry of a Man named Jesus. How could I be comfortable any more, bothered by the words "God so loved the world (and nothing about it being a black or white world) that he gave . . . ," or "Come unto me, all ye . . . (who are white? or Southern?), or "Inasmuch as ye have done it unto the least of these (the least rich, least educated, least white?), ye have done it unto me."

So on and on—the demanding, impossible ethic of Christ. And I try to escape it, and cannot, and that is my mistake.

The ministry carried me into the Army Chaplaincy of World War II, to stamp out the last great prophet of the "Master Race" (that is, before Faubus, Eastland and company). And deep in the Hurtgen forest, in the Belgium Bulge, I watched a Roman Catholic doctor give captured German blood plasma to a Southern Negro American rifleman, and I looked as the Jewish medic assisted the doctor by cleaning the stump of what had been the Negro's leg. And the clean, white teeth flashed up at him and demanded, "Look at it—my blood—it's red, you bastard!" And somehow it didn't sound like profanity at all—more like the echo of a Holy Book that teaches "He hath made of one blood all men to dwell upon the earth."

And I saw, and I believed, and that was my mistake. For back at home the little Hitlers, the supermen, still shout their patriotism and measure it by the hate they can arouse to insure elections.

Even so, I made a greater mistake. For I believed that, when we saw what race hate could do in Dachau and Buchenwald and on a thousand battlefields, the people who call themselves Christian would never rest until the big, beautiful words were translated into flesh.

And I turned to the Church, the fountainhead of all these great Judeo-Christian truths men hold to be self-evident. And there, in spite of the agony of many sensitive ministers and laymen, too often the Church (or rather the caricature we make of His Holy Body on earth) became molded and shaped by pious prattle, mouthing its love of the Supreme Law Giver and Lover of All Life while dragging behind the Supreme Court in human relations. Publicly it could pass great resolutions yet privately pass the word along: "Don't rock the boat; keep everybody happy; say nothing controversial, but say it beautifully," and the greatest of crimes is to offend one of these not least but loudest councils.

Have we, ministers and members, become "Killers of the Dream" in our futile desire to avoid the cost of awakening? Can our silence be "golden" only because it is "yellow"? And the questions keep coming, to haunt us as we sing:

> Dear Master in whose life I see
> All that I would fail to be
> Let Thy clear light forever shine
> To shame and guide this life of mine.
> —John Hunter

And I awake in the night—to ponder the words of the noted Ralph McGill, editor of The Atlanta Constitution, as he wrote about "The Agony of the Southern Minister" (*New York Times Magazine*, September 27, 1959). And I know the agony of which he writes—of the pressure brought to bear, of programs blocked, of silent curtains—and I know the truth of seeing my fellow ministers and my people being haunted by the presence of our brother whom we deny.

We sing: "Faith of our Fathers, living still," and we try to believe it, and that is our mistake. Hear my confession, please.

But the greatest mistake of all, the most terrible confession I must make (and here you, and you, and you, must join me at the confessional) —*our* greatest mistake was to teach the Negro that we believed this heritage of ours, this Judeo-Christian faith in the Fatherhood of God and the Brotherhood of Man. And believing, we find ourselves bound, whether we like it or not, in unbreakable ties.

271

For the Negro *is* my brother, whether I like it or not, or whether I ever choose to act like a brother to him. He is *my* brother, for God, *our* Father, gave him birth, even as He did me. He chose him—and me—and you—to be born at this particular time, to our particular parents, in this particular land, to live as one people before Him.

Whether I turn to ancient Proverbs (1:1) or to a later prophet (Matthew 5-7), I am reminded that it is not my opinion that counts but the inescapable judgment of God, our Father. I have made the terrible mistake of teaching the Negro these truths, so now it is the Negro who has the ultimate weapon which they provide—non-violent love. Against such there is no defense.

So I confess. I am hurt, and puzzled, and bewildered. This is my dilemma: My whole life, time, country, family, community, school, church, has taught me *to be a brother*. But now they say I cannot act as a brother should act. Can I believe them? Hear my confession, please!

Sermon Thirty-six

THE KEYNOTE OF THE REFORMATION

THE RIGHT REVEREND HENRY I. LOUTTIT, D.D.

*Bishop of the Diocese of South Florida of the Protestant
Episcopal Church, Winter Park, Florida*

Bishop Louttit traces the development of the Protestant Reformation and indicates its significance for the Western world during the last four hundred years. He discusses our Christian heritage and shows how best to enjoy it properly.

Henry Irving Louttit was born in Buffalo, New York, January 1, 1903, attended public schools in Buffalo, then graduated from Hobart College. He took his theological studies at Virginia Theological Seminary and was ordained to the priesthood in 1929. He began his ministry as vicar of All Saints' Church, Tarpon Springs, Florida, in 1929, was called to be curate of Trinity Church, Miami, and in 1930 became rector of Holy Cross Church, Sanford, Florida. In 1930, he became rector of Holy Trinity Church, West Palm Beach. From there, in 1941, he was called to active duty with the Armed Forces of the United States and was assigned as chaplain of the Thirty-first Infantry Division. He remained with this division throughout the war and rose to be assistant division chaplain. He was awarded the Bronze Star for his service in the South Pacific.

While still in the Armed Forces he was elected Suffragan Bishop of the Diocese of South Florida and was consecrated May 23, 1945. In April of 1948, he was elected Bishop Coadjutor of the Diocese, with headquarters in Orlando. Since January 1, 1951, he has been the Diocesan. His own preaching is stimulating, vigorous.

The Bishop was one of the founders of the Florida Council of Churches and served two terms as President. At the present time he is President of the Fourth Province of the Episcopal Church and is a member of the National Council Department of Christian Education. He is also Chairman of the General Commission on Chaplains.

THE KEYNOTE OF THE REFORMATION

"Stand fast therefore in the liberty wherewith
Christ hath made us free."

Galatians 5:1a

In that text is the keynote of the Reformation and of the churches of the reformation world. On October 31, 1517, Martin Luther, Augustinian monk, nailed his ninety-five theses on indulgences to the church door at Wittenberg. The normal way in his day and time to invite debate on matters of public interest, his challenge raised ultimate questions of the very nature of the Christian faith and the Christian Church. In so doing, it led inevitably to the opening of the flood gate releasing the pent up forces of reform, hence, as nearly as anyone can pinpoint social movements, that date marks a momentous turning point in the history of the Christian religion.

There began then that movement known as the Reformation, which was in fact a series of reformations in the several parts of the Western Church. The first three, although emphasizing the scriptures, preaching, and personal religious experience, were essentially conservative both in doctrine and in their views on church, worship, and sacraments.

Luther led the way. His basic break with the medieval church lay in his insistence that man is saved by faith alone, that good works can not earn salvation. To him it is the living Word of God, mediated through the scriptures, preaching, and the sacraments, that saves. Hence, he stressed the priesthood of all believers, true apostolic succession lying in the individual Christian who, filled with grace, proclaims to another the word of salvation.

Of the second generation is John Calvin, lawyer, theologian, organizing genius. His massive system of theology also begins and ends in scripture, its authority resting on the Holy Spirit witnessing to its truth in the hearts of men. His faith is theocentric; his cry, "To God alone be the glory." On the sovereignty of God rests his doctrine of predestination, our salvation is a result of God's will and grace, in nowise touched by our frailty or strength, and quite unmerited.

Even later is the reformation of the Church of England. Unlike the continental reformations, it had no single great man of God as leader but

274

was the result of the intellectual ferment and the social pressures of the times. Accepting the Reformation principles that the scripture contains all doctrine required as necessary for salvation, the need for preaching, and the emphasis on personal experience and responsibility, still it strove to maintain its position in the church catholic by its valuation of the church, its creeds, its doctrine, its tradition, its worship, and its ministry. Historically mayhap a compromise to preserve peace in the realm of England, theologically it embraced comprehension in an effort to preserve the whole truth of the Gospel.

The fourth of the reformations of the Church, the heir of widely scattered and varied dissent, was revolutionary. Termed sectarianism, it was to the earlier reformers as much the enemy on the left as Rome was the enemy on the right. Probably it has had more effect on present day Protestantism than they. To the sectarians true religion was always intensely personal, their watchword, "Liberty of conscience." To them the Church is where two or three are gathered together in His name, hence, the freedom, authority, and democracy of the local congregation. The indwelling Word, the Holy Spirit, the Inner Light loom larger in authority than either the church or the Bible.

The fifth of these reformations, too often overlooked, is the reformation of Rome itself by the Council of Trent. On the whole, the abuses in practice of the medieval Church were corrected, but, on the defensive, its theological basis was reactionary. The Church as the authority ends in papal infallibility. The Apostolic Ministry from being essential to the Church, becomes in fact *The* Church. The need for a mediator, or mediators between men and God, ends in the Mediator Supreme, the Blessed Virgin Mary, Queen of Heaven, who in effect replaces our Blessed Lord in personal devotion.

All these, plus fifteen centuries of earlier Christian history form our religious heritage. From the Reformation stem both gains and losses. The gains in part are these: The freedom of the Christian man. Man made in the image of God, fallen through sin, by his faith in the mighty works of our Lord and Savior Jesus Christ is saved, not by his own works but by God's redeeming grace. "By whom also we have access by faith into this grace wherein we stand, and rejoice in the hope of the glory of God." (Romans 5:2) This freedom in the relationship of man to God betokens a personal responsibility for the conduct of life both in moral living and in acts of mercy. "What doth the Lord require of thee, but to do justly, and to love mercy, and to walk humbly with thy God." (Micah 6:8b) The acceptance of the Bible, the supreme revelation of God, as the final authority in faith and morals, and the making of it available for every man. "And ye shall know the truth, and the truth shall make you free." (John 8:32)

The losses, though quite as impressive, are not so commonly recognized. In part they are these: In spite of the earlier reformers' insistence that the Church as the community of believers is essential to the Christian faith, Protestantism too often equates the Christian religion with the individual's relationship to God. To this we owe the fragmentation of the church into myriad sects and denominations. The rightful stress on freedom of conscience has led in effect to a loss of all authority. Too often the proclamation of the Gospel degenerates into an expression of personal belief. "I think" and "in my opinion" become weak substitutes for the older formulae: "The church teaches" and "Thus saith the Lord." Again the loss of a sense of community and fellowship has impoverished public worship. Modern Christian congregations have largely become audiences, spectators at the Mass or auditors of preaching.

Our hope lies in our freedom. Heirs of the Reformation must ever be reformers, apt to follow the guidance of the Holy Spirit who bloweth where He listeth: "Every scribe which is instructed unto the Kingdom of Heaven, is like unto a man which is an householder, which bringeth forth out of his treasure things new and old. (Matthew 13:52)

The most important gift of the Reformation is not any specific reform or precise doctrine, but rather what might be termed "The Protestant Spirit" which can stand outside of the immediate situation to see God's judgment on men and on His Church. Thus cometh His grace and His salvation. Before God we all have failed. Catholic and Protestant but feebly reflect His glory. This too is a day for reformation and we must face understandingly the paradoxical nature of the Christian faith.

The vast outreaches of God's revelation cannot be comprehended by the mind of man and frequently can be stated only in paradox, that is, in logical contradiction. For example, on these, concerning the nature and being of God, we are all agreed. We proclaim that God is transcendent, outside and above His universe, and in the same breath we proclaim also that He is immanent everywhere throughout His universe. "In Him we live, and move, and have our being." (Acts 17:28a) So likewise we would insist that He has revealed Himself as three persons, Father, Son, and Holy Spirit; and insist likewise that these three persons are but one God. Accepting Him as Savior, we believe that He shall come to be our judge; believing that in some real sense in His judgment lies our salvation.

On these instrumentalities, practices, values in the Christian religion there is less agreement. The evangelical would stress the Bible, preaching, and personal religious experience as the foundations of the Christian life. The Catholic would emphasize priority of Church, worship, and sacraments in the practice of the Christian religion. Ultimately we must face the fact that all are essential. What we need, all of us, is a "both—and" rather than an "either—or" religion.

The hope for Christian unity in the ecumenical Church lies not in compromise for the sake of peace, a lowest common denominator religion, throwing overboard the real values in our several traditions for the uniformity of practical nothingness; but in comprehension for the sake of truth, the rich diversity of our several streams of insight and of emphases commingling in the mighty ongoing stream of the Christian faith and the Christian community. In sum, the earmarks of "the coming great Church" must be in essentials, unity; in non-essentials, diversity; in all things, charity.

Lest this be seen as an impossible ideal, always we must remember the union we seek is but bringing to full fruition the unity we have. This was the wisdom of Archbishop Temple, "We could not seek union if we did not already possess unity. Those who have nothing in common do not deplore their estrangement." We share, all of us, in our common history as Christians; in the mighty acts of God, which is the story of His saving relationship to man; in the redeeming gospel of Jesus Christ, our Lord, whereby not merely are we saved, but whereby the Christian community is constituted that He may save the world.

Never let us forget the Church is already one. Hence, St. Paul to the Church at Ephesus could say, "I therefore, the prisoner of the Lord, beseech you that ye walk worthy of the vocation wherewith ye are called. With all lowliness and meekness, with longsuffering, forbearing one another in love; Endeavoring to keep the unity of the Spirit in the bond of peace. There is one body and one spirit, even as ye are called in one hope of your calling; One Lord, one faith, one baptism, One God and Father of all, who is above all, and through all, and in you all." (Ephesians 4:1-6)

We need must learn humility, all of us. All stand under the judgment of Almighty God. Here Paul Tillich's definition of the Protestant principle is of tremendous help to us. "The central principle of Protestantism is the doctrine of justification by grace alone, which means that no individual and no human group can claim a divine dignity for its moral achievements, for its sacramental power, for its sanctity, or for its doctrine. If, consciously or unconsciously, they make such claim, Protestantism requires that they be challenged by the prophetic protest, which gives God alone absoluteness and sanctity and denies every claim of human pride. This

277

protest against itself on the basis of an experience of God's majesty constitutes the Protestant principle."

As we walk, and pray, and work together; as we converse with each other seeking understanding of and sympathy with each other's point of view and emphasis, always we must distinguish in our thinking the church as an institution, largely the work of men, and the church as fellowship, community, brotherhood, the whole household of God (which is the basic meaning of ecumenical) which to say, the church as the Body of Christ, which is the will and gift of God. As H. Richard Niebuhr has pointed out in *The Purpose of the Church and Its Ministry* there are two ecumenical movements in our time—first, the organizational effort to develop worldwide institutions; and second, the spiritual, psychological, intellectual, and moral common life transcending all national (and we may add denominational) boundaries which seeks institutions through which to express itself. Frustration that the former (institutional union) is not easily achieved with uniformity in organization and rites should bring us to an understanding that in the long last the latter (spiritual unity) may well be of greater import by far. Unity of spirit, or better, unity in the Holy Spirit characterized by *agape*, Christian love, is ultimately essential to any organizational union if it is to be more than the hollow mockery and sham of the attractive façade to an empty and abandoned building.

We must remember always that the Church is not the end, but God's means to a greater end—the salvation of His created world. Hence, like the apostle Paul, the Church must be "made all things to all men" (I Corinthians 9:22) that it might by all means save some. This means that in the unity we seek, as now, the Church needs must be on the one hand, reformed, protestant, and evangelical; and on the other, one, holy, catholic, and apostolic. These things are not contradictory but complementary. All are essential in order that the high priestly prayer of our blessed Lord may be fulfilled, "That they all may be one: as Thou, Father, are in me, and I in Thee, that they also may be one in us": and, if I may use the expression, here is the punch line, the meaning, purpose, and goal of all our efforts, "that the world may believe that Thou hast sent me." (John 17:21)

This then is the purpose of our liberty, wherewith Christ hath made us free; enlisted in His service we may so present Jesus Christ in the power of the Spirit, that other men may be won to put their trust in God through Him; to accept Him as their Savior, and to serve Him as their King in the fellowship of His church; that this tragic world—lost, doomed, damned, may yet be saved.

278

Sermon Thirty-seven

JONAH: A VERY MINOR PROPHET

REVEREND JAMES T. CLELAND, D.D.

*Dean of the Chapel and James B. Duke Professor
of Preaching, Duke University Divinity School, Durham, North Carolina; a Minister of the Presbyterian
Church*

In this sermon on Jonah Dr. Cleland brings humor and insight to an Old Testament story which has troubled people over the centuries.

Born in Glasgow, Scotland, in 1903, James T. Cleland attended school in Glasgow, graduated from Glasgow University in 1924, and served as assistant in three parishes of the Church of Scotland during his theological training. He was graduated from Glasgow University Divinity Hall in 1927, gaining distinction in ecclesiastical history, after which he came to America.

Dr. Cleland was appointed to the Jarvie Fellowship at Union Theological Seminary in New York, then returned to Scotland on the Black Fellowship at Divinity Hall, Glasgow University; from 1929 to 1931 he was Faulds Teaching Fellow at the University. In 1931 Amherst College called him to its department of religion.

In 1938, he was ordained a minister of the Presbyterian Church, U.S.A., and spent 1938 and 1939 on leave of absence in Europe and the Near East. In 1944-1945 he did graduate work at Union, and in 1945 he was appointed Preacher to the University and Professor of Preaching in the Divinity School at Duke University, Durham, North Carolina. In the summers of 1948 and 1955 he was guest Professor of Homiletics at Union Theological Seminary. In 1954 he earned the Th.D. degree from Union. He delivered the Frederic Rogers Kellogg Lectures, Episcopal Theological School, Cambridge, Massachusetts, in 1953, which were published as *The True and Lively Word*. He has contributed three expositions to *The Interpreter's Bible* and writes a bimonthly article for the *The Chaplain* under the heading "Preacher's Clinic."

During the winter months Professor Cleland preaches in many of the preparatory schools, colleges, and universities on the Eastern Seaboard. At Amherst and Duke he has had a hand, as assistant coach, in turning out consistently successful soccer teams. His preaching shows a fine understanding of the problems of man and a kindly sense of humor.

JONAH: A VERY MINOR PROPHET

The moment a minister announces "Jonah" as a sermon-subject, there is either mirth or tension in the congregation. The very word "Jonah" evokes laughter or wariness. At least, no one goes to sleep, right off the bat.

For one type of person, Jonah is a joke or the cause of minor merriment. We are told: "When you're down in the mouth, remember Jonah. He came out alright." Or, when we talk too much, or too dangerously, we are reminded of what Jonah said to the whale: "If you'd kept your mouth shut, we wouldn't be in this mess." My own chuckle over the book has nothing to do with fishy intestines or the problem of human life therein, but with the picture in 3:8 of every beast wearing sackcloth as a sign of repentance. A horse in sackcloth is a reasonable possibility. So is a dog. (They have been seen in mink jackets in the U.S.A.) But rats and mice in sackcloth, to say nothing of the wilder forms of Assyrian fauna, give me pause.

For another type of person, Jonah is a battleground, one of the arenas in which the Biblical literalist and the Biblical critic slug it out, toe to toe, with shouts of "Whales and the Word," and "I would believe Jonah swallowed the whale, if the Bible said so." Jonah inspires, excites and inflames the one-track mind, conservative or liberal; and there is always a whale on the track.

I hope it will be satisfactory to you if we ignore both of these approaches: the humorous and the literal. Let us ask, very simply, what Jonah says to those who read it. After all, the author did write for readers. And we are readers.

The best way, then, to begin to understand Jonah is to look at the story. The four chapters are four acts in one drama. In Chapter 1, Jonah was given a commission to go to Nineveh, the capital of the Assyrian empire, and preach there. Jonah had no use for the assignment and headed, by ship, in another direction. A storm arose. It was obvious that someone on board had incurred the wrath of some god. Jonah, in an unexpected burst of heroism, volunteered to be a human sacrifice to appease God. Against their will, the sailors were prevailed upon to throw him overboard. There Jonah was swallowed by a handy "great fish." It is a tale of disobedience redeemed by self-sacrifice.

In Chapter 2, Jonah wrote a psalm (perhaps by the light of whale oil) to pass the time and to give thanks to God for his deliverance. One wonders just why he thought he was delivered? To escape from threatened shipwreck by absorption into the innards of a sea monster is surely as awkward a predicament as to jump out of the frying pan into the fire. On the third day the fish deposited him on the seashore.

In Chapter 3, Jonah, at last, went to Nineveh, and preached God's judgment on the ample evil and magnificent wickedness of the imperial city. The outcome was stupendous. The whole place repented. Fasting and sackcloth were the order of the day. Even God was staggered by the size and genuineness of the conversion, and decided to spare the city. Jonah was indignant! His preaching had been, embarrassingly, too successful. He personally had hoped for, and desired, a divine and wholesale holocaust following on his warning.

In Chapter 4, God tried to explain to Jonah why He forgave the city. He pointed out that mercy is the attribute of deity. Jonah said he knew that, but was personally against it. He preferred death, even his own, to such colossal good-will. We don't know what happened to Jonah thereafter. James Bridie in his play *Jonah and the Whale* leaves Jonah muttering the whimsical thought: "It is horrible to think that Jehovah may have a sense of humour."

Do you see the question we are left with? Why did the author write this Book of Jonah? Let us try to answer, very briefly. With the teaching of the scribe Ezra and the canonization of the Law, around 400 B.C., one wing of Judaism decided that God was the God only of the Jews; that salvation was for the Jew alone; and that, one day, God would annihilate the heathen for the benefit of the Jews. It was a religious-political viewpoint, born in nationalistic pride and resulting in a self-satisfied aversion to all that was non-Jewish. Here was an enthusiastic arrogance, a devout self-esteem, which was uniquely dangerous because it was rooted in religion.

With this point of view the author of Jonah was at odds. He was a universalist. His God was the God of all people: of Nineveh, that wicked

281

city, as of Jerusalem, the holy city. Therefore his prophet Jonah was not the hero of his book. God was the hero. Jonah was the villain. Maybe that is stating it too strongly. Let us soft-pedal the criticism and put it this way: Jonah does not rate very highly in the thought of the narrator. He is a very minor minor prophet. He is less than a minor prophet. He is a minimus prophet. He may even be a minus prophet. The author's God is not Jonah's God. The author's theology, as Professor McFadyen of Glasgow pointed out, is akin to that of John 3:16: "God so loved the world" —Jerusalem, of course, but Nineveh, too. Jonah is a pamphlet written by a man with a large view of a great and merciful God. It anticipates the teaching of Jesus.

Do you see one ever-recurring truth at the heart of this Old Testament story? Isn't it something like this: It is perfectly possible for a religious person to misunderstand the nature of God and to disagree with His ways with man.

Jonah was not irreligious. The author admits that he was a prophet. That we must accept, in good faith. But Jonah did not understand the God he served. He did not grasp what the universality of God really meant. He actually thought he could escape from the presence of God by going in the opposite direction from the way God ordered—to Tarshish instead of to Nineveh. James Bridie, in the play previously mentioned, has the whale—of all the dramatis personae—point out the absurdity of this! After a whimsical discussion of the implications of natural theology, the whale comments: "In the meantime, I implore you to remember this: it is a useless, undignified, irrational and utterly preposterous action for the leading citizen of Gittah-Hepher to run away from God." That describes the situation. For an intelligent religious person to think he can dodge the universal God is useless, undignified, irrational and preposterous.

Worse than that, Jonah thought he knew better than God what God ought to do: blast Nineveh, don't spare it. Jonah didn't ask much of God. All that he asked was that God would agree with Jonah's estimate of God. Jonah made God in Jonah's image. God had made man in God's image; Jonah returned the compliment. He wanted to serve God, but it had to be in Jonah's way, or else nothing doing.

It is extremely difficult for man to let God be God. Man wants to cut God down to size, to man's size, in all fields of endeavor: personal, political, ecclesiastical. He wants God to behave as tradition, environment and ac-

282

cepted morality feel that God ought to behave. And high religion says "No." It invokes the veto in the name of the noblest idea of God. High religion does not make God in man's image. It embarrasses, harries, reconstructs man so that he may be transformed into conformity with the will of a high view of God, whether man likes it or no.

Isn't that what Jesus was teaching? Isn't that why religious folk, like Jonah, put Jesus to death? Our Lord believed in a universal God: one who had a place in his love for the detested Samaritan; for an officer in a foreign army of occupation; and for the despised "people of the land"—the proletariat of Palestine—who couldn't or wouldn't keep the Jewish Law. And if you had asked Jesus why he backed these people against the temple supporters and synagogue adherents, he might have scratched his Jewish head and said: "I suppose it is because God loves them."

The struggle didn't finish with the author of Jonah and with Jesus. Just over a hundred years ago, in Scotland, McLeod Campbell of the parish of Rhu was expelled from the ministry of the Church of Scotland, because he said that Jesus died for all men and not only for Presbyterians. On the centenary of his dismissal a memorial window was unveiled in the church at Rhu, in atonement, by a Moderator of the General Assembly, who said, in his sermon, that while it took courage then to be unorthodox, now it took courage to be orthodox. I was present at that memorial service. The text that I would have preached on is Matthew 23:29-31: "Woe to you, Scribes and Pharisees, hypocrites! for you build the tombs of the prophets and adorn the monuments of the righteous, saying, 'If we had lived in the days of our fathers, we would not have taken part with them in shedding the blood of the prophets.' Thus you witness against yourselves, that you are the sons of those who murdered the prophets." It's in the genes!

" 'Tis old, yet ever new." The good is not only the enemy of the bad. It is the enemy of the better.

Now, we shall miss the point of all this if we think that Jonah and the Pharisees and the General Assembly of the Church of Scotland were knaves or fools. They were not. Jonah, for example, was a prophet, of a sort, a very minor prophet of a particularistic point of view. Yet let us be fair with him and to him. He had one admirable moment: his behavior during the storm, resulting in a voluntary self-sacrifice; or, so he intended. It is interesting, and surprising, to note that he was willing to try to save the lives of non-Jews on the ship, though he would be damned if he would save the lives of non-Jews in Nineveh. He could not, in cold blood, generalize what he offered to do in a time of crisis. This is the kind of per-

283

son God constantly has to work with: Balaam, Jonah, Peter, and us. God has eternity, however, and can have patience!

Do we now see the ever-recurring truth at the heart of that Old Testament story? It is perfectly possible for a religious person to misunderstand the nature of God and to disagree with His ways with man.

Do I need to apply this to our own time, to us, who have been favored with centuries of the Biblical message? There are so many areas where Jonah is opposing God, and the Pharisees are opposing Jesus, and the elect are opposing McLeod Campbell.

Take the matter of church membership, be it across denominational lines or caste lines or class lines. I was at a great men's meeting in a church not one hundred miles from Durham, North Carolina. There were 300 men meeting in Christian fellowship. I asked them how many were Trade Union members—the church was in a union town. Do you know how many? Two. I told this to a lay leader in another North Carolina church. He took me to the window of the vestry and said: "Do you see that factory? Our church is on the edge of the factory district. We don't have a single ordinary worker in our congregation, though we have lots of managers and some of the owners." Two caste churches. What will remedy this? Just one thing: a real, active, elbow-to-elbow belief in the universality of God, as the one God of all men in a down-to-earth, existential situation. Do you know why I say that? Because it was affirmed by a man who tried it in a different, but comparable, situation. The Church of South India was created by the merger of several denominations. A bishop of that church was asked if, given his choice, he would prefer to be a Presbyterian missionary in South India or a Bishop of the South India Church. He replied: "A Presbyterian missionary." He was reminded that he voted for the union of the churches. Do you know his answer? "I personally was against it. But I believed that God was for it. So I went along." That is what leads to change for the better: a willingness to vote with God even when we personally prefer no change. A real belief in the universality of God can work wonders for the person who yields to it. But it isn't always easy to yield. We have to allow God to fight us to let God conquer. Paul called it being a "new creature."

So the struggle goes on in our time, for us, here, there and everywhere: environment versus conviction; tradition versus truth; culture versus Christianity; a contemporary Jonah versus God. But here and there someone sees God, recognizes His truth, believes it with conviction and ceases to be a Jonah, a Pharisee, or even a Scots Presbyterian. A minor prophet can even become a major disciple.

The Book of Jonah is a book for our times.

The end of the Book of Jonah does not tell us what the poor wee minor prophet did. Do you know why? The problem was not Jonah's. The problem was the reader's. Do you see what that means? The problem is ours, who read the book. Are we willing to face the embarrassment of a high religion? Are we willing to allow the battle of spiritual values to be a real war within ourselves? Supposing we are not, what then?

Let me tell you a story. It comes from Bruce Marshall's novel: *The World, The Flesh and Father Smith*. It is of a young priest trying to persuade a dying sailor to confess his sins so that he may receive absolution and the last rites of the church. But the old sailor has a courageous honesty. He's not sorry for all the Jezebels he knew in foreign ports. He had enjoyed them and he wouldn't deny it. But the priest, despite his youth, was wise. He asked the sailor if he was sorry for not being sorry for having known all these women? The old sailor said "Yes," and he was absolved.

Are we sorry that we are Jonahs? If not, are we sorry for not being sorry that we are Jonahs? Yes? Good. That gives God a chance to move in.

Sermon Thirty-eight

THE HEART HAS ITS REASONS

REVEREND ROGER HAZELTON, PH.D., D.D.

*Dean of the Graduate School of Theology of
Oberlin College, and a Minister of the United
Church of Christ, Oberlin, Ohio*

Dr. Roger Hazelton has participated in international church conferences in Holland, Switzerland, Germany and India. In 1938 he studied at the Nietzsche-Archiv in Germany on a Carl Schurz Scholarship and in 1951 and 1952 was a Fulbright Research Professor at the University of Paris.

He studied at Amherst College, took his divinity degree at the Chicago Theological Seminary, his M.A. at the University of Chicago, and his Ph.D. at Yale. The honorary D.D. was conferred upon him by Amherst in 1951 and by the University of Chicago in 1960. He has been chairman of the Department of Religion at Pomona College, Professor of Religion at Claremont Graduate School; tutor in religion at Olivet College; Dean of the Chapel at Colorado College; Professor of Philosophy of Religion and Christian Ethics at Andover-Newton Theological School, and Abbot Professor of Christian Theology at Andover-Newton. He has lectured in colleges and universities in various states, and has been a member of the summer school faculties of Southern Methodist University, Boston University School of Theology, Garrett Bible Institute, and Union Theological Seminary.

Dr. Hazelton is a member of the American Theological Society and the National Council on Religion in Higher Education. Between 1957 and 1959 he was a member of the commission to prepare a statement of faith of the Congregational-Christian Churches of the United States. He has also served on the Hymnal Committee of the Congregational-Christian Churches and has worked with the National Council of Churches on the message committee.

THE HEART HAS ITS REASONS

Some of you, I am sure, will recognize where the title of this baccalaureate sermon comes from. Not from the Duchess of Windsor, or her ghost writer, who used it for her memoirs a few years ago; but from Blaise Pascal more than three centuries earlier, who wrote it in his unfinished work called the *Pensées*, "The heart has its reasons which reason cannot know." That is probably one of the most famous and cherished sentences in modern literature because it says something deeply and luminously true about the misery and the grandeur of man.

My sermon also has a text from the Bible. You may find it in Psalm 51, "Behold, thou desirest truth in the inward being; therefore teach me wisdom in my secret heart." It is with this biblical word that I shall begin.

When the Bible, or Pascal for that matter, speaks about the heart it does not mean what our modern romantic notions tend to mean—the imperious drive of emotion or desire, what William James called "the feeling side of life." The other day on the radio I heard a woman singing one of those throaty German songs in three-quarter time which freely translated went like this, "Tonight I'll give my heart away; tomorrow is another day." According to this modern idea, the heart and reason are in constant conflict with each other and the victory of the heart would mean the triumph of feeling over intelligence, of passion over reflection, of impulse over thought. When Elizabeth Barrett Browning wrote, "My heart beats in my brain" she pointed to this kind of displacement and victory. But Pascal and the Bible mean something very different from all this. There is a truth of the inward being, a wisdom of the heart, which is both God's own gift and man's own task.

A baccalaureate sermon is as good a place as any to be saying this. The heart of man, in biblical terms, is not a part of him but the whole of him, that is, the gist and kernel of him. The heart not only feels, or feels in place of thinking, but thinks, "As a man thinks in his heart, so is he." Or in Jesus' words, "Where your heart is, there will be your treasure too." So when it is a question of my heart it is a question of myself, my own true self, the self that thinks, decides, and acts as well as feels. To have a heart is the same as to be a fully human self. And there is a truth and wisdom far beyond our reasoning that men and women need to learn if they are to become actual, authentic selves. All this must have something to do with higher education, and with the uses to which it may be put. That is what I want to make clear in this sermon.

Now we may as well admit, to start with, that truth of the inward being and wisdom of the heart do not come easily and are far more a matter of living than of learning only. There are people who never achieve the kind of wholeness and lucidity of being to which these biblical phrases point. Certainly a college experience cannot guarantee that this will happen, but can only stir and beckon you toward achieving it. Here we have been more concerned, day in, day out, with knowledge than with truth or wisdom in the biblical sense. But even knowledge, as John Dewey said once, is not a glassy eye beholding a ready-made reality. Really to know something is to enter into it, to let yourself be open to it and be reshaped by it. A handy assortment of facts and quotes is not knowledge, much less truth and wisdom. I suppose we all would grant this, but it needs to be made emphatic ever so often, especially when looking back upon the pilgrimage called higher education.

Yes, the heart has its reasons which reason cannot know. That is because human selfhood is and remains a mystery, even after our hardest thinking and most thorough knowing have been done. It is as if I put my questions to the world only to have the world put to me a more difficult question which then I find that I must ask of myself. Who am I, really, and what does being me mean? "Man is a great mystery," said Saint Augustine, "and the hairs of his head are more easily to be numbered than the motions of his heart." If you have not been faced with this mystery in yourself, if you have not become a question to yourself, no matter what your grade point average may be, then the sort of education in which our colleges believe has simply not come off. We have only been conspiring together to prevent its happening in you.

But if, on the other hand, you have really felt the questioning mystery of selfhood, then whether you are what the world calls an "achiever" or not will not very much matter, because your education will have truly and deeply begun—and it is a safe bet that it will never be concluded. For a person to enter into his own depth, to be at home with himself, is as Thomas à Kempis said "a most praiseworthy manly thing." All education depends upon it, but no form of education yet devised can do anything but urge and prod us toward it. No amount of busy-work in courses can suffice, no sharpening of wits, no smooth performance of a schedule of duties, no slick manipulation of the tools and techniques of learning. To reason with the heart, that is, to do your own thinking humbly and honestly about matters of an ultimate concern, becomes possible only

289

within the human context of encounter and response. "All real life is meeting"; so is all real education at whatever level or range. So true is this that all of us in places like Claremont are always both teaching each other and learning from each other, which is exactly as it should be. If your teachers have ever treated you as disembodied intellects, or worse, as emptinesses to be filled with data and then processed into a certain pre-arranged shape, they owe you a profound apology. For it is really truth in the inward being, wisdom of the heart, that they have wanted and purposed to share with you, or at any rate to make more fully possible for you. What is more, they would not hesitate to tell you that this self-discovery and self-enlargement ought to be, and in some measure are, your gifts to them as well as theirs to you.

This brings me to a second point. There is a risk in the sort of search I have been describing—the rather considerable risk that what you find you may not like very much. Isn't it always easier to go skimming over the surface than to go in search of yourself? Of course it is, and that is why so many of us keep so busy looking elsewhere, forgetting that the proper study of mankind is man. Our very activism then becomes a kind of escapism, a way of putting off indefinitely the sobering, disquieting revelation of ourselves to ourselves. We would rather not be reminded of the real self that acts in our actions and thinks in our thoughts. It is as if we knew all the time that an unpleasantness waited for us at the center of our being; no wonder that we avoid such an embarrassment as coming to ourselves would cause.

Yes, there is always the risk that the most real thing about us may turn out to be our unreality, that is, our heart's tricky way of fooling ourselves about our real goals, needs, powers, and limitations. Do I love someone else chiefly because I love myself more, because I love being loved? And when I study is it knowledge and learning I am after, or status and approval? God would like to know, even if you or I would not. The melancholy Jeremiah wrote these words about the heart's amazing capacity for self-delusion, "The heart is deceitful above all things, and desperately corrupt; who can understand it? I the Lord search the mind and try the heart, to give to every man according to his ways, according to the fruit of his doings." And here is the more sprightly Pascal again on essentially the same subject, "Man is neither animal nor angel, and the pity of it is that in trying to act the angel he usually only behaves like an animal." The reasons of the heart are mostly rationalizations, our all-too-human ways of making the worse appear the better reason. I think I shall not go on laboring that point. It is enough to say that being human is very largely just a matter of becoming humble.

I hurry on then to my third point. Although the sort of truth and wisdom we have been thinking about is hard to come by and it is perhaps understandable that we should want to avoid it, nevertheless, there is no higher wisdom, no more imperative truth. All the great faiths of the world really agree on this. And all the schools and colleges of the world, when all is said and done, do the same. A liberal education must be a humane education, that is, the liberating of a sleeping self. The arts and sciences to which we are exposed, the ways of viewing and of working into which we are invited, have just this liberation of the self or heart of man as their intent and aim. No matter how painful it may prove to be, no matter how risky, it is worth everything it costs; otherwise we should not have spent this time together.

This shared task has a peculiar urgency in our own period. Here are some words of Paul Tillich which help to make this clear, "Twentieth-century man has lost a meaningful world and a self which lives in meanings out of a spiritual center. The man-created world of objects has drawn into itself him who created it and who now loses his subjectivity in it. He has sacrificed himself to his own productions. But man is still aware of what he has lost or is continuously losing." And therefore Tillich issues a call to courage, the "courage to be as oneself," which we might define as thinking ourselves back into the world, or in Pascal's terms as reasoning with the heart. Confronted by so many claims to conform—to look and act and believe—just like everyone else, that call to courage must be heard and heeded before today's dream becomes tomorrow's despair.

That kind of courage will require faith. Let me say quite precisely what I mean and do not mean by this. I do not mean that you should allow the Church, or its creeds, or its theologians, to do your thinking for you; that is not faith but irresponsible credulity, just one step removed from unthinking superstition. Real faith, on the contrary, is always something very different. It means the venturing and sending forth of the human heart, unworthy and broken as it is, upon the wide, deep seas of a reality that is both intimate and ultimate. It may mean giving up merely doing and having for the sake of *being*. And it will certainly mean accepting man's own task of selfhood as God's own gift, gracious and free. It is God, after all, who desires truth in our inward being and wisdom in our secret heart; and finally only God can give this to us, if we but open ourselves to Him, letting Him have His way with us. And so I conclude with a further word from the Bible, which is also a word from my heart: "Keep your heart with all vigilance, for from it flow the springs of life."

291

Sermon Thirty-nine

THE ESSENTIAL ABSURDITY
AND THE CHRISTIAN MESSAGE

REVEREND DAVID O. WOODYARD

*Dean of the Chapel, Denison Univer-
sity, Granville, Ohio, and a Minister
of the American Baptist Church*

David Woodyard early decided that he wanted to work with college students in the field of religion and studied toward this end. His courses at Denison University and Union Theological Seminary, New York, were mainly focused toward work in the college chapel. At Union he studied homiletics with Dr. Paul Scherer and wrote his thesis for graduation on "Myth and Preaching."

After college at Denison, he was Danforth Intern and Assistant Chaplain at Pomona College, Claremont, California during 1956 and 1957. He was appointed director of the University Christian Association at the University of Connecticut in September, 1958, then was called to Denison University to be Dean of the Chapel and to teach religion and counsel students.

THE ESSENTIAL ABSURDITY
AND THE CHRISTIAN MESSAGE

> "Or those eighteen upon whom the Tower in
> Siloam fell and killed them, do you think they
> were any worse offenders than all the others who
> dwelt in Jerusalem?"
>
> Luke 13:4

The Parisian newspapers bore a one-word headline: "Absurd." The story is now familiar. Nobel Prize Winner, Albert Camus, intended to take a train into Paris. The chance comment of a friend led him to drive. Within a few hours, Camus' mangled body was sprawled in the back seat of the car which attempted a curve at over ninety miles per hour. The brightest light in French literature was extinguished. "Absurd" was the only word for it, one which the novelist and playwright himself made famous.

Throughout his literary career, Albert Camus developed the theme that "at the center of man, dominating the great moments of his life, there is an essential absurdity." What he meant by this is that our experience of life will not yield itself to rational coherence, that life is riddled with incongruities, that it fails to measure up to our expectations, that it doesn't seem to make any sense. This theme emerged from the experience of a sensitive spirit whose integrity would not permit him the luxury of optimism or the self-indulgence of despair. And for that reason it calls to mind realities in my life, and I am sure in yours.

I think immediately of a college chaplain with whom I was associated in California. Some months ago he went into the hospital for a minor operation. They discovered cancer and had to amputate his entire leg. Now he is crippled with pain which nearly drives him out of his mind. Or again, there was a close friend in graduate school. Several years ago he joined the faculty of a Baptist College with full expectation of years of teaching. Headaches led to the discovery of a brain tumor. Today his whole life is telescoped into a few weeks within which he will make a torturous descent into death. Then there was a classmate at Denison. We had both been closely associated with the minister at the Baptist Church in Granville, both attended seminary, and both entered a ministry to students. The other day I picked up the *Alumnus Magazine* and read on one page of my appointment at Denison and on another of his death at the hands of a merciless disease.

Who among us can bear realities like these in mind and not understand what Albert Camus is talking about? Perhaps he is right when he speaks of "The absence of any profound reason for living." There is at the heart of life an "essential absurdity."

I

When we turn to the Bible, we might expect some relief from this nightmare. But the first thing we come up against is that the absurd is conspicuously evident. Think of Job. We read of him, "that man was blameless and upright, one who feared God, and turned away from evil." He had a loving wife, ten children, and abundant wealth. Job was a faithful servant of God, and a man richly blessed. But then things began to happen. Thieves fell upon his oxen and asses and stole them, fire consumed his sheep and servants, and a band of marauders made away with his camels. His worldly possessions were gone. Then his children were taken from him by a "great wind" which leveled their house while they were making merry. Next Job was afflicted "with loathsome sores from the sole of his foot to the crown of his head." As if that were not enough, his three friends descended upon him with words of condemnation. The man of faith had taken from him his worldly goods, his beloved children, and the support of friends. He lies on an ash heap and curses the day he was born.

Archibald MacLeish sketches a modern Job in his play J.B. Though it is weak and false in its resolution, the pinch of the absurd is still there. In bewilderment and despair brought about by cruel turns of fate, J.B. cries, "Look at me! Every hope I ever had, every task I put my mind to, every work I've ever done annulled as though I had not done it. My trace extinguished in the land, my children dead, my father's name obliterated in the sunlight everywhere . . . love too has left me." J.B. is experiencing the absurd.

"Well, that's the Old Testament," you say. So it is. But you come off no better in the New! The absurd reaches a climax on a cross at Golgotha. God had determined that the time was ripe for a full and final disclosure of Himself. He sent His Son to make real His love and forgiveness. Nothing like that had ever happened before. "In him was life, and the life was the light of men." But you turn a page or two and it is all over. Love gets crucified. How can you draw any other conclusion than that life is absurd, that it doesn't make sense?

The Bible is ruthlessly faithful to reality as we experience it. There are no concessions to our yearnings for a happy ending. There is no attempt to conceal the absurd. Scripture maintains a posture of real integrity before life.

II

But we need to move beyond this tough-mindedness and realism. The Bible is equally careful to profess the mystery of life which will not yield itself to easy answers. A crowd to whom Jesus was speaking one day was well aware of eighteen men who had met a senseless death. They had been working on the tower in Siloam which was a fortification of the city. The tower caved in and crushed them. Many said it was because they were sinful or engaged in a project displeasing to God. Jesus would have none of their simple solutions. He steadfastly refused to offer any explanation.

Some months ago the Dean of Union Seminary preached in morning chapel following the death of the most beloved member of the faculty. "Our thoughts are filled this morning with a sense of great loss," he said, "and this cannot be balanced by such human consideration as the thought that the one whom we have lost had already finished his work or by the thought that death was a release from suffering." Dean Bennett would not content himself with cheap answers to a costly loss. He refused to penetrate the mystery of life and death, to engage himself in human considerations or divine accusations.

This is a posture which Albert Camus will not assume. In his novel, *The Plague*, a Catholic priest stands with Dr. Rieux before a dying child. While admitting that the spectacle is revolting, the priest says rather limply, "Perhaps we should love that which we cannot understand." With emotion and determination the doctor replied, "No, Father, I have another idea of love. And I shall refuse until death to love that creation in which children are tortured." Camus at this point agrees with Arthur Koestler who said in *Darkness at Noon*, "as long as chaos dominates the world, God is an anachronism." But this is every bit as much a refusal to respect the mystery at the heart of life, as the contentment with easy answers. And it leads as surely to ultimate despair.

Psychoanalyst Erich Fromm makes a significant point: "One who has never been bewildered, who has never looked upon life and his own existence as a phenomenon which requires answers and yet, paradoxically,

296

for which the only answers are new questions, can hardly understand what religious experience is." None of us can live simply on the basis of answers to answerable questions. The truly religious person takes "the risk of resolving his life about some unanswerable questions." He is willing to live with mysteries which he can neither penetrate nor dissolve, with wounds which remain open.

Many of us are familiar with the name of Martin Niemoeller, that great German pastor who spent eight years in a concentration camp. Just before Christmas in 1944, one of his daughters had attempted to visit him in prison. Because she was only sixteen, the Nazis refused her permission. Shortly thereafter she became sick with diphtheria and died. Niemoeller was informed of this by a guard who said, "Ha, one of your children is dead." The pastor asked, "Would you have the grace to tell me which one?" Finally he was permitted to talk with his wife on the phone. After their conversation Mrs. Niemoeller, shattered by grief, returned to her room. There she found that their son had placed a photo of his dead sister on her desk. Underneath it he had copied a verse from the Book of Job. It read, "Hitherto shalt thou come and no further." Mrs. Niemoeller bowed before the mystery of life and death and wept. She was willing to live with an open wound, to risk resolving her life about some unanswerable questions.

III

We have said this much: the Bible takes account of the absurd, refusing to shield us from its reality; and it bids us live with the mystery at the heart of life, refusing to engage ourselves in answers which can only lead to despair. But we need to move deeper. In the face of the absurd and in the midst of the mystery which enfolds life, there is the presence of the living God.

Towards the end of his ministry, Jesus was preparing his disciples for his fate and their reaction to it. "The hour is coming, indeed it has come, when you will be scattered, every man to his home, and will leave me alone." But before he can be shattered by the tragedy of his own lot, he adds, "Yet I am not alone, for the Father is with me."

When easy answers are a mockery, when cheap words of comfort are an offense, when a hollow optimism is but a nightmare, there is one comfort alone which will satisfy—the presence of One whose love is so near we cannot touch it, whose mercy is so broad we cannot comprehend it, whose compassion is so full we cannot imagine it. So real was this to

Pascal that his last words were a cry of anguished hope, "May God never abandon me"

The testimony of the Bible and of the Church through the ages is that God never does abandon us. He is with us at all times, and no less so in the presence of the absurd.

But Albert Camus chooses something else. His one great affirmation of hope was this: "In the midst of winter, I finally learned that there was *in me* an invincible summer." For all its nobility, what a small comfort—that there is something "in me." Unless you or he are made of different stuff than I, what is "in me" is hardly enough. The sheer frailty of it is reflected in the answer John Gunther gave to the question "in what do you believe." He said, "I believe in myself," but then added "with fingers crossed." When life is hovering between terror and horror, it is not what *is* "in me" but what is "with me" that comforts and heals. Only the gentle firmness of His everlasting arms can support and uphold.

This was the great affirmation of Job. At the peak of pain and agony, he forsakes his plea for acquittal and relaxes into the care of God. "For I know that my Redeemer liveth; and at last shall stand upon the earth; . . ."

But we need to remember that his is not a posture which Job sustains for long. He soon lapses back to his protest of innocence. The Bible is intensely realistic at this point. Trust in God's grace escapes us and slips away. But once we have known it we can be content with nothing less.

Some one hundred years ago, a young man of unusual talent entered Glasgow University. The promise of academic excellence and a forthcoming marriage raised high his hopes. But then his fortunes turned; he became blind and his fiancée rejected him. His world was dark in more ways than one. In spite of this he graduated and became one of the greatest preachers in the Church of Scotland. His moments of pain, loneliness, and suffering were countless; he lived with the absurd daily. But in the midst of it, he was sustained by the vision of a God who clings. Out of the ashes of his own life he wrote the hymn which begins, "O love that wilt not let me go, I rest my weary soul in The. . . ."

The experience of the absurd is with each of us. And our one comfort is this: that in the face of the essential absurdity and in the midst of the mystery of life, there is the presence of the living God, the One whose love wilt not let us go.

298

Sermon Forty

THE SAINTS AND THEIR CHECKBOOKS

REVEREND CARROLL E. SIMCOX, PH.D.

*Rector, St. Mary's Episcopal Church, Tampa,
Florida*

Dr. Simcox was born in North Dakota. He graduated from the University of North Dakota, took his divinity degree from Oberlin and his Ph.D. from the University of Illinois in Classical Philology. He began his ministry in Minnesota, was Episcopal Chaplain at the Universities of Illinois and Wisconsin, became Rector of Zion Church in Manchester Center, Vermont, and taught Latin and Greek at Bennington College for Women. He was then called to be Assistant to the Rector of the famous Saint Thomas's Episcopal Church on Fifth Avenue, New York City. In 1958 he became Rector of St. Mary's in Tampa.

Dr. Simcox was book editor of *The Living Church* for several years, and is a frequent contributor to Forward Movement Publications of his Church. He is the author of *Living the Creed, Living the Lord's Prayer, Living the Ten Commandments, Understanding the Sacraments, The Words of our Worship, The Promises of God, They Met at Philippi, An Approach to the Episcopal Church,* and *Is Death the End?*

THE SAINTS AND THEIR CHECKBOOKS

"Remember the words of the Lord Jesus, how
he said, It is more blessed to give than to receive."

Acts 20:35

The young parson had just finished preaching his first sermon. He was very nervous and rattled, and he wanted to give out the offertory sentence to launch the collection. He tried to say "Remember the words of the Lord Jesus, how he said, 'It is more blessed to give than to receive' "; but those words didn't come. What came out instead was, "Remember the words of the Lord Jesus, how he said, 'A fool and his money are soon parted!' " We hope that his congregation did not take him too literally. Too many Christians take a niggardly attitude toward their monetary offering to the Lord, and we are going to think about it frankly this morning. Today is the Feast of All Saints. On this wonderful holy day the preacher is tempted to talk about the saints in very lofty, ultra-spiritual terms, dressing them up in haloes and flowing white robes. I propose to by-pass the haloes and robes of the saints and to consider with you their wallets and checkbooks.

One of the masters of the art of writing biography is Philip Guedalla. He once lectured on the difficulty the biographer has of finding out what kind of person his subject really was. He described what he had done when he was preparing his biography of the Duke of Wellington. Where did he look for evidence of the Duke's true character as a person? In the Duke's old checkbooks, of all places. He went through the stubs and the cancelled checks, and there he found what kind of man Wellington was. For there, you see, he could find what were the deepest concerns of the Duke. You spend the most money on what matters to you most; and what matters to you most is the real index of your innermost soul. That is what reveals your true self. To put it another way: You are, you increasingly become, what you care about most.

If a biographer who knew his business wanted to write a book about you, he would want to get his hands on your old checks. They would tell him the truth about the real, ultimate you. They would tell him, among other things, what kind of person you are. He could find out without looking at your checks that you are a member of the Church, that

300

you attend regularly, that you serve on boards and committees. But suppose that in looking through your checks and other records he learned what your income is, and he learned that you spend in a typical year one per cent of your income for the support of the Church and six per cent for such items as cigarettes, liquor, and luxuries. Would he, or would he not, be justified in saying about you something like this? "On the evidence that we have, it appears that our subject loved the Lord in the amount of one dollar per week, and loved his personal luxuries in the amount of six dollars per week." Would this be fair and just? You may think not, but in that case it is up to you to state why not, and I'm afraid I can't help you.

Let us think, then, about the saints and their checkbooks. First we had better clear up what we mean by this word saints. Forget all the stained-glass pictures of saints you've ever seen. Forget all about the church's procedures of canonization which have resulted in some people's getting the honorary degree of saint. In the New Testament, the basic Christian idea of a saint is that he is a person who is living as a Christian. St. Paul reminds us that we are all called to be saints. So a saint, as we are now using the term, is a Christian who is trying to live worthily of the name he bears. I like to think that I am preaching now to a whole congregation of saints, and I believe that I am. I am assuming that each one of us is a Christian who wants to be a better Christian.

Well, how do we go about it? Where do we go from here?

There are a lot of things to be done with yourself, of course. You can look at your personal qualities as they are and ought to be and find plenty of room for improvement. You need more patience, more loving-kindness, more charity, more courage, more faith. You can take your own self-inventory and say to yourself, "Here thou ailest, and here, and here." But there is something more fundamental than all these things, something that fits us all, without exception, and it is that we all need to be better givers.

The great saints are the great givers. This can be said without any qualifications or exceptions whatever. The great saints differ from other men in the way in which they give of what they are and what they have in the loving and joyful service of their Lord and their brethren. You will not find one person deserving of the name of saint of whom that cannot be said. But here's another thing about the saints; they give all, but they throw nothing away. They have a purpose in all their giving, and that purpose was expressed by one of the strongest of the saints, David Livingstone. Said he, "I will place no value on anything that I have or possess except in relation to the kingdom of Christ. If anything I have will advance that kingdom it shall be given or kept, as by giving or keeping it I shall best promote the glory of Him to whom I owe all my hopes both for time and for eternity."

This should be the rule for every Christian, not just for the Livingstones and the Schweitzers, the Peters and the Pauls. Try now to apply it to yourself. You will value whatever you have—of money, or time, or talent, or anything else—only in terms of what it can do to help establish the rule of Christ in the world. If Tampa needs better hospital facilities and you have some money you can give toward that end, you will ask yourself whether it is the Lord's will that we should have better hospitals. You value your money only as it can be put to His service. We should not think of Christ's kingdom on earth in exclusively churchly terms. He carries on His rule not only through churches but through schools, hospitals, good housing, good recreation, anything and everything that enriches life for all the children of God. A true Christian, devoted to spreading Christ's kingdom, is concerned about all these things. Whatever is good for people belongs in Christ's kingdom. When we work for, or give to, any genuinely good cause, we are working for and giving to the kingdom of Christ.

To all of us this poses a problem of choice. The United Fund appeal comes to us making a real and inescapable claim on our generous support. Many of us feel a special responsibility for some particular charity or agency of the common good. Many of us are trying to help needy individuals. But then there is also the Church. Where shall we put that—first, last, or somewhere in between?

I do not see how any Christian can be in much of a quandary about this. If we are living members of Christ's body, that body—the Church—comes first. We will first do all that we can for the Church; then we will heed all those other calls. There are many things that could be said in support and defense of this proposition. I shall mention only one. The Church is the mother of all charities and good causes. The unique business of the Church is to create people who will always put the works of love and of light first in their lives. Only as the Church is able to do this will these good causes find good human soil in which to grow. It is only as we give and work and pray for the strengthening of the Church that we can hope to roll back the darkness and to create a world in which there is less darkness and misery and more light and happiness and well-being for all.

In that passage of Livingstone, which I quoted, the point is made that in all our giving we are to ask where our gift will do the most to advance the rule of Christ in our own lives, in our neighborhood, our community, our world. These check stubs of ours should show evidence of clear thinking and wise choosing on our part. They should show to that hypothetical biographer a hundred years after our death that we, in our day, gave sacrificially, joyfully, unstintingly, wholeheartedly, for the support and strengthening of Christ's Church—that we put that *first*, and that we then took good generous care of the other needs which seemed to us to be dear to the heart of our Lord.

I have devoted this sermon on the saints very largely to the subject of money, and this may be offensive to some of you. I do not apologize, but I want to explain. If you suppose that the true saints of the Lord ignored or despised money as something beneath their spiritual concern, I beg you to do some research into that. You could start with St. Paul. The fifteenth chapter of his first letter to the Corinthians is an exalted discourse on the resurrection of the body. Do you say that this is the kind of thing that claims the undivided attention of the saints? Well then, read on into the next chapter, which begins, "Now about that collection for the saints, I want you to do what I ordered the churches of Galatia to do." One moment Paul is talking about the resurrection, the next moment he's talking about what Christians should do with their money. He makes that shift without breaking his stride. The resurrection is most important—what we do with our money is most important. That's how he sees it, and Paul was an eminently representative saint. Do you suppose that our Lord Jesus took a dim or disdainful view of money? Then why do most of His parables deal with how we are to use our material possessions? We may remember that St. Francis of Assisi gave all his money away and embraced holy poverty with glad abandon. He did; yet not because he despised money, but because he loved the poor. It just isn't true that Christ and His saints regard money as worthless. It just isn't true that the Bible teaches that money is the root of all evil. It teaches (I Timothy 6:10) that selfish, covetous craving for money, for one's own sake, is the root of all evil—a very different thing indeed.

Your money, be it much or little, is one of the things God puts in your hands commanding you to use it in His service, to His glory. The saint is he who strives to use all that he has to God's glory. So I close by putting this question on your mind and conscience, for you to answer before God.—One year from today, will your check stubs show progress, or regress, in your life as a Christian?

Sermon Forty-one

THE MODERN CHRISTIAN AND SUNDAY

REVEREND LESLIE D. WEATHERHEAD, PH.D., D.D., LITT.D.

Minister, City Temple (Congregational), London, England, and Honorary Chaplain to Her Majesty's Forces

In "The Modern Christian and Sunday" Dr. Weatherhead discusses the use and abuse of the Sabbath and its ancient historical and religious meaning and presents his own view of a Christian Sabbath.

Leslie Weatherhead was born in London in 1893, studied at Richmond Theological College, London University, and Manchester University. During World War I he served as a Second Lieutenant in India, Mesopotamia, Kurdistan and Persia. In 1919 he went to Madras, India, for the English Methodist Church and in 1922 returned to Manchester and Leeds. After serving as Methodist Minister of Wesleyan Methodist Churches for some years, he was called to be the minister of City Temple in 1936 and remained there until he retired in 1961. After City Temple was destroyed during World War II, Dr. Weatherhead kept the congregation together for eleven years in rented quarters. In 1958 the congregation moved into a new church building.

Dr. Weatherhead has published a number of significant religious books, including *After Death, Psychology and Life, Jesus and Ourselves, How Can I Find God?, Why Do Men Suffer?, Personalities of the Passion, Discipleship, A Plain Man Looks at the Cross.* He was honored with the doctorate by the University of Edinburgh, Pacific School of Religion, and the College of Puget Sound.

Dr. Weatherhead has been popular as a preacher in England, the United States, and everywhere he has spoken. He has always had the ability to bring fresh meaning to religion and new faith and encouragement to his hearers. His style is simple and sincere, his word choice excellent. The originality of his sermons has made him one of the great preachers for a quarter of this century.

THE MODERN CHRISTIAN AND SUNDAY

One of our members, who has a young family growing up in his home, asked me recently to preach a sermon on how the modern Christian should keep Sunday. "I was always made to go to church twice and to Sunday school twice," he said, "but they want to motor to the coast or play tennis. If I don't give way, then as soon as they are old enough, they will go off and enjoy themselves and the family unity will be broken. Can you give any help?"

Well, I can only help by thinking aloud. It is not for me to lay down the law as to how others should behave in regard to Sunday. I may be quite wrong. I certainly should not deny the title "Christian" to those who keep Sunday differently from the way I hold to be best. They may have problems of health or loyalty about which I know nothing.

It says something for Sunday observance that the day has been regarded as "different" for over three thousand years. When Moses, armed with notebooks and pencil—as we should say today—went up into the mountain to think out those rules for the well-being of his people which would help them to live together with a minimum of friction and a maximum of good health—those rules which now we call the Ten Commandments —he borrowed from the older Babylonian code of Hammurabi (2100 B.C.) what is now the fourth commandment: "Remember the sabbath day to keep it holy." [1] The word "sabbath" comes from an old Babylonian word meaning: "Stop doing what you normally do," and the word "holy" means "healthy." The root of "hale," "holy," "heal," "healthy," and "whole" is the same, and, to anticipate, I do think that the ideal Sunday is one on which we stop doing what we normally do and promote the health of the body, the mind and the spirit.

The Jews, by the time Jesus was born, had interpreted the Mosaic Law in a ridiculous code of meticulous and finical rules. No wonder Jesus condemned them! Keeping the Sabbath had become an intolerable burden.

For example, "No work," was interpreted as "No carrying of burdens." But this again was interpreted finically as, "No ribbon *pinned* on the dress—that is a burden. It must be sewn on—then it is part of the dress."

---

[1] Exodus 20.8.

306

The matter became farcical. False teeth must not be worn on Sundays. That is bearing a burden. Some of the Jews cannot have looked their best on the Sabbath! A woman must not use a mirror on Sundays. She might espy a grey hair and, if she did, she would want to pluck it out. If she did this, it was officially "reaping," and that was breaking the Sabbath! [2]

No wonder Christ called the Pharisees hypocrites and exclaimed: "The Sabbath was made for man, not man for the Sabbath."

In Victorian days in England things could be very dull on Sundays, as Mr. Peter Fletcher showed recently in his most readable book, *The Long Sunday*. Dickens in *Little Dorritt* wrote of a man who hated church bells because they reminded him of hateful, dull, depressing Sundays, and Ruskin said that Monday morning was the happiest time in the week for him because then there were six clear days before Sunday came round again. He is the only man I ever heard of who liked Monday mornings!

I have read of Scottish homes in which the blinds were kept down on Sundays just in case anyone should get too cheerful, and even in my own Scottish Presbyterian home novels on Sunday were frowned upon. I remember my sister being rebuked for putting a novel on top of a Bible, and I got into trouble myself for reading a "secular" book on Sunday. I even remember the book. It was a book by Henty about pirates and much more attractive to a boy than the pious books children were then expected to read, like *Eric*, or *Little by Little*, or *Jessica's First Prayer*.

Yet, I hasten to add, Sunday in my home was not miserable. There was much joyous laughter and eager discussion, particularly about sermons and their preachers! It never occurred to us to do anything but go to church and Sunday school. There were no cars and no one dreamed of picnicking, but, of course, for us boys a walk was allowed after Sunday school, and I remember that there were some nice girls who went to Sunday school too!

How different things are now. Much more freedom and much more advantage taken of it. No one now would succeed in getting through Parlia-

---

[2] Further examples of these stupidities can be found in the volume, *Philo-christus: Memoirs of a Disciple of the Lord* (London: Macmillan & Co.), p. 12 ff.

ment a law prohibiting Sabbath-breaking, though there was such a law once. And the new freedom is a move in the right direction.

At the same time Jesus remains the wisest guide and truest authority. Did He not call Himself the Lord of the Sabbath Day? Look at two of His sayings:—

(1) I take one from an incident not recorded in the gospels, yet, in my opinion, of undoubted authenticity.[8] At a time when a man could be stoned for breaking the Sabbath, Jesus saw a man working in his garden on Sunday morning. He spoke to him thus: "Man, if thou knowest what thou art doing, blessed art thou; but if thou knowest not, thou art accursed and a transgressor of the Law."

This I interpret to mean, "If you are digging your garden deliberately, intending to go to the synagogue later, but doing this to protest against the finical nonsense of the Pharisees, good luck to you. But if you just don't care about the value of Sunday at all, then you are doing wrong."

So—to interpret for the modern man of today—let a man give due place to corporate worship in some church or other (God knows there are enough to choose from), and then let him get fresh air or exercise as he will, so long as his action does not interfere with others. Let him have his tennis or golf, but don't let him treat Sunday as a matter of indifference. Worship is essential to the health of the spirit, as fresh air and food are essential to the body.

(2) Many Sabbath-breakers quote for their comfort Christ's words, "The Sabbath was made for man, not man for the Sabbath." But the saying should be contemplated in the light of the answer to the question, "What is man?" If he is only a body; if he is a parcel of carbon, phosphorus, iron, water and the rest, let him not bother about spiritual values. Let him take no heed of God.

Someone has called him "a mental machine that works only for wages." Well, if that is the whole truth about him, it is not worth doing anything save making the machine work as well as possible and attracting the highest wages possible.

But if man is an eternal spirit, made for communion with God, made for love and faith and hope and the inspiring of his fellows, let him remember that however busy he may be, he *must* attend to the health of the soul or it will atrophy and could perish.

Religion may be universal and it may have—has, I believe—some of its

[8] Taken from the Codex Bezae (6th century M.S.) now in the University of Cambridge.

roots in the instincts and the instinctive emotions, but desire for God is not instinctive like eating. Miss a few meals and you will be ravenous. Miss out prayers and no instinctive drive will urge you back to God. Leave out eating and you will want food more. Leave out God and you will want Him less. It is part of God's respect for personality that we must choose Him and cultivate communion with Him, not be driven to Him as a starving man for bread.

The Sabbath was made for man. Here is the golden opportunity to keep the soul alive. Here is the chance in a busy world to meditate and pray and visit the lonely and the sick and the imprisoned.

In regard to Sunday games I am no spoil-sport, but I would say two things.

(1) If our fun and recreation take Sunday from another, we must think things through, mustn't we? Tennis in your own garden, yes. But remember that on the day on which the London County Council permitted Sunday games in the parks, the Underground Railway ran one extra train every five minutes. For A to enjoy his Sunday, B had to lose his, and though he had another day instead, and was paid more, he could not meet his relatives, let alone worship with his family on another day. Many of you have come to church by Underground Railway, but the driver in your case is doing what I am doing, trying to help you to worship, even if he does not know it.

(2) The second thing I would say is this. Let us imagine the English village with its village green and parish church. On Saturday afternoon, cricket is in full swing. Splendid! But will the boys come to Sunday school and Bible class if the cricket is repeated on Sunday? Cricket is splendid. But what chance has the vicar on Sundays if he has to compete with cricket or Sunday afternoon cinemas? And which is the greater contribution to the life of the nation? I know much has to be done to make religion attractive to youth, but do not forget the recent words of a London magistrate, that no one had ever come before him who had been for any considerable period a member of a Sunday school or Bible class. Is there no connexion between the decline of the Sunday schools and the rise of the Teddy boys and girls?

Near my home in a London suburb, there is a little park. Formerly it was just the grounds of a gentleman's house and the Borough Council has taken it over and made it into a very pleasant little spot. There are lovely flower-beds, beautiful lawns, shady trees, a rock garden and a little pool where two rather tired ducks make the best of the muddy water. A large notice often makes me smile. It says "No Fishing." You would think that but for that notice someone might land a sizeable salmon or half a dozen trout! Nevertheless, I am not in the mood to sneer at this little oasis in a London suburb. The action of our Borough Council is to be commended. It has railed round this little park with iron railings and it is locked at night. There are notices which say, "Please do not pick the flowers," and, in a few places, "Please keep off the grass."

One might say, "Why the palings and the prohibitory notices? Why not leave people free to do what they like?" But I am quite sure that the answer to that is this: that if there were no notices, there would soon be no flowers, and if there were no prohibitions, there would soon be no little park for anybody to enjoy at all. Many people, of course, would respect that little haunt of peace where one may sit on a quiet, sunny afternoon and meditate, but many others would not. The Borough Council has even appointed a stalwart guardian who assumes a fearsome demeanour, especially to little boys who disregard the notices, and as a resident in the Borough I would support the appointment of this friend, and I would support the maintenance of the palings and the notices, and they give me just the parable I want.

Sunday is a little park in the noisy din of our hectic week. Sunday is a little oasis in the desert of our monotonous and unnatural life. But I believe that, human nature being what it is, Sunday must be protected and guarded by a number of "Thou shalt nots," or else, very soon, there will be no Sunday for anybody to enjoy. As I say, if you take no action in this generation, two generations hence there will be nothing to take action about. Sunday will have gone, and those who sneer at some of us and call us narrow-minded old fogies who are trying to hold back the wheels of progress, may then ask whether it really was progress, and whether the pace of life has not brought the population, at least of great cities, to the verge of insanity. It is not far from that now.

No one wants to return to the old restrictions and gloom. But unless our actions on Sunday are so private that they obviously affect no one else—a desert-island life, for instance, or a regiment far from home—we may have to act in a way that *looks* more narrow-minded than we ourselves feel, just as we vote for railings round a park which, to safeguard our own behaviour, we ourselves do not need.

And though I do not want to bring back solemn, pompous Puritans, I recall some fine things about them. They knew the difference between right and wrong. They had high moral ideals. They had a great sense of duty and example and obligation. Their thinking was not superficial. Having no "telly" or radio they even read serious books! Better these things, even if accompanied by gloom, than the butterfly whirl of meaningless inanities in the senseless round of which some young moderns appear to giggle away their days.

Let me finish with one picture. Some time ago I was called to see an old man over eighty years of age who was dying and who was very frightened of death, as some old people are. And when, as tenderly as I could, I tried to talk to him about God and religion and the soul, he said, very bitterly and brokenly, mumbling as he said the words, "I have led a very busy life. I have never had time for that sort of thing. . . ." But he had had four thousand Sundays!

Sermon Forty-two

THE WONDER OF WORDS

REVEREND H. EUGENE PEACOCK, D.D.

*Pastor, Dexter Avenue Methodist Church,
Montgomery, Alabama*

This sermon reveals the importance of words in daily life—in love, work, social life. Words are, after all, the tools with which a minister works, the chief means of communicating thoughts and ideas to others.

Born October 11, 1919, in Kincey, Alabama, Eugene Peacock graduated from Millsaps College, and Candler School of Theology of Emory University, and received the D.D. from Birmingham-Southern College. He held a Sherwood Eddy European Seminar, 1951.

He was Pastor of Fairlington Methodist Church, Arlington, Virginia, 1944-1946, of St. Francis Street Methodist Church, Mobile, Alabama, 1946-1961, and became Pastor of Dexter Avenue Methodist Church, Montgomery, Alabama, in 1961. He is active in the American Red Cross, Child Day Care Center, Association for the Blind, Goodwill Industries, is a member of the Society of Biblical Literature and Exegesis and Association of Biblical Instructors.

He has been a contributor to the *Alabama Methodist Advocate, Christian Century, Christianity Today, The Pulpit, Upper Room Pulpit, The Christian Advocate,* and has been a delegate to the Southeastern Jurisdictional Conference and General Conference of the Methodist Church, World Methodist Council, and was a former member of the Methodist Commission on Church Union.

He is married and has three children. He is a frequent speaker on preaching missions, at conventions, and on college campuses.

THE WONDER OF WORDS

"The tongue is a fire."

James 3:6

The more I ponder the mystery of life the more I am impressed by the wonder of words. The capacity for speech surely identifies man as a child of God. Its importance for life is underlined by the fact that the main thrust in modern philosophy is an analysis of the meaning of words. Perhaps we can approach the marvel of words best by thinking about the poverty which would overwhelm us were we deprived of the use of words. Some things, of course, are, as we say, too deep for words; but life would lose much of its luster were we to lose the use of words.

Take romantic love as an example. I have some recollection of the tenderness of teen-age love when nothing was quite so thrilling as to sit by the side of a lovely young lady and hold her hand in silence, but all who have gone on beyond adolescent love to the deeper, richer love of maturity have found that love has its own vocabulary and we would be much the poorer were we to lose the wonderful words of love between a man and his beloved. Who would be willing to surrender such words as these:

How do I love thee? Let me count the ways.
I love thee to the depth and breadth and height
My soul can reach, when feeling out of sight
For the ends of Being and ideal Grace.
I love thee to the level of everyday's
Most quiet need, by sun and candlelight.
I love thee freely, as men strive for Right;
I love thee purely, as they turn from Praise.
I love thee with the passion put to use
In my old griefs, and with my childhood's faith.
I love thee with a love I seemed to lose
With my lost saints,—I love thee with the breath,
Smiles, tears, of all my life!—and, if God choose,
I shall but love thee better after death.

Consider, also, the wonder of words when applied to patriotism. In these times, when world issues seem to have lessened patriotism for some, there remain many whose love for country is deep and genuine, who are not chauvinistic, but truly patriotic. Their hearts leap with pride when they hear the rousing strains of the national anthem. The sight of the flag brings tears of gratitude to their eyes. For all whose love of country is of such quality, such words as these comprise a part of their treasure:

> Breathes there the man with soul so dead,
> Who never to himself hath said,
> This is my own, my native land!
> Whose heart hath ne'er within him burn'd,
> As home his footsteps he has turn'd
> From wandering on a foreign strand?

If the raptures of romance and the pride of patriotism are immeasurably enriched by words, religion is doubly so. The Holy Bible is a collection of words with inspired meanings. The new Testament writers, searching for a symbol to represent the Savior, called him "the Word of God." The mystic may claim that religious experience at its best is a mysterious union of the human soul with the divine spirit as a flame is absorbed in a blaze of fire, but most of us must be satisfied with some other expression of our sense of the reality of God and we search for words whose meanings give voice to our devotion. To all such, the words of the psalmist contain a special wonder:

> The Lord is my shepherd, I shall not want;
>   he makes me to lie down in green pastures.
> He leads me beside the still waters;
>   he restores my soul.
> He leads me in the paths of righteousness
>   for his name's sake.

Whether we turn to romance or patriotism or religion or some other basic area of human experience, words are important; they may not say everything, but our lives would be woefully impoverished were we deprived of their wonder. You may gather from this that I love words, and you are correct, for I do love words. Indeed, I honor and respect them as sacred ships designed to carry cargoes of meaning and purpose. As a preacher of the gospel, words are my tools. Their proper use to tell "the old, old story of Jesus and his love" is both a craft and an art. It hurts me deeply, therefore, to see words debased and put to harmful use. Indeed, the very freedom we enjoy in the use of words is, if anything, more of a wonder than words themselves, for words, more than any other power we possess, can either bless life or make it wretched. The happiness of a whole life can turn on the use of a single word. For instance, a person called his minister in the middle of the night and asked him to come to him at once. When the minister arrived, the person said, "Had you said 'No' instead of 'Yes,' I was prepared to take my life."

The power of words is at one and the same time thrilling and terrifying.

When one considers the creative power that words place in his hands, he is thrilled to share this power with God. When he considers the destruction that words can work, the responsibility of their proper use terrifies him. New meaning comes to the ancient prayer: "Let the words of my mouth, and the meditations of my heart, be acceptable in thy sight, O Lord, my strength and my Redeemer."

Why is it, then, that so many, even among those who regard themselves as Christians, use words in cruel and careless ways that leave heartache in their wake? I suspect that the reason often is that we do not understand ourselves as well as we think we do and we are not as Christian as we suppose. There remain areas in our lives that have never been brought under the purifying and controlling love of Christ. They remain as hidden citadels of evil in us from which evil influences issue to warp our words to evil purposes. Let us consider some of these harmful influences on the use of words.

Take that very common evil that we find in the lives of so many people —a feeling of inferiority. Felix Adler, the famous psychiatrist, believed that the traumatic experience of birth left every person with a deep-seated feeling of inferiority and this became the basic motivation in his personality. Whatever the cause, no Christian ought to feel inferior. I am not suggesting that Christians should abandon the virtue of humility, but I do believe that it is unchristian for us to make either favorable or unfavorable comparisons of ourselves with others, for our purpose is to accept ourselves as the children of God and to recognize that he has made a place for each which cannot be filled by any other. The failure to accept oneself as a child of God in this sense, leaves one in the grip of a feeling of inferiority which causes much pain and unhappiness.

Sometimes this feeling of inferiority expresses itself in very odd ways. I once knew a young lady, for instance, who had better than average natural endowment but who lived in the grip of a strong feeling of inferiority. She was a Sunday School teacher and potentially a good one, but she refused to take any training courses or read any books that would improve her teaching skills. Moreover, she discouraged others from seeking additional training. The reason for her unusual attitude was that she feared that her engagement in special training would be an admission of inferiority and her insecure ego would not agree to that. Her use of words, therefore, was destructive and harmful.

The old green-eyed monster of jealousy is an expert in robbing words of their creative wonder. It is traditional in churches to make jokes about the choir and to call it the "war department of the church." This, of course, is greatly exaggerated. People are no worse or better in the church choir than in any other department of the church. They are just more in the spotlight and, hence, their virtues and vices may be more noticeable than those of others in less conspicuous places. In a certain small town church, for instance, there was a woman in the choir who had served faithfully as a soloist until the years had taken their toll of her voice. In her better moments, she realized this and observed that she would like to retire. In fact, she declared that she would retire as soon as some one came along to take her place. Finally, a lovely young lady with a beautiful, trained voice did join the choir and true to her word the older woman graciously retired. The first few Sundays everything was lovely. The young lady sang beautifully and the older woman rejoiced in her singing. Before long, however, she began to miss the plaudits she had received for so many years from kind people in the congregation. A little dragon of jealousy began to grow in her heart and she began to make small criticisms of her youthful replacement. Before even she realized what was taking place in her life, the little dragon had developed into a great, green-eyed monster and she had launched a full scale attack on the new soloist. The consequences were bitter and painful. A conflict ensued that reached out into the congregation and eventually caused the young singer to leave the church altogether. Jealousy had poisoned the words of a woman who had forgotten their wonder.

A feeling of inferiority or the poison of jealousy are bad enough in their power to change words from messengers of love into poisoned darts of destruction, but worse even than these is a sense of unforgiven and unshriven guilt in the human heart. Of all the devils that hide in the caverns of the soul, none causes more damage and wreaks more destruction than guilt unconfessed and unforgiven. Such guilt blocks the flow of spiritual powers in the soul. It transforms the heart from a haven of peace into a hall of horrors. Macbeth with bloody hands could not even pray: "When I had most need of prayer, 'Amen' stuck in my throat." Psychologists say that we tend to project our frustrations and our vices onto other people. Guilt which has not been submitted to God for forgiveness and removal takes words and twists them into ugly, frightful missiles that blight and blast human life.

I have cited some of the causes that rob words of their wonder and turn them into evil things. There are others we might mention, but these should awaken us to the perils that threaten us all and put us on guard against them. My real purpose is to awaken you to the wonder of words and their potential for making life happy and good. Jesus commissioned

INDEX

This index has been prepared for clergy and laity alike, but particularly with the needs of the busy pastor-preacher in mind, to be suggestive, helpful, convenient, for the man in search of sermon ideas and illustrations. The reader is advised to add other words and pages as he finds them useful for his own reference. All the possible entries under the heading of God, Christ, Salvation and similar subjects are not listed in this Index because they are the basic subjects of all sermons in the book.

319

322

323

327

"And as ye go, preach."